CUMBERLAND HERITAGE

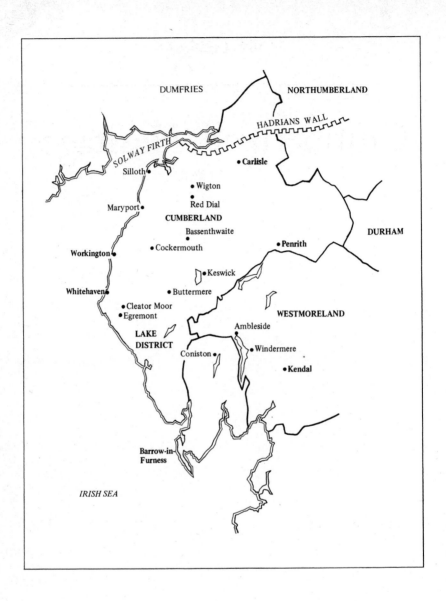

Molly Lefebure

Cumberland Heritage

ARROW BOOKS

ARROW BOOKS LTD
3 Fitzroy Square, London W1

AN IMPRINT OF THE HUTCHINSON GROUP

London Melbourne Sydney Auckland
Wellington Johannesburg Cape Town
and agencies throughout the world

First published by Victor Gollancz 1970
Arrow edition 1974

© *Molly Lefebure 1970*

*Made and printed in Great Britain
by The Anchor Press Ltd.,
Tiptree, Essex*

ISBN 0 09 908740 5

To Dr A. E. Clark Kennedy
't'owd lang doctor',
himself so much part of the Cumbrian scene.

CONTENTS

LIST OF ILLUSTRATIONS

ACKNOWLEDGEMENTS

A book of this nature could not possibly be attempted without a great deal of assistance from a large number of people. The author cannot hope to acknowledge all the generous help that she has received, particularly in the Lake Country itself. Some who have helped her are reticent by nature and have asked that their names should not appear. She would like to thank (not in any kind of order) the following:

Mr Kenneth Smith, F.L.A., City Librarian, Tullie House, Carlisle; Record Office, Carlisle Castle; Mr Warren Elsby and his assistants, County Library, Keswick; Mr C. Roy Hudleston, F.S.A., Editor of the *Cumberland and Westmorland Antiquarian and Archaeological Society Transactions*; Rev. J. C. Dickinson, F.S.A.; Brigadier J. W. Kaye; Mr and Mrs T. Grave; Mr George Bott; the late Mrs Bainbridge and the late Mr George Bowe; Mr John Edmondson; Mr Stanley Edmondson; Mr E. H. Shackleton, F.G.S.; Mr John Moon, F.G.S.; Mr M. Davies-Shiel; Mr W. Vickers; Dr A. E. Clark Kennedy; Mr Michael Finlay; Mr George Fisher; Mr A. Dawson; Mr A. Wainwright; Ordnance Survey; Area Surveyor, Cumberland County Council; Messrs Ward & Pridmore; Mrs A. M. Robinson; Manchester Corporation Waterworks; Miss Ann Meo; Miss Margaret Birkbeck; Mr David Hodson; Mr Brian Greenwood and Messrs Fred and David Tee, Cumberland Pencil Works; Victoria and Albert Museum; British Museum; Mr Dudley Hoyes; the late Mr Fred Williamson; the late Miss Winnie Burns; Routledge & Kegan Paul Ltd, Publishers, for permission to quote from Samuel Taylor Coleridge's *Notebooks*; *Drapers' Record*; *Encyclopaedia Britannica*; Mr Fred Mills; Mr J. Ashbridge; Mrs Mary Marshall; Mr Ronnie Porter; Mr Albert Benson; Mr and Mrs Isaac Wilson; Rev. Waterhead-Dixon; Rev. Geoffrey White.

Particularly the author wishes to thank her very dear friends and former neighbours at High Snab, not only for extensive assistance over matters of local lore and expert help in unravelling the dialect intricacies of old Braithwaite's road surveyors, but also for innumerable other kindnesses with which they have eased her path.

Finally, she thanks her own family for their good-natured toleration of her works and wadd.

". . . The Country although it be somewhat with the coldest as lying farre North, and seemeth as rough by reason of hilles, yet for the variety thereof it smileth upon the beholders and giveth contentment to as many as travaile it. For after the rockes bunching out, the mountains standing thicke together, rich of metall mines, and between them great meeres stored with all kindes of wildfowle, you come to prety hilles good for pasturage, and well replenished with flocks of sheepe, beneath which againe you meet with goodly plaines, spreading out a great way, yeelding corn sufficiently. Besides all this the Ocean driving and dashing upon the shore affourdeth plenty of excellent good fish . . ."

Camden writing of Cumberland,
Britannia

CUMBERLAND HERITAGE

The Stream Still Roaring . . .

CUMBERLAND IS ABOVE all notorious for its rain. Seathwaite in Borrowdale boasts the highest annual average fall in England, 123 inches as opposed to London's 23. The dalehead and surrounding fells are consequently murky, or, as Cumbrians put it, clarty.

Seathwaite, for the true Lakeland *aficionado*, is the essential heart of the district. This sky-lowering and peaty-hued dalehead, where the clouds dangle in dark fragments like the tatters of Tamburlaine's tents, full of threat and poetry; where water and stones are the two staple features of the scene, each vying to deluge the other; where everything smells of sheep; where spring shines with icicle-sticks on Jenny Banks; where summer falls in solid sheets of rainstorm; where autumn is gentle, golden and crepuscular and winter gleams hard and beautiful, has, for the greater part of its very long history, been a busy place. Today, for much of the year, there are cars parked by the intakes and hikers plodding in droves through the farmyard, going or returning from the Sty. In the old days Seathwaite was the stopping place for the pack-pony wool trains; here the Wastdale-bound drovers balanced loads, adjusted halts (a pair of strong wicker hampers joined by the pack-saddle) and tightened girths, getting all secure for the steep pull up the pass. Here, on their return, they refreshed themselves with a sup and a crack before driving their train down Borrowdale. Here, too, lodged many of the Old Men: miners from the wadd holes, slate-quarrymen from Honister (Old Men being the regional name traditionally given to the early miners and quarrymen). Here paused for rest weary foot-travellers: itinerant workers, packmen, soldiers home from the wars, beggars of all kinds. The Sty, as described in Chapter One, has always been an important highway.

As well as being an historical departure point and arriving place for travellers, Seathwaite has been, from time immemorial, an important sheep-farm, the home of Cumbrian statesmen, descendants of the Norse settlers. It has changed hands frequently: the popular notion that ancient statesmen families have occupied the same ancestral farmstead, century in, century out, is quite erroneous. Although it is possible that statesmen families occupied their same holdings for generation after generation in the medieval and Tudor periods, an examination of the movements of selected Cumbrian statesmen families within a circumscribed district and over a period of time dating from the mid-seventeenth century, reveals a surprising degree of mobility; to find one family occupying the same farmstead, for centuries on end, as in the case of the Graves of Skelgill, whose history is recounted in Chapter Four, would seem to be exceptional. For instance, parish registers tell us that Gatesgarth (like Skelgill and Seathwaite, one of the oldest and best known sheep farms in the region) was, in 1613, in the tenancy of Tickells, in 1708 of Greens, in 1762 of Robinsons, in 1798 of Mummersons, in 1806 of Peter Grave, in 1812 of the Vicars (or Vickers) family. By 1879 the Tysons, who followed the Vicars, had in their turn left Gatesgarth and the celebrated Mr Edward Nelson was there (the Nelsons coming from Undercrag, Mungrisedale); he was succeeded in 1934 by the Richardsons, who originated from Seathwaite and who are at Gatesgarth still today.

Miners and quarrymen have always been as symbolic of the Lake Country as shepherds. Seathwaite, over the centuries, has been as much a mining community as a pastoral one. Wrapped in fog and obscurity, high on the steep eastern slopes of Seatoller Fell, overlooking Seathwaite, lie the ancient wadd holes, from which came the once celebrated Borrowdale plumbago, or black-lead, as it was incorrectly but popularly called. For several centuries these holes were the only known source of pure plumbago in the world. Considering their one-time fame and their historical connections with the pencil industry, it is surprising to discover that these Seathwaite mines are enveloped in an obscurity not solely climatic.

The recorded history of wadd is patchy and largely unreliable, as is the case, too, with Keswick's famous pencil industry. Seatoller Fell, both literally and figuratively, is mist-distorted: distant rocks, looming through the fog like Peruvian pinnacles, dwindle, when approached, into stones a few feet high; Greenland bears become sheep; wadd, an established commercial commodity for over 300 years, proves amazingly elusive. The quest for its story, which readers will find in Chapter Three, developed for the author into an almost Alice-like adventure; the nearer she drew to wadd, the further did wadd recede.

The Cumbrian high country lives amongst clouds and the landscape is therefore never fixed; it changes from one moment to the next. Coleridge's description of the Lake Country sky as a non-stop theatrical performance was a very true one. After an early springtime morning of sunshine, violent hail and snow, you may find yourself walking, in sunshine again, over, say, Maiden Moor, with a snow-rimmed Helvellyn to the left, a sloe-coloured Great Gable to the right and the Langdale Pikes, blue and translucent, directly ahead. A bank of cloud broods over the Scafells. Before you have reached High Spy a large portion of this cloud bank has advanced to Dale Head and has settled there, solid as a load of bricks. The wind blows chilly, the cloud starts rolling down Dale Head toward Lobstone Band. Your route leads in a direction which implies head-on collision with this avalanche of cloud. Here it comes rolling, a white engulfing monster, swallowing the landscape whole. Stones and boulders protrude for a moment, like flotsam from a wreck, then they too are gone. The yawning space beneath Eel Crags whirls and eddies with coils of mist. The terrifying moment of being swallowed is immediately here; and then you are in the cloud; a moist and impenetrable world, cold on the face and smelling curiously of something definite, yet undefinable. You continue over descending ground; the mist grows thicker every moment. The track, always vague here, gets lost completely. Then a cairn appears; a vast one. Marvellous. Make for that! You make for it. The vast cairn proves an optical illusion, nothing more than a small and meaningless collection of stones that nature, not man, has assembled. The clouds drift and billow like net curtains swiftly drawn, one after the other, across an open window; between them another cairn is glimpsed. This time it must be genuine; so after it you lope. Odd how you never reach it! A mad sprint, a desperate dive; that cairn shall be reached! The cairn breaks into a wild, lolloping canter, like a loose-covered chesterfield on the run. It gives a frightening bleat, reveals itself as an idiotic old Herdwick ewe fleeing in terror.

There is only one thing to do and that is to stand immobile, listening. If you can hear the beck you will get your bearings. But positively nothing may be heard: no beck running, no scree trembling, for the moment no wind even. The universe is featureless, colourless, and you are totally alone in the centre of it. Out of the void the mist swirls, like the day God made the world. Then, suddenly, a rent is torn and there is a port-hole to peer through: black crag, screes, a breast of green fell-side with a spangle of sunlight moving across it. All this is clear, abnormally so; sharp in detail like a dream, but where exactly is it? The mist closes in again. Cautiously, one recommences walking downwards and presently the beck is heard, noisy after the melted snow:

> I have been here in the Moon-light,
> I have been here in the Day,
> I have been here in the Dark Night,
> And the Stream was still roaring away![1]

The streams of the region, with their eternal roaring, symbolised for Wordsworth the eternal voice of the truth of the region. The physical landscape of Cumberland is all too often cloud-concealed, indistinct and unreliable. The historical landscape of the fells bears remarkable resemblance to the physical; it is frequently obscure, with long passages of groping mystification, interspersed by sudden, intriguing revelations. Somewhere, nonetheless, is the truth; here buried underground, there obliterated by the mosses, now walled under stone, now dropping in a bright and deafening cataract, now murmuring in a little voice down an ancient syke, now swirling and singing in broad daylight. The artist or writer, groping for the essence of Cumberland, the truth about this region, must listen, like the traveller in the cloudy fells, for the voice of the stream.

The high country abounds with physical relics of the past; old roads and tracks, old walls, intakes, sheep-folds, farmsteads. It also abounds with old mines, quarries, mills: the sites of ancient industries. A mine-level or quarry is as essential a feature of this region as a sheep-fold or farmhouse, but whereas the latter will be universally looked upon with delight, there are still far too many people who deplore, even try to screen, what they insist upon calling "unsightly industrial scars". To the genuine lover of the region and to the artist, such scars are not only deeply interesting but also beautiful. They are an integral part of the Lake Country and to ignore them, or to attempt to ignore them, is a sentimental whim. For too many people the Lake Country is a kind of prettily nostalgic Never-Never Land; it is the reality which counts and which must be found and preserved before it is too late.

We, as a nation, are astonishingly unaware of our historical industrial achievement. Much more thought should be given to preserving something of the efforts of the early industrialists for the interest of generations to come and the sheer satisfaction of caring for a vital part of our national heritage. Industrially, the Lake Country, and especially Cumberland, is of immense importance, but the romantic school has for too long made the region its favourite (and virtually sacred) playground; shepherds are delightful, their old homes are lovely and should be cared for, but industry is ugly and rather vulgar, so old pits and quarries and mills should be forgotten, allowed to fall into neglected decrepitude as fast as possible, if necessary screened from the eye. Out of sight, out of mind. Let us concentrate upon wandering clouds and daffodils. Poets are charming men, miners are not.

The Cumbrian landscape cannot be seen in its truth all at once; it is not a giant mural in tasteful colours, or a Lakeland-at-a-glance modelled map, like that of Joseph Flintoft. The chiaroscuro of this region is subtle, complex, unique, as too is the Cumbrian character: one does not get to know this country, or its people, in one picturesque August fortnight. Perhaps the attempt to capture the truth of the region is futile: but every artist who works here, whether painter or writer, feels it necessary to commit to canvas or paper at least some impression of Cumberland as it is now, clear evidence of its past synthesised with its present, the two not divorced but part of a living reality, before the country is changed out of all recognition, as it may well be in the near future.

To do this, the artist can also employ a technique of synthesis, hoping to combine certain significant elements and ingredients into a revealing whole. The Cumbrian high country faces the writer with particular difficulty, for he cannot deal purely in shapes and colours and abstracts; he requires facts. Some are there to be seen with the naked eye; others have to be sought in the past, through books and records.

The industrial enterprises of the Cumbrian high country are but scantily recorded and documented. This is not altogether surprising, for the region remained inaccessible, remote, virtually unknown, for longer than any other county in England. Those who ventured to visit it and wrote about it produced work which was often misleading, rather than illuminating. Within the region itself some written records were doubtless made, but all too often they have not been preserved. It is significant that among the few surviving documentary records of old mining enterprise available today the most efficient are those of the sixteenth-century Germans of the Mines Royal Company! John Postlethwaite, who wrote comprehensively, in 1877, of the region's mines in his classic *Mines and Mining in the Lake District*, drew heavily upon John Clifton Wards's geological survey of 1876. Postlethwaite clearly used some other contemporary material too, which seems to have been provided by mining and quarrying companies active at the time, but this material appears to have become largely dispersed and lost, so that one cannot augment his pages with personal examination of those records which must have been at his disposal.

The records preserved at Millbeck in connection with its eighteenth and nineteenth-century woollen industry, described in Chapter Five, are unique; the region abounds with ancient mills which were formerly engaged in water-powered industry of various kinds, yet their ledgers and records seem all to have disappeared. The greater part of the records of the historic Keswick pencil-making firm of Banks & Co were destroyed by fire; some ledgers and day-books survived and are preserved in the County Archives office at Carlisle. These are the only known existing records of Keswick's boom period as a pencil-making centre.

Fox-hunting, a most important part of Cumberland's old, indigenous way of life, dates much further back in this region than is generally appreciated and has always been such an integral part of the daleman's existence that the study of it is not irrelevant. It has, however, gone almost wholly unrecorded. The bulk of the material in Chapter Eleven, "John Peel and the Blencathra", came either from veterans of the chase with whom the author had long and detailed interviews, or from Hugh Machell's definitive biography of John Peel, the substance of which Machell obtained first-hand from descendants of Peel and his hunting contemporaries.

The study of high country roads and tracks, a most essential feature of the landscape, takes the investigator over very clarty terrain indeed. Low-country roads of the region have been well written about in the invaluable *Transactions of the Cumberland and Westmorland Antiquarian and Archaeological Society*, but the tracks, trods, roads and mountain highways of up-country have been curiously neglected. Many people do not even realise that the greater part of these high-country routes were originally wrought, not simply by the basic process of walking over them, but in considerable part by roadmen, this construction work undertaken by the parish or township responsible for that particular locality. The account of high-country roads in Chapter One is drawn from various sources, including, largely, what might be termed the author's own field-research, while the detailed and fascinating evidence in Chapter Two, "Roads and Road-makers of Braithwaite", comes from a book of eighteenth and nineteenth-century road surveyors' records, preserved by the Bowe family, who most kindly and gener-ously put this unique old book at the author's disposal.

Much of that which, in the Cumbrian high country, is advanced as solid historical fact evaporates, cloud-like, upon close scrutiny into unsubstantial legend. A great deal of it must be relegated, however reluctantly, to the realm of folklore. Here, however, a problem arises. The hearsay regional lore that has been passed down from one genera-tion to the next has, somewhere in the obscure past, an origin founded, however shakily, on fact. This cannot be forgotten and to dismiss every tale as myth is pedantry of the most offensive kind! Myth in itself can be important: but how much myth is pure myth and how much is founded on distant historical fact, and where this fact lies buried, and how it can be got at, is the sort of problem which bedevilled the Old Men when they searched for silver in the Newlands fells.

Cumberland is a country of long memories; people have a habit of vividly describing, as if dealing with incidents of the previous week, events that happened a century or more ago. In some ways intensely revealing, so that for a brief moment one has the thrilling sensation of being truly in touch with the past, this can also be confusing, for invariably no dates are appended to these vibrating little fragments of history. These dateless, teasing anecdotes are like unidentified cairns, breaking into view through the mists of a cloud-submerged ridge.

Sometimes the anecdote carries a clue, evokes a memory of something else heard or read, so that it may be possible, with concentrated tracking, to pin it down at last to hard data. Sometimes one carries the tale in one's mind for months, years even, at last to encounter a similar isolated fragment of information which makes sudden sense of the first.

The late Mr George Bowe, who was in his nineties at the time, was kindly discoursing to me upon local lore in general, and his lengthy family tree and ancient statesman lineage in particular when, suddenly, he stopped short in his conversation and turned to me with a face of distress. "Have you heard about the terrible disaster up at the mine?"

"Which mine is that?" I asked, alarmed.

"Why, Stoneycroft mine, up yonder." He nodded in the direction of Barrowside and Stoneycroft Gill. "The early morning shift all lost; not one man saved!"

"How dreadful!"

"The main working yonder is in the gill bed; the shaft is in the bed of the beck itself, like. They built a dam upstream so that the water flowed aside, through a channel cut in the rock."

"Yes, I've seen it."

"Well, the lads had just gone down the mine on the early morning shift when the dam burst. The water poured back into its old course and down the shaft; every poor lad below ground was drowned. Every one. Nothing could be done to save 'em." He paused, his agitation great. He repeated, "Every one drowned. Not a thing could be done to save 'em."

His sister, almost as old as he, echoed his words, "All drowned. All drowned."

They stared at me with the faces of those who have lived in a community which has known tragedy. Mr Bowe continued, "They couldn't reach the bodies. Never so much as got one body out. Aye, it was a bad business. A black day for Newlands."

There was a melancholy silence in the little parlour. Miss Bowe, sighing, mournfully poked the fire in the range. Mr Bowe repeated yet again, "Aye, every poor lad drowned."

I had read about this disaster in Postlethwaite, who gave it no date. His account was a scant, dry, three or four-line reference, in no way comparable with Mr Bowe's, which bore all the stamp of the first-hand. Intrigued, I asked my host, "You don't remember this disaster, do you, Mr Bowe?"

"Nay, nay; well before my time. It was our father told us about it."

"He often spoke about it," said Miss Bowe. "A dreadful day in Newlands."

"Was it in your father's time?"

Mr Bowe reflected. "That I couldn't say for certain. I think it was, but I couldn't say for certain. It might have been in his father's time and he handed it down, like, but whenever it was that it happened, my father knew about it well. How the morning shift went down and then, almost directly after, the dam broke. It had been raining all night and there was a lot of water coming down at the time."

Here, then, was a tale of a local mine disaster, clearly originated from an eyewitness account that had been handed from one generation to the next. No official record of the disaster had been preserved; even the approximate date had been lost. Mr Bowe was quite unable to assist with suggestions for a possible date: father's time, grandfather's time, a remote possibility that it might even have been in his great-grandfather's time. He ruminated, sighed, shook his head, smiled apologetically. I was offered home-made raspberry cordial and short-cake biscuits.

According to Postlethwaite both the Stoneycroft Gill lead mine and the neighbouring Barrow mine dated back to the late sixteenth century. Both were worked, therefore, by the Old Men; Barrow mine mostly by tributers, e.g. lone prospectors who raised ore on their own account and paid a certain percentage or tribute to the proprietors of the mine. These old, lone miners made little piles of ore and then hid them for safety in a working. Sometimes the miner died before he could sell the ore and then the knowledge of his cache died with him. Between 1848 and 1865 two such storehouses were discovered in Barrow mine, together with old tools. The Keswick Mining Company worked Barrow mine intermittently, for the last time during the period 1848 to 1865. (It was reopened by the Barrow Mining Company in 1883 and proved quite profitable. It seems finally to have closed during the eighteen-nineties.)

Stoneycroft mine seems not to have been worked into the modern period, but to have been exclusively a province of the Old Men; which would bring its activity to a close by mid-eighteenth century, at the latest—"Old Men" being a term reserved for sixteenth, seventeenth, and early eighteenth-century miners. Postlethwaite makes it quite clear that it was the Old Men who dammed Stoneycroft beck (or Smelt Gill beck, as it is locally called—from the smelting works built in the gill in 1790 or thereabouts, when the sixteenth-century Newlands mines at the foot of Dalehead were reopened) and cut the channel through which the diverted water flowed. This dry channel, in the rock on the right-hand bank as one faces the gill from the bridge, may still be seen; the site of the burst dam, too, is discoverable upstream. The ancient workings in the gill bed are, of course, under water.

Since Coleridge made no mention of mine shafts and workings in the gill when he visited it in September 1800 (he only remarked upon the ivy growing on the picturesque old bridge, whose parapets were so low, he noted, that they came no higher than his ankles) we may take it as pretty certain that the disaster had occurred, and the flooded workings abandoned, some time before that date. All evidence considered, the early eighteenth century would seem the most likely date for the disaster. Mr Bowe's handed-down eyewitness account may have originated with his great-great-grandfather, or earlier.

The Cumbrian low country, not surprisingly, is far better documented and researched than the high. The Solway coast on Cumberland's side of the Firth and the plain inland is redolent with the spirit of eighteenth and nineteenth-century industrial boom, relics of industrial archaeology and enterprise adorn the scene in every direction: spoil heaps and mines, rows of miners' cottages, silted harbours, industrial architecture which is being ruthlessly pulled down by people who are in a fervour to escape from the clutch of the lost past and stagnant present in an attempt to embrace a newly booming future. In many respects the west Cumberland coastal belt is strongly reminiscent of parts of Brittany; Silloth, Maryport, Whitehaven and Millom contain whole streets and squares which might be Breton. Here one feels oneself in St Brieuc, there in a corner of St Malo as it was before the war. Allonby and its long beaches are strangely akin to the coast east of Ploumanach, while between Silecroft and Millom one might be travelling between Batz, Le Croisic and Guérande; which is not surprising, for both regions are ancient salt-pan lands. Yet Millom, once one is away from its main square, so curiously French, is full of astonishing visual excitements which could only be West Cumberland: the long, straight, rigid little streets of nineteenth-century industrial cottages, leading slap into a brooding, rearing mountain of slag; the slag-heap hard beyond the street, the Duddon estuary hard beyond the slag-heap, Furness beyond the estuary, the enormous sky over and beyond Furness. Whitehaven, in parts pure Côtes-du-Nord, lying deep in a basin among cliffs, could only be Cumberland when one glances up and sees a huge factory on the cliff-top, its tall chimneys waving enormous billows of purple, blue and amber smoke, the snow-topped mountains of the Copeland Forest rising inland, shining and mysterious, as the Solway gleams beyond the dark quays and sea-walls of the port and the Scottish shore broods beyond the Firth.

West Cumberland is crammed with visual delights and delicacies; a shop perched in a row clinging defiantly to the steep gradient of a hill, a window full of clogs of traditional pattern, some large for adults, some tiny for children, made, sold and worn today as they have been made, sold and worn since West Cumberland first had quaysides and work-floors.

In another shop window, this one overlooking a cobbled square, gleam row upon tiered row of glass sweet-jars, each jar packed with brilliant-hued sweets, a gorgeous sight no longer seen in swinging parts. And here is a rain-sodden, windswept little promenade with spiky ornamental trees looking dismally out of context and iron-banconied boarding-houses, like a fragment of Menton which has been wrenched North and undergone subtle, yet mortal change. Here is a long finger of quayside with a square harbourmaster's house and a great round rusted German mine plonked down beside at the end of it; here a drab-fronted, dusty-doored working-man's club with a single eye-shaped window in its wall; over there, on the tide-abandoned shore, glisten the stumps of an antique forest, while along a ridge of windswept land reclaimed from the shore straggles a Victorian cemetery and behind it a disused pit, with spoil-heaps, derricks and a gaunt, red-brick building with a black roof falling in.

This must be one of the most visually stirring stretches of coastline anywhere in the country, with its juxtaposition of sea, mountains and stark industrial landscape. It has produced important contemporary artists, among them Norman Nicholson, the poet, and Sheila Fell and Percy Kelly, painters.

Everyone who knows and loves the Solway will have a favourite industrial relic. The author confesses to a great fondness for the old Carlisle canal. Its history so well typifies the spirit of the burgeoning industrial and technical age: its tragedy, its comedy, its gusto, optimism and vitality. The canal's remains possess in marked degree the integrity and elegiac beauty which industrial archaeology of that period so significantly possesses for our plastic age. Some aspects of the story of this canal are given in Chapter Eight.

A very different aspect of Carlisle is given in Chapter Seven: the citizen's-eye view of the occupation of that city by Prince Charles Edward Stuart in 1745. Carlisle typifies the frenetic and often bloody history of the Border and also Cumbrian intransigence; the story of the occupation, of the City Militia, of the ambitious Whig Chancellor of the Diocese, Dr Waugh, and his indefatigable curate who was left behind in the occupied city to protect the Chancellor's plate, hay and wine-cellar, is one of Trollopian comedy and stark tragedy.

Carlisle is a fine capital for Cumberland. Although its city walls have long since gone Carlisle has retained character, individuality even, in the face of an era of conformist cities. One cannot yet mistake it for Wolverhampton or Slough; in Carlisle one is in Carlisle. The castle still stands, with its violent memories; the cathedral preserves some of its Norman magnificence.

The Cumbrian, it should be noted here, has a genius for rugged individuality, independence of spirit, inspired bloody-mindedness in short, which may have a desperately disconcerting effect upon the natives of lesser counties. If he decides that he wishes to pursue a different course from yours, or perhaps that he wants to be rid of you altogether, he will either go about it with a directness which can be pulverising or alternatively employ a delicacy of touch which makes swansdown seem a harsh substance. He is subtle, with a sublety which is deeply and dangerously underestimated by southerners. He is above all master of the speaking silence. André Maurois found the English a people who were at their most eloquent when they said nothing. His masterpiece, *Les Silences de Colonel Bramble*, is an unparalleled study of this national idiosyncrasy. The ancient Norse must have had the edge on the English in this, for in Cumberland non-conversation has been perfected to a degree which requires at least a decade of study for true appreciation of the art. "Aye?" can mean *no* to an extent to which the southern *no*, for example, can never aspire. "Oh aye?" can mean the entire Oxford Dictionary. But "Aye" uttered alone, or prefixed by the "Oh", must be judged, weighed, interpreted by the silence which precedes it and, even more important, the silence which follows, before the next verbal eloquence is embarked upon.

Yet the Cumbrian, once his words do start to flow, is the most articulate conversationalist in the kingdom. Here is true speech. But no gushing.

Cumberland, even today, remains a uniquely different and deeply satisfying country (it is more than a mere county). Cumbrians, it must be confessed, watch television, but they are still capable of switching off. "Dowse yon bugger," said a neighbour of mine, tersely, after several insufferable minutes of a certain television personality. The personality was accordingly dowsed. Cumberland has not yet been hypnotised.

The battles which rage there today are not of the bloody sort but of the aesthetic, and they are mainly fought by offcomes (the Cumbrian term for the not-bred-and-born Cumbrian). The great Thirlmere controversy is the subject of Chapter Nine. The proposed A66 road through the heart of the National Park is the great battle being waged at the time of writing.

Of all the offcomes who most delighted in and understood Cumberland, Samuel Taylor Coleridge must hold pride of place (although in Chapter Six he is examined as a fellwalker rather than an addict of Cumbria, his love and addiction may be spotted shining through his strenuous exploration of the tops). Time and again in his letters and journals one finds him repeating Cumbrian conversations, turns of speech, reporting customs, dwelling affectionately upon Cumbrian idiosyncrasies. He recalls the old man of eighty who remarked to him, "I hope in God's Mercy that He won't cut me off short in the midst of my Days." The old woman of seventy who pointed out a mountain-track, gave the poet the approximate time in which she thought he would climb it, then appended the time in which she, the septuagenarian, would do it, adding that she'd "gang like a daisy".

The journal entries in which Coleridge describes his fellwalking also contain long accounts of the conversations he had with the local people whom he met on his travels. He, a marvellous talker, had no difficulty in getting these people to talk. Particularly he loved to collect local place-names; always a sign of the true *aficionado*. On 12 September 1800, he climbed Grisedale Pike from Braithwaite, "over Heaviters and Long Ridge". These names he had got from shepherds; Heaviters—Heavysides—Outerside: the name can be traced through to the one which we use.

He expounded upon that fell which we now so lovingly know as Cat-bells, a name that seems not to have been used in his day. The Catbells ridge was then always referred to as Skelgill Bank and the highest point of Skelgill Bank was Howthwaite. The name Skelgill Bank is still in use, Howthwaite has dropped from usage; Skelgill Bank is now reserved for the Skelgill side of the neese of Catbells, while Brandel-howe lies on the lake side; here we meet with the "howe". Perhaps Coleridge was confusing Howthwaite with Yewthwaite (the combe reposing on the Littletown side of the fell), or perhaps Howthwaite is derived from Yewthwaite or, as seems more likely, Yewthwaite is a mispronunciation of Howthwaite; for we still have the hause over the saddle between Catbells and the commencement of Maiden Moor, and hause was sometimes in the old days written as "hawse", or even "howse", and by the lake we have Hawesend, which must be derived from How-thwaite, and Howthwaite may so well come from Hausethwaite, the thwaite of the hause! Of cats there are no early signs, but 'bields' are shelters, and on the Newlands side of Catbells is Martbield Crag; this fellside was once a great place for marts or martens and must have been so long after wild cats had disappeared from this area (the wild cat was extinct by the early nineteenth century, but the mart survived for nearly another century). But marts were an unknown quantity so far as tourists were concerned, while everyone knew about cats; so mart bield became cat bield and this in turn became Catbells. Therefore Catbells must be supposed, with however much reluctance, to be a tourist name and of fairly recent origin.

But Coleridge, as we learn from his journals, had an eye for much else besides place-names. "On a man's coffin, 'Died in his 208th year'. Bless me!—I enquire—he was 28 when he died—"

And of a character in Keswick; "Old Willy Bank has a passion for old antique Cupboards & Drawers & at different Sales of the old farms of the Country, he has bought 19— Now, how to reconcile this with his avarice?— Why, he lets them out to poor people at a shilling a year

each & they are to keep them in repair—he gets them 15 to 20 percent
for his money as few have cost him more than 3 or 4 shillings."

Another journal entry reads: "A large round of Beef. Sirloin of
Beef—a Ham, 4 Geese—4 Fowls—a Hare—2 Giblet Pies, 1 Veal Pye—
12 Puddings—Vegetables of all sorts. 1s 6d a head, at an annual Hunt-
Feat[?Feast] at Calthwaite, 7 miles from Penrith, on the Thursday before
Martinmas, 28 persons present." Ale, Coleridge added, was included.

Lavish feasts have always been a part of Cumbrian life. We are given
a description of a wedding feast by Robert Anderson, a pattern drawer
for calico printing who in his day (1770–1833) had a reputation as a
dialect poet:

THE CODBECK WEDDING

(To be sung to the tune of "Andrew Carr")

They sing of a weddin' at Worton
    Where aw was feight, fratchin' and fun';
Feegh! sec a yen we've hed at Codbeck
    As niver was under the sun:
The breydegruim was weaver Joe Bewley,
    He com frae about Lowthet Green,
The breyde, Jwonny Dalton' lish dowter,
    And Betty was weel to be seen . . .

Furst thing Oggle Willy, the fiddler,
    Caw'd in, wi' auld Jonathan Strang,
Neist stiff and stout, lang, laeme and lazy,
    Frae aw parts com in wi' a bang:
Frae Brocklebank, Faulders, and Newlands,
    Frae Hesket, Burkheads and the Height,
Frae Warnell, Stairnmire, Nether Welton,
    And awt 'way from Eytonfield Street . . .

For dinner, we'd stew'd geuse and haggish,
    Cow'd-leady, and hot bacon pie,
Boil'd fluiks, tatey-hash, beastin' puddin',
    Sant salmon, and cabbish, forbye
Pork, pancakes, black puddin's, sheep trotters,
    And custert, and mustert, and veal,
Grey-pez keale, and lang apple dumplin's—
    I wish every yen far'd as weel! . . .

Come bumper the Cummerlan' lasses,
   Their marrows can seldom be seen;
And he that won't feight to defend them,
   I wish he may ne'er want black een.
May our murry-neets, clay-Daubins, races,
   And weddin's aye finish wi' glee;
And when ought's amang us worth nwotish
   Lang may I be present to see.

('Cow'd-leady', or 'cowd-lword', was oatmeal pudding made with suet; 'boiled fluiks' was boiled flounder; 'beastin' puddin'' was a great delicacy—a kind of rich batter pudding made with the first milk of a cow newly calved, this milk being named beastings, or beastlings. 'Grey-pez keale' was dried-pea broth.)

The fellwalker new to the district is unaware than Cumberland is full of ghosts: not the variety locally known as "boggles", but the sort who survive in regional memories and tradition, figures who became part of the landscape in life and have left an imprint of themselves for posterity, gradually taking their place amongst local lore and legend. Some of these are explored among other matters mythical, and not so mythical, in Chapter Ten. The newcomer to the Lake Country sees only the scenery and feels himself to be wandering amongst it in delightful solitude, lonely as a cloud; he gazes happily at the open fell-sides, silent valleys, bare crags and windy horizons and the fewer people that there are about the more he congratulates himself upon having escaped from the crowds. But as the years pass and his visits to the region mount in number and his knowledge of the Lake Country increases in proportion, he discovers that he can never be alone, for processions of characters from the past, and not so distant past, throng the fells and frequent the dales. One such ghost is that of Coleridge himself; that agile, rather sprawling figure, bursting with youth and high spirits, bounding over the tops, afire with the joys of fellwalking. The shades of fox-hunters also roam, and legions of Old Men and generations of statesmen-shepherds. Here comes an eighteenth-century roadman to scrape a gutter; there toils a farmer's wife in her kilted petticoats, cutting peat; up the fellside climbs a quarryman with a sled.

These are figures in the mind's eye; very real nonetheless. When, two or three summers back, a farmer took to building a new fence by Scale Beck, beyond Crummock, conveying the fencing-materials across the fellside on a horse which he led by the bridle, his dog running at his heels (the ground being too soft for him to use his tractor for the job) it was hard to tell whether he was a man of today, or a vision from the past.

> I have been here in the Moon-light,
> I have been here in the Day,
> I have been here in the Dark Night,
> And the Stream was still roaring away. . . .

CHAPTER ONE

High Country, Low Country

GREAT DIVERSITY OF scenery and mood is Cumberland's salient characteristic. The Solway mosses and the pits and foundries of the West Cumberland plain and the bloodstained battlements of Carlisle hold as vital an essence of this region as do the screes of Great Gable, the pastoral peace of Loweswater, the birches and crags of Borrowdale. Tourist Lakeland is not Cumberland; merely a medley of high country beauty-spots glimpsed through daffodil-tinted spectacles. The fell-walker, as often as not, is as ignorant of the real Cumberland as the motorist; the region being for him nothing more than a series of tops over which he tramps enjoying what might be termed a strictly boot's-eye view. Occasionally he pauses on some western height to stare down at the coastal plain; he sees distant towns and water-towers and pit-heads and smoke-stacks and turns away with a shudder.

The distinction between high and low country in this region is a dramatic one, the mountains rising almost without preamble from the flatlands which curve from the estuary of the Duddon in the south to the dunes and marshes of the Solway Firth in the north, extending inland as a plain dominated by Carlisle, frontier, garrison and cathedral city. This plain reaches northwards to Longton on the English side of the Border, and Gretna just over it, and to Kirkcambeck lying below Cumberland's most northerly town, Bewcastle, sheltering in the foot-hills of the Cheviots. To the south the plain embraces Brampton and Wetheral under Cold Fell on the north-western flanks of the Pennines and thereafter merges into the rolling agricultural landscape of the Eden valley, guarded by Cross Fell to the east and Penrith to the west.

Beyond this old market town the mountains leap up in echelons; the successive battalions of Skiddaw, Helvellyn, Newlands and Coledale, the Scafells, the Gables, Pillar and the Copeland Forest, their heights enfolding narrow valleys, some with glacial lakes. The central barrier of this high country, the Scafell *massif*, rears like a wall between the landlocked north-eastern side of the region and the coastal belt of the south-west; a wall breached only by the Norsemen's famous pass, the Sty.

The Norse invasion of the region was a penetrating one, cutting as deeply into the Cumbrian dales as the ice that had first hewn them from the rock. The appearance of the Norse on Solway shores had been preceded by the heathen Danes, who, under Halfdan, had in 875 sacked Carlisle with such brutality that it lay derelict for the next two hundred years. The stay of the Danes in Cumberland was a comparatively fleeting one; they moved on, northwards and eastwards, into Northumberland and Yorkshire. The Norse arrived in 925, coming up the Solway in a steady infiltration, not directly from Norway but having sojourned for a considerable time amongst a Gaelic-speaking race, whose language had to some extent affected their own and from whom they had learned something of Christianity. From the tenth to the twelfth century these Norse immigrants arrived, gradually building up a dense settlement of the flat Cumbrian coastal belt. In due course the Norsemen penetrated into the mountains of the hinterland where, their inclinations being pastoral rather than agricultural, they and their descendants settled as sheep-farmers. They lived in scattered farmsteads and small hamlets, draining and clearing the marshy daleheads to provide sheltered low-altitude pastures and crop-bearing land which they enclosed with stone walls; thus over the course of time producing the valleybottom landscapes of today with their farms surrounded by patterns of walled intakes.

Other races had thought these mountains theirs before the Norsemen. Stone-age men searched among them for flint-beds. Bronze-age fell-settlers succeeded them, to be in their turn followed by the celebrated Brigantes, or hill-men, whom the Romans found so difficult to subdue. That these people, and the British of the post-Roman kingdom of Strathclyde, must from time to time have used the pass which we call the Sty may be accepted as something more than mere conjecture; it was the only route available.

Hederlanghals[1] was the name which the Norse colonisers gave to this natural highway in its entirety: a name deriving from the Icelandic *Heidar-lang-háls*, the long pass of the heath or wild fells, *heidar-vegr* being a track over fells and moors, *lang* long, and *háls* a pass, a steep way over or between, a "hause" in fact, such as we commonly meet with throughout the Lake Country (Newlands Hause, Hause Point, High Hause Gap and so on). As truly descriptive a name for the pass today, one would say, as when the Norse first used it. Yet the name *stigi*, a ladder or sharp ascent, which they reserved for the opening section of the pass (the climb up from Stockley Bridge) is the name which we give now to the entire route from Seathwaite to Wastdale Head; the Sty, or as older local people more correctly pronounce it, the Stee.

From Styhead branches, on one side, the long rake of Esk Hause, leading the traveller to upper Eskdale by Ure Gap, or down Rossett Gill to the Langdales with their access to Windermere, Coniston and Furness; on the other side, the cleft of Aaron Slack between Great and Green Gable takes one away to Ennerdale and Buttermere, the Lorton fells and the north-western coast. In short, Styhead is the hub of a system of mountain highways, trodden since time immemorial.

The specific aim of the Romans when they arrived in the region was military subjugation. For this they required speedy and well-fortified routes of communication and to this end they built and used a road system which encircled, rather than cut through, the main mountain mass of the area. Their conquest of Britain was gradual and there was no real attempt at a northward thrust beyond the Trent until Petillius Cerealis, one of Vespasian's ablest generals, made great progress during the period A.D. 71–74 with the conquest of the Brigantes in Yorkshire. His successor, Julius Frontinus, had by A.D. 77 probably advanced as far north as York. He was succeeded by Agricola and under his governorship the Roman conquest of the North began in earnest.

In A.D. 78 he advanced northwards by a road driven from Chester (Deva) to Carlisle (Luguvallium); in that same campaign garrisons were placed between Solway Firth (Ituna Aest) and Tyne. Consolidation of these northern gains was achieved by further campaigns of A.D. 79 and 80, the action being concentrated upon the eastern routes of advance. A line of forts was established between Clyde and Forth. In A.D. 81 a northwards advance was made along the west coast from Chester via

Lancaster to Solway Firth and Dumfries: an invasion of Ireland was possibly planned (although never carried out) since this west-coast campaign included the establishment of military posts along the coast facing Ireland. A.D. 82 saw Agricola's advance into Caledonia and the following year, in Perthshire, he shattered the army of the Caledonian league. The words of Calgacus, one of the leaders of the Caledonians (whom today we would describe as a guerrilla-fighter leader) reach us with a timeless, partisan ring, as he describes the Romans as, "Brigands of the world . . . East and West have failed to glut their maw. They are unique in being as violently tempted to attack the poor as the wealthy. Robbery, butchery, rapine, the liars call Empire; they create a desolation and call it peace."[2]

The Romans failed to follow up their Grampian Hills victory over the Caledonians; they pressed no further north. At the close of this campaign Agricola was recalled to Rome and his northern military successes were followed by a period of peace, or desolation, not broken until late in the reign of the Emperor Trajan (A.D. 98–117) when the Brigantes revolted, during the course of this revolt destroying the famous Ninth Legion. Hadrian, Trajan's successor, built his celebrated wall along the line of Agricola's forts from Carlisle to Newcastle; according to Tacitus, "It was observed by experts that no general had ever shown a better eye for ground than Agricola. No fort of his was ever stormed, ever capitulated or was ever abandoned."

Thereafter the northern tribes submitted, without further serious defiance, to Roman rule. The Brigantes became comparatively civilised; the less aggressive developed agricultural interests, while the belligerently inclined were recruited by their military masters as auxiliary troops. (These auxiliaries, recruited chiefly from provinces that were new and warlike, were often permitted to use their native weapons but were wisely employed in service away from their homeland. They obtained Roman citizenship upon discharge.) Trading towns were developed, Carlisle becoming a particularly prosperous example in our region, and settlements grew up near the larger forts.

The Romans had as their chief Cumbrian ports Maryport (Uxellodunum) and Ravenglass, which was guarded by the fortress of Glennaventa. A coastal road round Furness and along the fortified southern shore of the Solway linked up with Carlisle, whence ran both the walled highway to the Northumberland coast and a road southward to the important fort at Brocavum (today's Brougham, near Penrith). At Brocavum commenced the major Roman mountain highway of the region, which travelled over Barton Fell and along the ridge between Martindale and Bampton commons, descending at last to Troutbeck (Windermere); nigh on thirty miles of sustained and very aptly named High Street. This mountain route connected, at the fort of Galava at the head of Windermere, with the road via Little Langdale, Wrynose and Hardknott (where stood another fort, Mediobogdun) and thus down Eskdale to Glennaventa.

Roman occupation of the area terminated at the opening of the fifth century, after a period lasting more than three hundred years. At least parts of the Roman road system were still in use in the Lake Counties at the close of the Middle Ages; the monasteries made additions to the existing mileage of Roman roads to suit their own needs. One such road, for instance, traces of which have been found near Ulverston and Millom, is thought to have run round Furness and the south Cumberland coast as an extension of the Lancaster road over the Kent and Leven estuary sands. Other medieval roads were the "street" from Appleby to Tebay in Westmorland, the Brampton "streitte" to Appleby, the "great street" (*magna strata*) from Kendal to Shap and the "ordinary road through to Bassenthwaite" mentioned in a grant to Holm Cultram abbey about 1317.[3] These monastery-developed roads, it has been said, were "less thoroughly constructed, but enough like Roman roads to be mistaken for them". (However, one authority on early roads, Mr R. L. Bellhouse, doubts whether monasteries were active in building metalled roads.[4])

These were low country and foothill thoroughfares. The routes through the *massif* followed the natural passes that are still in use; routes which for centuries would have been no more than rough pedestrian trods. When animals were introduced for pack-carrying, the better frequented of these trods became accepted pony tracks; in due course, as pack-pony traffic increased to the point where trains of ponies were regularly used, these tracks needed to be, at least in part, causeyed and surfaced in order to prevent the terrain being reduced here to shilly-bed, there to quagmire.

Examples of such time-honoured routes include the track across Burnmoor, also renowned as a corpse-road (a road along which bodies were borne by horse or pony from a community which possessed no burial ground to a community which did); the old fell road from Hard-knott to Dunnerdale via Grassguards (pronounced Grassgars, a true Norse name for this isolated farmstead which originated as a *saetr*, or summer high-altitude fold); the road from Eskdale Green to Ulpha across Birker and Ulpha Fells, as well as the ancient track which branches off from this, to pass along the southern shore of Devoke Water, descending thereafter by Barnscar, Birkby Fell, place of cairns (borrans) and lost civilisation of which Coleridge, unsuccessfully searching for ruins, sighed, "*Albinus omnino nihil*," adding, to encourage himself, "However, the view is very fine. Sauce better than the fish . . ." This track in former times led to the ford over the Esk at Waber-thwaite, thence to Ravenglass.

The pass of Coledale Hause, connecting Lanthwaite Green, where there was an early British settlement, with Braithwaite and the Derwent fells, must be as ancient a way as the Sty itself. The track from Wast-water to Ennerdale, via Nether Beck and Tewit How, a nowadays much-neglected pedestrian route, was for centuries a favoured pony track, saving the traveller a long journey round the great mass of the Copeland Forest; a similar track, cutting across a great mass of upland country, which would otherwise have had to be encircled, was the track over Skiddaw Forest via Whitewater Dash, Skiddaw House and Burnt Horse, connecting Bassenthwaite and Threlkeld. A well-used time-saver, too, was the partly causeyed route from Buttermere via Dubs Bridge and Scale Beck over Floutern to the open country below Ennerdale Water. The track from Thirlmere by Harrop Tarn, Long Moss, Watendlath Fell and Watendlath, from there either descending to Rosthwaite or, alternatively, continuing by Ashness Bridge and Derwent Water to Keswick, was a pack-animal route long associated with the wool-trade. All these (to name but a few) are traditional short-cut routes; all must have been in use since men first began to frequent the high country. Attentive examination of them reveals that many are in certain parts causeyed and metalled and/or in other ways constructed: such road construction is unlikely to date before mid, or late, seven-teenth century.

The drift (Icelandic *edrift*) roads of the Norse-descended sheep-farmers are among the earliest roads of the high country. These were the tracks along which flocks passed from a farmstead or small settlement up to the *heaf*, or grazing stint, belonging to that particular farmstead.

Such drift roads abound throughout the district and are still regularly used by the sheep and shepherds of today. One good example is that which gives the sheep of Grange in Borrowdale access to the grazing grounds of Maiden Moor and Scawdel Fell; this ascends by Swanesty How to an old sheep-fold above Cockley How and thence climbs between Nitting Haws and Blea Crag on to the open fell, here a dreary waste of quagmire, moss and peat-holes. It is, for sheep, the only way up and through this precipitous fellside, although it holds no joy for fellwalkers, being specifically purpose-created for flocks and flockmasters. Wainwright correctly gives it as a "tedious ascent".[5]

Other primitive early roads were the peat-roads, which remain well marked, as they were frequently used by carts, as well as by sleds and ponies. The most fascinating of these is surely that which crosses Threlkeld and Matterdale commons between Hill Top, St John's in the Vale, and High Row, Dockray. Although this road is marked on Ordnance Survey and some other maps as an old coach-road, there is no authenticated evidence, or local legend either, to support the claim that such was ever its purpose. Clearly, wheeled horsedrawn vehicles have used this road over the centuries and some of these may well have been local transport carts of various kinds, but it is extremely improbable, to say the least, that coaches ever regularly passed this way. On the other hand, there is much local testimony to show that this was a well-established peat-road. Its earliest origins possibly reach back to the ancient British, who had a settlement on Threlkeld common. Thus, as well as being a peat-road, this thoroughfare must rank as one of the region's oldest general transport routes.

Many of the region's best surviving causeyed and metalled routes are those built specifically for the transport of quarried stone and mined ore. Some of these mine roads are of very ancient origin: silver and lead, for instance, were mined intermittently in the Alston Moor region even before 1133, while foreign experts such as Thomas of Almayne in 1324, Tilman of Cologne in 1359 and others in 1478, were engaged in prospecting and mining. The Society of Mines Royal, formed in 1561, involved the formation of a considerable network of high-country transport routes; these mine roads may therefore be dated with certainty at the end of the sixteenth century and early decades of the seventeenth.

Particularly good examples of such roads are the old road from Grange to Honister, with its finely preserved causey beneath Castle and Gate crags and its partly causeyed link-road from Longthwaite; the pack-pony route from Threlkeld to Brigham, especially well discernible in the neighbourhood of the ford at Brundholme (at Brigham were the Mines Royal smelting works); and the marvellous network of Mines Royal ore roads in the Newlands-Manesty region. Well worth exploration, too, are the old sledgates and quarrymen's tracks of the Honister district.

However, the date of actual construction of the Sty and kindred general transport routes of the high country is shrouded in obscurity. Archaeological study of them is unlikely to be rewarding, since unworked local stone was used and this is quite undatable. There is chronicled indication that the track from Stockley Bridge up Grain Gill, which joins Esk Hause just above Sprinkling, or, as it was formerly called, Sparkling tarn, was established as a causey by the thirteenth century, but to what extent this may have been a constructed causey, if at all, we do not know. Examination of constructed routes indicates that they were wrought only over ground that was particularly rough, miry or steep. The Sty seems to be unique amongst the pack-animal routes of the region inasmuch as it was a built road virtually for its entire distance, which is some indication of its importance.

The Sty causey commenced just beyond Seathwaite farm and proceeded from thence to Stockley Bridge, following the left-hand side of the beck, the infant Derwent. Thirty years ago one could still perceive quite easily that this track had once been an elevated and metalled way, but the procession of hikers and the celebrated Borrowdale floods of 1966 have now, in combination, all but wholly obliterated this first section of the causey (indeed this dalehead is steadily deteriorating into a desolation of stones, worsening every year). Stockley Bridge, a fine example of a small Lake Country pack-pony bridge, was also damaged by the floods but has been carefully restored.

Beyond Stockley Bridge comes the veritable *stigi*; now a clambering maze of rough pedestrian tracks with the causey almost vanished, although there are traces of it directly above the bridge. The comfortable section of paved way, contouring on the left, halfway between the bridge and the gate in the wall, which has been hailed as "a splendidly preserved stretch of the ancient pony-track", is, in fact, the work of Mr Vickers, a roadman who, some thirty years ago, constructed this length of cobbled way as a gutter to carry down water from the drains which served this part of the pass.[6]

The maze of pedestrian trods converge at the gate in the wall into a single route. The actual causey can be discerned again a short distance beyond the gate, zig-zagging above the present route, which it rejoins just above Taylor Gill Force, and from thereon it may be followed by the attentive observer all the way to Styhead tarn. Several sections of this upper reach of road are very distinct; there are two particularly good expanses which nobody can miss. The causey crosses the beck, which the Norse named Ederlange and which we call Styhead beck, two or three yards above the present wooden footbridge; today's pedestrian track is touchingly faithful to the old route.

The causey throughout the greater part of its extent upon this Borrowdale side of the pass was elevated, with a ditch or syke on either hand; a very necessary precaution considering that the beck runs immediately beside the causey and is prone to bursting into spate at the slightest provocation. Over the wet peaty ground near Styhead tarn the old route becomes less easily traceable and concentration is required to follow it along the right-hand shore of the tarn to the mountain rescue-post which today marks the head of the pass. Tradition maintains that here was once a rude stone shelter.

From the rescue-post the pony route takes a fairly level, diagonal course for a hundred yards or so in the direction of Round How, then commences a most skilfully contoured and, in its first stage, cairned descent to Spouthead Gill, which it crosses, to continue down to cross Grainy Gill. Then further down it crosses Spouthead Gill again at its junction with Piers Gill (that most awesome and indeed gothic chasm into which, during the nineteen-twenties, fell a Mr Cornelius Crump who broke his ankle and lay in the gill, without food but with water mercifully at hand, for three weeks before he was found, weak but alive, an incident which will never be forgotten in Wastdale Head). Piers Gill and Spouthead Gill unite to become Lingmell Beck. The pony-track continues down the right-hand side of this beck to level out in the dale bottom. There it joins the old pedestrian trod which traverses the flanks of Great Gable in descent from Styhead and which, originally developed as an alternative to the pony-track in order that travellers might not be held up by the slow-plodding trains, is today the accepted and much shorter and speedier route this Wastdale side of the Sty. Pony-track and pedestrian trod, once united, then proceed to the intakes of Burnthwaite.

The Sty's branch road, Esk Hause, also reveals sections which were formerly causeyed, especially in the neighbourhood of Sprinkling and Angle tarns, while the zig-zagged pony-track in Rossett Gill gives evidence of careful contouring and construction. At the highest point of the Hause is a pile of boulders, possibly the final remnants of the shelter which once was here and which some maps still mark, most misleadingly, as being in existence today.

The solitary modern pedestrian given to musing too enthusiastically upon the past while returning, say, over the Sty on a rainy evening in the back-end (autumn), when the summer's tourists are all forgotten and the fells are their lonely, evocatory selves again, will find it easy, in the misty failing light, to start hearing and seeing things: rough, shouting voices snatching on the wind, a striking of hooves against stone, the jingling of pony bells and harness—all the sounds of a pack-train coming up the pass. Staring nervously back down the track the twentieth-century traveller will see boulders detach themselves and move, shapes gather and define, so that soon a whole eighteenth-century procession of ponies and men will appear; the ponies each wearing a halt and the men carrying long staves. This pack-train, every instant becoming more clearly visible, climbs steadily up the pass, the voices of the drovers, the snorting of the ponies, the clatter of hooves and jingling of bells increasing in volume; there is even a smell of pony! At this point the lone pedestrian either turns and flees, regardless of sprained ankles, convinced that a procession of ghosts are on his tail, or, too paralysed by consternation to move, remains rooted to the spot, watching and waiting, finally to have the pack-ponies resolve into a straggle of sheep, the men into boulders and shadows, the voices, hoof-echoes and bells into a natural combination of those wind-sounds which forever wander and sigh among mountains, while the smell of pony identifies itself as wet Herdwick, wet self, wet rock, wet everything.

Hallucinations of this sort, while totally unknown to some persons, are common enough to other, less rational, souls; the half-light of early morning and late evening being especially conducive to encounters with everything and everyone, from mammoth elephants miraculously survived from the Ice Ages, to the Abbot of Furness riding out on circuit upon his mule, or William Wordsworth taking a stroll.

It is frequently suggested that the monks of Furness Abbey originally constructed the Sty causey. Furness had a manor in Borrowdale which included pasturage, several *saetrs*, a grange, a cornmill and the saline springs at Manesty (the monks may perhaps also have worked the wadd holes at Seathwaite, but this is very uncertain). Furness also had a large *saetr* at Throstlegarth in upper Eskdale, forests and bloomeries at Coniston, grazing in the fells above Dunnerdale and it used the seaports of south-west Cumberland, to mention but a few of its interests and activities; thus the Sty and Esk Hause would have been obvious routes of communication and transport for the monks. No mention, however, has been found of causeys in the Furness documents and it must therefore be regarded as very doubtful that the Sty causey is of pre-Reformation origin. The most acceptable theory is that it was built by the parishioners of Borrowdale on the one side and Wastdale on the other, as part of their ancient local government obligation to construct and maintain necessary roads. Since no effective system of road maintenance can be said to have existed before 1555, one would hesitate to place the building of the Sty causey before the latter half of the sixteenth century at the earliest; probably the safest date to hazard would be late seventeenth century.

As for the likely date of the commencement of the Sty's decline, the great days of the pack-pony trains ended during the second half of the eighteenth century and it was for the pony trains that the causey was built and maintained. Housman's map of 1802 shows a road over Styhead; it is true that maps of that period were highly misleading about roads, but there can be little doubt that there was a much better route over the Sty in 1802 than in 1970!

Even when the pack-pony trains had dwindled almost to nothing, the mountain highways continued to be well used by travellers. The years of the closing eighteenth and opening nineteenth century saw, in the Lake Country, a varied and comparatively large itinerant labour force; the isolated farms, hamlets and quarries, mines and mills rendered it necessary for workers to travel long distances on foot, pursuing employment. From various sources we obtain glimpses of these people treading the high country roads and tracks: quarrymen and miners, drovers, wallers, charcoal-burners, bobbin-makers, weavers, wool-combers, bone-setters, tailors and tutors (who stayed weeks, sometimes months at a time, working for one household before journeying to the next), fiddlers-cum-dancing masters, turners, joiners, basket-makers, chair-menders, tinkers, mole-catchers, faith-healers, scriveners, salvers, pedlars and packmen, general labourers willing to turn a hand to anything and, finally, beggars of all descriptions, many of whom had a regular beat, or lait as it was called; to go laiting being to beg, to collect or seek (Wordsworth's poem, "The Old Cumberland Beggar", is very informative upon this subject).

These travellers were the news-carriers of the day to the statesmen and cottagers living within the recesses of the fells. Persons who lived near a well-frequented route were never short of information (albeit garbled), but if one dwelt in some remote spot far from a road one might become badly out of touch. Coleridge and the Wordsworths were fond of quoting the (perfectly authentic) story of an old spinning woman who lived near Bampton; talking to the gentlefolk one Good Friday when conversation turned to the subject of the Crucifixion, she sighed, "I hope they haven't killed the poor gentleman— Well, it is so long ago and so far away, that I hope it is not true— O well—we live up under the Hill here—we do never hear a bit of news!"

Today's traveller over the Sty, looking down into Wastdale Head, sees a scene closely resembling that which those earlier travellers saw; the dark Icelandic gleam of Wastwater, the narrow, deep vale with its intricate patterns of stone-walled intakes, the claustrophobic involvement of fells, lake, screes and patch-worked pasturage giving way to open plain and sea, Cumberland's coastal belt.

This low country is of great and subtle beauty in which industry, much of it of very ancient origin, and natural landscape have together produced a fascinating synthesis. Here, in medieval times, salt was produced by evaporation of sea-water in coastal salt-pans; this industry, however, was far in decay by the reign of Elizabeth I and evidence of it now is only to be found in some of the place names, e.g.; Silecroft, Silloth. The region between Seascale (celebrated now for atomic power) and Maryport was a source of iron and coal; iron was worked in the Egremont district from the early twelfth century and coal dug in the Whitehaven district before 1272, though neither iron-working nor coal-mining really attained dimensions worthy of the title 'industry' until the seventeenth century. By the early eighteenth century Egremont, Cleator, Whitehaven, Distington, Harrington, Workington and Maryport were thriving industrially in the fullest sense, while textile production flourished at Cockermouth, Dalston, Carlisle, Wetheral and Brampton. Pottery and clay pipes were made at Dearham and Little Broughton, and sailcloth and rope in the district about Whitehaven, where there was also an eighteenth-century tobacco manufacturing industry. Much of West Cumbrian industry dating back into the past is now quiescent, but there are several flourishing new ventures in the region, which doggedly believes that there is an industrial renaissance awaiting it in the near future.

The political history of Cumberland is largely Border history and therefore is restless and bloody.[7] The flavour of the turmoil and violence of this country reaches us with particular clarity in the music of the famous *Kinmont Willie*, a traditional ballad, thought to have been largely rewritten by Sir Walter Scott:

> O have ye na heard o' the fause Sakelde?
>   O have ye na heard o' the keen Lord Scroope?
> How they hae ta'en bauld Kinmont Willie
>   On Haribee to hang him up?

Harraby is Carlisle's traditional execution place, Lord Scroope Thomas, tenth Baron Scrope of Bolton, Warden of the West Marches of England, and Kinmont Willie (William Armstrong of Kinmont), a noted Scots freebooter, "broken-man" (outlaw) or "moss-trooper" (the three titles being synonymous).

The Border abounded with such lawless individuals, who flourished against the background of traditional raiding, feuding and skirmishing in which both sides, Scots and English, participated equally. Southern opinion lumped them all together under the derogatory name, "The Bad Borderers". Moss-trooping, romantic as it sounds, was nothing more than a system of professional robbery, its chief exponents being certain virtually outlawed families, of whom the Grahams of the

English West Marches, Armstrongs of Liddesdale in the Scots Middle Marches, the Carletons and Giffords were the most notorious.

Kinmont Willie was arrested by the English authorities in March 1596 while he was (technically) protected by a trew (Border truce meeting). The Kinmont was handed over to Mr Salkerd ("the fause Sakelde"), Scrope's deputy, who immured Kinmont in Carlisle castle. Lord Buccleugh, after trying unsuccessfully to parley for Kinmont's release, rode out at dead of night on 13 April, with 500 horsemen of his own clan (Scrope's estimate) and a party of the Kinmont's friends (whom Buccleugh later asserted to have been the Grahams and Carletons), broke into the castle and carried Kinmont Willie away.

The Scots' estimates of the size of Buccleugh's party vary from three-score to ten-score; the ballad tells us that with forty marchmen, all of whom save one, Sir Gilbert Elliot, were kinsmen of his, Buccleugh set forth in spurs and armour, green gloves and blue feathers. Ten of his men, again so says the ballad, were arrayed like huntsmen, ten as fighting men (including, it seems, the laird himself), ten like a mason gang, carrying tall ladders and the rest like broken-men or outlaws, which of course was precisely what they were.

> And as we crossed the 'Bateable Land,
> When to the English side we held,
> The first o' men that we met wi'
> Whae should it be but fause Sakelde?

Salkerd, continues the ballad, questioned them as to their mission. The huntsmen parried the question by saying that they were off to hunt an English stag that had trespassed into their country, the fighting men said that they were out to catch a man who had broken faith with Buccleugh, while the mason lads tactfully explained away their ladders by saying that they were "gang to herry a corbie's nest." But when the broken-men came to be questioned their leader, one Dickie of Dryhope, of whom we are succinctly told that "never a word of lear (learning, lore) had he", made no attempt to evade the interrogator with verbal subtleties but, objecting both to being stopped and to being addressed as a "row-footed outlaw", thrust his lance through fause Sakelde without ado, after which the party rode on.

Then we held on for Carlisle toun,
   And at Staneshaw-bank the Eden we crossed;
The water was great and mickle of spait,
   But the never a horse nor man we lost.

And when we reached the Staneshaw-bank
   The wind was rising loud and hie;
And there the laird garred leave our steeds,
   For fear that they should stamp and nie.

And when we left the Staneshaw-bank,
   The wind began full loud to blaw;
But 'twas wind and weet, and fire and sleet,
   When we came beneath the castle wa'.

We crept on knees, and held our breath,
   Till we placed the ladders against the wa';
And sae ready was Buccleuch himsell
   To mount the first before us a'.

He has ta'en the watchman by the throat,
   He flung him down upon the lead—
Had there not been peace between our lands,
   Upon the other side thou hadst gaed!

'Now sound out, trumpets!' quo' Buccleuch;
   'Let's waken Lord Scroope right merrilie!'
Then loud the warden's trumpet blew—
   O wha dare meddle wi' me.

O wha dare meddle wi' me, an ancient fighting refrain, inflamed the rescue party:

Then speedily to wark we gaed,
   And raised the slogan ane and a',

And cut a hole through a sheet of lead,
　And so we wan to the castle ha' . . .

Wi' coulters, and wi' forehammers,
　We garred the bars bang merrilie,
Until we came to the inner prison,
　Where Willie o' Kinmont he did lie . . .

The Kinmont was lifted up by Red Rowan, "the starkest man in Teviotdale" and borne down the ladders. During this descent Kinmont Willie shouted derisive messages to Lord Scrope, bidding him farewell and promising to pay him rent for accommodation in the castle when next they met the other side of the Border. Lord Scrope, not ready to let his prisoner escape, gave chase with a party on horse and on foot. Buccleugh and his men plunged again into the Eden, now flowing full spate after the wild night's rain; they reached the safety of the opposite shore. Lord Scrope preferred not to follow.

The Grahams were at all times a thorn in the flesh of Lord Scrope, who referred to them as "caterpillars", a "viperous generation" and "malignant humours" (*Border Papers*, Scot. Rec. Pub. vol ii, 114–5). After the Kinmont Willie episode an effort was made to have strong measures taken against them but, to Scrope's annoyance, Elizabeth refused to sanction such action. The moss-troopers used certain techniques of intimidation which seem familiar enough to us today, including the levying of blackmail, as it was called. Persons were carried off from their homes by the outlaws, in other words kidnapped, and kept until redeemed by ransom. The Grahams openly referred to this "black maile" (the term coined by the victims of the racket) as "protection money or a reward *pro clientela*". Occasionally they referred more euphemistically to the "protection money" as "Defence moneys".

Ultimately the over-confident Grahams went too far. While James I was at Berwick on his way south to London and coronation as the first monarch to unite England and Scotland, the Grahams led a destructive foray, penetrating Cumberland as far as Penrith. Following this, the Border Country (referred to now as the Middle Shires) was placed under the jurisdiction of a royal commission and governed as a Crown colony. Sir Wilfred Lawson was elected governor in 1605. The commissioners were above all else determined to be rid of the Grahams, 150 of whom were forcibly enlisted in the Army and sent to Flushing and Brill. Most of them returned home without leave. They were then ordered to be arrested and imprisoned; they vanished into the mosses and eluded the law. Finally the clan agreed to be transported to Ireland: thus 114 Grahams and 45 horses travelled to Connaught, wives following. Many, in due course, trickled quietly back.

Furthermore, even with the Grahams gone, other awkward families, including the aforesaid Armstrongs, Carletons and Giffords, remained to trouble the Border. Lord William Howard, who was recusant and therefore unable (officially)to hold a post under the Crown, was renowned as a successful hunter of moss-troopers. King James turned a blind eye to the recusancy and employed Lord William as a very effective influence against Border lawlessness.

Cumberland was Royalist during the Civil Wars, and afterwards Commonwealth placed the county under the governorship of Sir Arthur Haselrig. The region experienced a period of great poverty and recession, but the old intransigency clearly survived. Following the Restoration it became necessary for Charles II to pass an Act "preventing . . . theft and rapine upon the Northern Borders of England", for the work of "lawless and disorderly persons, commonly called moss-troopers" had "increased since the time of the late unhappy distractions". A crude police system was established, consisting of an officer called the Country Keeper and twelve men, for the purpose of hunting thieves and bringing them to justice. By Act 18 Charles II c. 3, ". . . great and notorious thieves and spoil takers in the counties of Northumberland and Cumberland shall suffer death as felons without benefit of clergy, or may be transported for life by order of the judge and assize". Bonds of the Country Keepers continued to be registered with the clerk of the peace at Carlisle until 1756, at about which time the justices ceased to have the Act renewed.

The numerous surviving fortified homesteads of the county intensify further our sense of the recurrent violence which flickered and exploded along the Border, never allowing the region fifty consecutive years of quiet until after 1745. These fortified, larger houses were built not only along the Border itself and upon the sea coast, but even were necessary in the Eden valley: here the houses on the edges of the agricultural land, where it met the open fell, were strongly fortified, although in the sheltered heart of the vale fortification was considerably lighter. The earliest surviving fortified houses are the pele-towers (pile-towers): defensive structures of fire-resistant stone, built in the fourteenth and fifteenth centuries. Their defence was of a passive nature, depending mainly upon the solidity of the building. When the beacons warned the region that attack was imminent the local humble populace hurried to their lairds' pele-towers for protection, placing their livestock in a walled and guarded corral.

After physical violence had ceased to torment the region, the low country enjoyed a long period of industrial expansion and prosperity. The histories of the Senhouse, Curwen and Lowther families admirably illustrate the abundant and aggressive energy of the region during the eighteenth and nineteenth centuries.[8] Inaccessibility and remoteness enabled the high country to retain its regional characteristics and traditionally isolated way of life for considerably longer. Tourists, however, gathered progressive impetus from the mid-nineteenth century onwards, inevitably effecting marked, albeit gradual, changes in the Lake Country. The visitors sought simplicity, the unspoilt, the sublime, the picturesque. William Wordsworth, himself largely instrumental in attracting them, saw in the annually increasing crowds a warning for the future. As early as 1806 he was complaining at the numbers of visitors and the extraneous note which they introduced into "the calmest, fairest place on earth". In a letter to Sir George Beaumont, written in August of that year, the poet describes two young men who had rented a summer cottage in Grasmere and who, exceedingly elegantly dressed, paraded their poodle up and down Grasmere village, exclaiming in constant rapture over the unspoilt rusticity of the scenery. "One of them we suspect to be painted."[9]

Tourism, however, as the region is at last beginning to realise, like all other industries must be organised. Properly planned and controlled, it can contribute enormously to the prosperity and development of the region; the laissez-faire approach can only ultimately destroy what the visitors came to find. It is no exaggeration to say that survival as a viable region (not as a mere depopulated peepshow for motorists) is the stark problem facing the Lake Country today: it is in very real danger of deteriorating into a scenic amusement park, complete with tamed shepherds and sandwich-fed sheep, in which every inch of land below a thousand feet will be cut up with motor-roads and crammed with car-parks, cafeterias, public lavatories, post-card and soft-drink kiosks and a lavish sprinkling of caravans; a fun-place seething with tourists for three months of the year, while lying aridly quiescent for the remaining nine months, apart from invasion by motorists every week-end; it will be emptied of all local labour (and ultimately of most of the native population as a result) except for the necessary complement of car-park and petrol-pump attendants, soft-drink and ice-cream vendors and litter-wardens. Once the valley-bottoms have been destroyed for the convenience of visiting motorists, then all real life will have gone from the Lake Country, for it is from the valleys, and not the tops, that the indigenous life of this region springs. Future generations will curse us for destroying entire countrysides and communities because of our insane obsession with the motor-car.

The school that passionately opposes the *laissez-faire* deterioration of the Lake Country into a motorists' fun-place, seeks instead the planned development of a National Park, pre-eminently for walkers, climbers, campers, naturalists, geologists, general fell-wanderers and all similarly inclined persons (of whom there will be more in the future, thanks to wider education and stimulation of interests); where the region's wild life may be conserved and where the young may learn the vital lessons of ecology, and the responsibility for the legacy of a beautiful country. Attractive centres, good hotels and restaurants, as well as hospitable farmhouse accommodation and landscaped camp-sites will encourage profitable tourism that contributes to the region rather than hastening its destruction.

At the same time, no country which depends exclusively upon tourism for its existence can hope to maintain any kind of real, indigenous character, neither can it hope for a sustained high rate of local employment. Thus the Lake Counties need to create for themselves all-the-year-round industrial enterprises quite distinct from the industry of tourism. The synthesis of scenic beauty, farming, wild life conservation, tourism and hard industry can be achieved with skilled planning. Cumberland may solve the problem (a vital one for the country at large, not simply for the Lake Counties) because Cumberland is fortunate in possessing a low country with a prosperous industrial past and an equally good, indeed better, potential. There is unlimited scope for low and high country to work together to create an exciting and rewarding future in which expertly planned zoning will enable the region to progress simultaneously on several fronts. Such is the thinking of forward-looking Cumbrians today.

The visitor, however, does not feel himself concerned by such problems. He simply wishes to enjoy beautiful scenery. Much of what he sees strikes him as so wild that he can scarcely believe that this Cumbrian landscape is largely man-made. But such is the case; he is enjoying an inheritance from the old Cumbrians. The kind of Cumberland that future generations will inherit is a decision for all of us.

CHAPTER TWO

Roads and Road-makers of Braithwaite, 1769–1859

E ARLY IN THE year of 1769 John Tyson, yeoman farmer of Stonycroft, Newlands, appointed surveyor of the highways of Braithwaite for that year, purchased for the sum of 1s. 8d. an accounts book. On the first page he wrote in ink with a quill pen, in a scholarly, beautifully neat hand:

> The Accounts of John Tyson of Stony Croft Surveyor of the Highways for the Precinct of Braithwaite for the Year 1769. Containing the number of Inhabitants within the said Precinct liable to perform Statute Work upon the Kings Highwayes according to the late act of Parliament in that case made and provided, and also showing how the Statute work was performed.[1]

The village of Braithwaite lies at the foot of the Coledale fells three miles west of Keswick. A township, or constablewick, in the ward of Allerdale-below-Derwent, together with the neighbouring township of Thornthwaite, it was formed into an ecclesiastical parish in 1841; until that date it belonged to the ancient parish of Crosthwaite. The individual manors of Braithwaite and Coledale, Newlands and Portinscale, in all comprised the great manor of Derwent Fells.

The obligation of the inhabitants of a locality to keep their roads in good repair dates back to earliest times, being reinforced by Acts of Parliament in 1555, 1562 and 1575, whereby a definite system of road maintenance was created. A salient feature of this system was the appointment in each parish or township of a surveyor of highways, holding office for a year. These appointments were made with the assent of the justices of the peace. The surveyor was unpaid and was not required to have any technical qualifications. The office of road surveyor, like that of the parish constable, seems to have been looked upon as a somewhat irksome responsibility which parishioners, out of a sense of fairness, shouldered in turn. Under the direction of the road surveyors the householders of a parish or township might be compelled to turn out for six days a year to work on the roads, but they could, if they wished, send others to work in their place or pay composition money instead. Failure to keep roads in good order could result in a community being summoned before quarter-sessions and fined.

It might be helpful at this point to take a quick glance at the system of local government prevalent in Cumberland in the sixteenth and seventeenth centuries and later: government by select vestry, a body consisting of twelve, sixteen, eighteen or twenty-four members (survival of the ancient "four and twenties").

The history of the eighteen sworn men of Crosthwaite, Cumberland,[2] throws considerable light on the appointment and functions of such a body. A royal commission set up in 1571 ordered that the eighteen sworn men and the churchwardens of Crosthwaite be elected annually on Ascension Day by the vicar of Crosthwaite, the outgoing eighteen, the outgoing churchwardens, Sir George Radcliff, officials from the Keswick Mines Royal, the bailiffs of Keswick, Wythburn, Borrowdale, Thornthwaite and Brundholme, and the forester of Derwent Fells.

The eighteen men were "to enjoy and exercise so full, large and ample authority as heretofore they by lawful and laudable custom either have or ought to have had and exercised". From this it is clear that the body of eighteen men in Crosthwaite was of some antiquity; the ruling of the commission merely effected changes in the method of its election. The oaths of appointment were taken on the first Sunday following Ascension Day; the eighteen to be responsible for the parish stock and money, also in part responsible for the salaries of the parish clerk and the schoolmaster. An innovation was made by the commission in regard to these salaries; though every freeholder in the parish had, since time out of mind, paid 2d. a year towards the parish clerk's wages, the eighteen men were in future to pay him £2 6s. 8d. only, the residue to augment the schoolmaster's stipend. The accounts of the eighteen were to be rendered at the end of the year, to be audited by their successors and the vicar.

The churchwardens were required to present all offenders, to attend and to keep order in the church, to provide the bread, wine and necessary ornaments and to deliver to their successors all church money and goods in their hands.

From this it will be seen that the combined body of eighteen men and churchwardens formed a body of parish trustees, officially appointed and having both secular and ecclesiastical functions to perform. Through this body the parish fulfilled its duties, some of which were traditional, dating far back into the past, while others were contemporary measures imposed upon the parish by statute.

The system of road maintenance by townships and parishes under the supervision of the county justices continued through the eighteenth and early nineteenth centuries, but industrial expansion and an increase in the number of persons coming to the Lake Counties, either on matters of business or as tourists, necessitated revolutionary improvements in communications and transport. These improvements were accomplished by the establishment of turnpike trusts, which in this area began soon after 1750.

A turnpike trust was a body set up by Act of Parliament, to have charge of a specific section of highway on which the trust was empowered to place toll bars or gates in order to collect fees from road-users to pay for the maintenance of the road. The trusts, which were composed of gentry or professional people subject to a property qualification, began by borrowing money to be repaid with interest from the tolls. The construction of a turnpike road was let out to contract by a turnpike road surveyor acting for the trustees.

The first turnpike trust to be set up in the Lake Counties was in 1752 for the road running from Kendal through Kirkby Lonsdale to Keighley. Turnpikes did not reach Keswick until 1761, when by Act of Parliament a trust took charge of the highway from Kendal through Ambleside over Dunmail Raise to Keswick and from thence, via Braithwaite, over the Whinlatter to Cockermouth. This 1761 Act was the Act of Parliament referred to by Tyson in his preface to his accounts.

These local turnpikes transformed the way of life of the people of the Lake Counties, bringing about, it has been said, a greater revolution in their manners and customs than anything in the whole of their previous history. Before the turnpikes were built, the roads of the Lake Country were for the most part only narrow lanes designed for pack-animals. In the more mountainous parts of the region wheeled vehicles were rarely if ever seen; instead of carts sleds were used. With the turnpike roads all this was changed. The trains of pack-horses sharply declined, post-chaises were introduced, carrier's carts and waggons appeared and a stage-coach commenced its run from Edinburgh to London; a "flying-machine" that took a mere fourteen days for the journey! Medical men warned of the dangers of travelling at such high speed.

The cost of the new roads gave rise to considerable discontent and it was a long time before the inhabitants became reconciled to the innovation of having to contribute towards this modern transport system, although as its benefits gradually became apparent the grumbling decreased. Something of the attitude of remote Cumbrians towards the era of improved roads, speeded communications, industrial revolution, meddling bureaucracy and the encroachment of the nineteenth century in general may be gathered from the records of Braithwaite's road surveyors for the years 1769–1859 which, as already mentioned, have been preserved and handed down in the Bowe family.

The introduction of the turnpike trusts did not end the obligation of the parishes and townships to maintain their own highways, neither was the traditional office of parish or township road surveyor, as distinct from turnpike road surveyor, abolished. The degree of highways statute duty or labour for which each township inhabitant was liable varied according to the wealth of the individual. John Tyson's first list of persons in Braithwaite liable for statute work for the year October 1768 to October 1769 reveals that:

George Stamper, John Dungleson and Joseph Bowe, who occupied lands and tenements etc. rated at £50 per annum, were each liable to provide statute labour upon the public highways for six days, with two horses and carts; Joseph Bowe in addition had to provide two able men with each horse and cart, George Stamper and John Dungleson one able man with each horse and cart.

William Barker, Joshua Rawling, Edward Rackstraw and William Armstrong, who each kept a team, draught or plough, were liable to provide six days labour with one horse and cart and two able men therewith each day.

John Crosthwaite, Thomas Hodgson, Robert Litt, James Wilson, John Walker and George Fletcher, who each occupied lands and tenements rated at above ten pounds per annum and under twenty, Joseph Stamper, John Radcliffe, John Banks, Robert Smith, James Clark, James Stranger, Joseph Bowe, Joseph Simpson, George Barnes, Thomas Gilbanks, Thomas Bowe and Mary Graham, each occupying lands and tenements above three pounds per annum and under ten and Joseph Middlefield, Edward Baron, Benjamin Wilson, Daniel Hind and John Gibson, labourers, were each liable to provide six days labour with one able man each day.

Persons preferring to compound for their statute work had to give notice of their intention at Crosthwaite parish church on the first Sunday of January. In 1769 fourteen Braithwaite persons compounded:

Edward Baron, Joseph Stamper, Joseph Middlefield, John Gibson and Daniel Hind each compounded for the sum of two shillings; John Radcliffe, Robert Smith, John Banks, James Clark, James Stanger, Joseph Bowe, Thomas Gillbanks and George Barnes each for three shillings, John Crosthwaite for four shillings.

Composition money received in all amounted to £1 16s. Part of this money had to be paid towards the upkeep of the turnpike road (how much was paid in 1769 we are not told). The rest was spent on road work performed (in addition to statute labour) upon the other public highways in the precinct.

The various projects were 'let out' as the phrase went, being advertised by crier. Interested persons 'put in' for them and, when final agreement had been reached between the road surveyor and the man who had put in for the job, the contract was sealed with ale.

Statute work, according to Tyson, was performed on 16, 17, 18, 19, 20, 21 and 22 February 1769. Thereafter no further statute work was recorded until 16 October. Commissioned roadwork (meaning work other than that performed by workers under statute duty) was recorded for 23 February, thus:

| 23 Feby. | Agreed with John Gibson Robt. Smith & | |
| 1769 | Edward Baron for the sum of one pound five shillings and sixpence to cutt some rocks and burst some large stones in Little Braithwaite Lane ... | 1 5 6 |

Tyson recorded no road upkeep of any kind between 23 February and 14 September. The explanation for this in all probability lies in the nature of the community itself. These people were mainly hill sheep-farmers. Lambing in the Lake District does not occur until mid-April, but farmers become busy with their ewes by the end of February, gathering them into the intakes, giving them extra fodder, watching them for signs of early lambing and so forth and remain busy with their sheep and crop-harvesting right through until mid-September. These eighteenth and nineteenth-century hill farmers grew more crops than do their counterparts today, since they had to be almost entirely self-supporting. Thus between February and the back-end there was no time for road-making.

Then in September the road surveyor realised that in a month's time he was due to appear before the justices of the peace at Whitehaven there to swear that all necessary work had been performed on the highways and that his accounts of such work were correct and true. The result was an outburst of roadwork and a hasty (to judge by his handwriting) entering of details of the same in his book.

More rocks were cut in Little Braithwaite Lane, Braithwaite bridge was repaired and on 16 October Joseph Simpson and Robert Litt provided one able workman each (themselves?) to perform statute work of unspecified nature.

This, if the records are correct, was the extent of Braithwaite's road work for the year. It seems likely that not all the statute labour specified was in fact required. For instance, John Dungleson, who was liable to provide two horses and two carts and one able man to each cart for six days, provided them, according to Tyson's records, for four days only. George Stamper likewise.

The total amount of composition money disbursed on road-work came to £1 9s. 1d., leaving 6s. 11d. in hand. From this Tyson deducted the 1s. 8d. he had paid for the accounts book. This left him with 5s. 3d. Of this Barron and Smith received a further 3s. (possibly for ale, Tyson seems to have been very discreet on this subject) so that there remained in his hand 2s. 3d. These accounts were sworn at Whitehaven on 17 October 1769 before Henry Ellison and John Cooper, justices of the peace, and signed by them. Tyson also appended his signature.

He continued as road surveyor for the following year, 1769–70. Twenty-eight persons were entered as liable for statute labour, of whom ten compounded at a total of £1 6s. The highlight of the year, roadwise, was Braithwaite's trouble with the turnpike which, authority alleged, had not been kept in a proper state of repair. Tyson's entries speak for themselves:

	£	s.	d.
Midsummer Sessions 1770 paid to the Clerk of the Peaces the sum of two pounds two shillings being Braithwaite share of an Indictment on the Turnpike Road from High hill Turnpike gate to the village of Braithwaite. . . .	2	2	0
At the same times paid to Mr Barnes Attorney at Law three shillings and sixpence being Braithwaite share to him for moving a Court at the said Sessions to have the Indictment withdrawn. . . .	0	3	6
Spent with Mr Spedding when he certified for the road one shilling and fourpence.	0	1	4
Then also paid John Dungleson one shilling for a Journey to Cockermouth relating the said Roads	0	1	0
	3	3	10*

		£	s.	d.
7th Oct. 1770	Paid to Mr John Radcliffe Turnpike Surveyor the sum of eight shillings and eightpence being a third share of the Composition money collected of the Inhabitants of Braithwaite. . . .	0	8	8
	Do going to Easter Sessions to desire further time to repair the Turnpike Road then under Indictment shall only charge my own expenses which was six shillings. . . .	0	6	6

'John Dungleson of Uzeker' succeeded Tyson in 1771; Uzzicar is a small hamlet lying about a quarter of a mile distant from Stoneycroft in

* Incorrect in the original. See also pp. 78 and 89.

the vale between Swinside and Braithwaite. Dungleson's hand was a little less scholarly than Tyson's and his spelling frankly phonetic, in old Cumbrian dialect. It is worth noting here that the handwriting of all these early entries is remarkably good. The eighteenth-century inhabitants of Braithwaite were surprisingly literate, a tribute to local schooling. Only one recipient of money, unable to sign his name, had instead to make his mark; this was labourer Joseph Middefell, or Middlefield, who on 5 August 1771 was paid 11s. for cutting rock in Little Braithwaite.

Dungleson entered twenty-nine persons as liable to statute work, of these seventeen compounded. On 1 October 1771 John Radcliff, turnpike surveyor, was paid 19s. 6d., "one half of the composition money collected by Braithwaite". Dungleson did not write all his entries himself; an anonymous person with an angular clerky hand inserted some and so did John Tyson. Dungleson was obviously not of a methodical temperament; he seems to have written when he suddenly remembered to do so or the spirit seized him, fitting random entries in wherever he spied an empty space. For instance, there is this undated one, popped in unexpectedly at the end of persons listed as liable for statute work:

	£	s.	d.
Mondon of Stare Brigge	0	2	9
Mondon of wood Brigge	0	1	0
Sanding of Pow Brigge	0	3	0

The workmen that year received five quarts of ale, at a total cost of 1s. 8d. Tyson inserted after this, in his own hand, a note to the effect that £1 10s. 6d. had been carried forward, £1 19s. received in cash, £1 15s. 6d. disbursed, leaving 3s. 6d. in hand.

Tyson was probably helping Dungleson wind up the accounts in efficient style before they went to Whitehaven. On the next page came Dungleson's list of statute work performed. Following this list, close to the bottom of the page, we read, in the hand of the J.P.:

Sworn 3rd Oct. 1771
                    (signed)   Ant. Benn.

Then in Dungleson's hand:

	£	s.	d.
paid Mr Ben the warren one shilling	0	1	0
Do going to Wh'haven Sessions Coss	0	1	6
paid William Dixon mondin Wod Brigge Braithwaite	0	1	0

A full page more of afterthoughts followed:

	£	s.	d.
Oct. 10 Paid to Thomas Hodgson for Loadon of Stons to Hige Brddgg	0	3	4
Paid to Joseph Fisher mondon the Brddggs	0	5	4
paid to Stephen Fisher 33 foot of Wood at 10 per foot	1	7	6
7½ half foot of Wood att one shilling per foot	0	7	6

(signed) John Dungleson

	£	s.	d.
half a Day man and Horrs leoden of the wood to the place at poarr end (Powe End)	0	1	0
paid to John Tyson warrern Last year	0	9	9

This last figure of 9s. 9d. obviously represents a desperate attempt to reach a total for this page of odd entries, including a shilling for Tyson's warrant of the previous year. Dungleson was by now well tangled up. His good friend and neighbour, Tyson, once again came to the rescue on 2 November writing this final entry:

	£	s.	d.
paid to Stephen Fisher f Sanding Pow Bridge	0	1	8¼
Received by Tax and otherwise	4	9	5½
Disbursed in all	4	3	1¼
remains	0	6	4¼

How he arrived at these figures at the end of it all is a complete mystery. One thing is clear, the final financial situation for the highways of Braithwaite in 1771 bore no resemblance to the financial statement sworn before Anthony Benn at Whitehaven.

John Dungleson, understandably, declined to continue in office for a further year and so the book and the 6s. 4¼d. in hand were passed on to his immediate neighbour, Joseph Stamper of Uzzicar, who drew a heavy line under Tyson's final entry and started away, as road surveyor for Braithwaite for the year 1771–72, in an evenly flowing copperplate, with a list of thirty-three persons liable for statute labour, twenty-two of them performing it, the remaining eleven compounding.

Stamper, like Dungleson, made no attempt to enter his accounts in chronological order; once again he seems to have indulged in a frenetic outburst of record writing on the eve of his official trip to Whitehaven.

The literate inhabitants of Braithwaite undertook the position of road surveyor turn and turn about. The eighteenth-century accounts create an unmistakable impression of a community which did not perhaps take civic responsibilities quite as seriously as it should have done. During the years 1774–78, for instance, the number of persons liable to statute labour fell and the balance in hand dwindled from 8s. 11d. to nothing. James Wilson, who became road surveyor in 1779, writing his accounts in a tremendously large, loopy, careless hand, entered fourteen persons for statute duty. Seven shillings only was collected in composition money and all this was paid to the turnpike surveyor. Wilson was again road surveyor for 1780, but this year's accounts were even more meagre and badly written and were not taken to Whitehaven to be sworn (they are, in appearance, suggestive of having been written by a person in his cups). 1781 was missed entirely. In 1782 Wilson was clearly obliged to turn over a new leaf; he sobered up, sharpened his pen, took pains with his writing and produced quite creditable, if brief, accounts which were sworn at Whitehaven before William Hicks.

John Tyson became road surveyor once again in 1783 but even he had become considerably more lax in his attitude towards the township's highways, if we can judge by his accounts, which for this year were scrappy and somewhat untidy.

Next appear some distinctly odd entries. The first reads:

The A Counts of John Dungleson of Uzicker Surveyor of the Heyways within the Township of Brathwate for the year of our Lord 1784.
Containing the number of Inhabitants With in the said Township liable to do Statute Labour upon the sade Roads According to the late Act of Parliament in that Case made and provided and also shewing how the statute Work was performed and the Compshien moneys was Aplied

By me   John Dungleson

Then came a list of eleven names of persons liable for statute labour and the amount they were due to do. Checking of these names against later entries indicates that some of them, in 1784, must have belonged to quite young children! The list stops abruptly. There are no further entries of any kind after this until 1791, an interval of seven years.

Throughout this first part of the book (1769–84) there appear frequent scribblings and odd little interpolated entries which clearly do not belong to the main body of accounts. The first page of the book, bearing John Tyson's opening entry has been plentifully scribbled upon, most certainly not by Tyson himself! It appears at first glance to be headed *John Tyson Book* (but not in Tyson's handwriting) and under this, more strongly inscribed but by the same mysterious hand, *Gorge Stampar Book*. At the bottom of the page *John* has been faintly scribbled once or twice and *John Tyson* experimentally and haphazardly written three times, as if by a person attempting to copy John Tyson's handwriting.

At the top of the second page, squeezed in the margin, the person who wrote *Gorge Stampar Book* has experimentally written *Joseph Stampar* and the hand that scribbled the experimental *John Tyson* of the previous page has scribbled *Joseph Stamper*. Comparison with the entries written by the real Joseph Stamper as surveyor reveals that it was not he who wrote his name in the space at the top of the second page, above Tyson's meticulously tidy list of persons liable for statute work.

Various other scribbles adorn many subsequent pages. At the foot of the last page of Joseph Stamper's accounts the scribbling game becomes much bolder. The same hand (using apparently the same ink and quill) that wrote *Gorge Stampar Book* on the first page has here written, beneath the signature of Henry Ellison, J.P.:

> John Stampar Suravar,
> For the Township
> Brathate For the
> Township

Seathwaite, *circa* 1890. Note the woods behind the farm and further up the dalehead. These trees were cut down in 1916. *(Abrahams picture—George Fisher collection)*

Remains of old pony causey between Seathwaite and Stockley Bridge. (*Photo: Nicholas Gerrish*)

Vickers' gutter, Sty Head Pass. (*Photo: Nicholas Gerrish*)

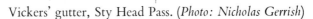

Braithwaite, *circa* 1885, looking towards Skiddaw. (*George Fisher collection*)

The account of William Barker of Mearings Surveyer of the Roads in the town ship of Braythwaite in the year one thousand seven hundred and seventy three Containing the number of Inhabitents within in the said Township liable to do Statute labour upon the said Roads according to the late act of parliment and also Shewing how the Statute Work was performd the Composition Monnyes applied and other moneyes Collected and Disbursed as after

And lift the Roade in Good Repare

By me William Barker

of Braithwate For the Year one thousand seaven Hundred Eighty & Seaven

God Save the King of Braithwate

Braithwaite road-surveyor's accounts: William Barker 1773, with interpolated entry "God Save the King of Brathwate" (see text). Quill pen. (*By courtesy of the late Mrs Bainbridge and the late Mr George Bowe*)

Mill hands and employees of Banks and Co., Greta Pencil Works, *circa* 1885. Henry Birkbeck, manager, on far right, top row; Mrs Birkbeck, seated, on far right, bottom row; Simon Birkbeck, seated, right, on ground. (*By courtesy of Miss Margaret Birkbeck*)

Wadd. (*By courtesy of Miss Margaret Birkbeck*)

Cumberland Pencil Company mill at Greta Bridge, Keswick (formerly the pencil works of Ann Banks and Co.), and earlier a woollen mill. Today these premises house a youth club. Picture taken *circa* 1910. (*Abrahams picture—George Fisher collection*)

Newlands, taken from Swinside, *circa* 1890. Skelgill in middle distance, left. This essentially pastoral vale is little changed even today. (*George Fisher collection*)

Sheep clipping. The two individuals in right foreground are wearing old jackets specially donned for the job; note the tears where the sheeps' horns have caught. One man holds a ewe steady, the other is smitting (marking) her with a smit-stick now that she has been shorn. *Circa 1885. (George Fisher collection)*

On the opposite page, in the space below William Barker's introductory paragraph (written by him when he became surveyor in 1773) the same hand that wrote 'John Stampar Suravar' etc has gaily inscribed:

And lift the Roade in God Repare
By me William Barker
of Brathwate For the
Year one thosand Seaven Hundrade
Eighty Fooar
God Save the King
of Brathwate

Two pages further on, at the foot of Barker's list of persons liable for statute work, the same hand has scrawled:

John Dunglson for
the Year of our Lord

These random scribbled entries (with the exception of some interpolated dates, which belong to a much later period) are entirely of a nature which suggests that they were the idle play of two or three children, distinctly under the impression that the book was not going to be used officially again and therefore might be scribbled upon with impunity. They were children old enough to be of mid-school age and thus able to write a good hand, but still young enough to get a kick out of imitating the signatures of their elders and scrawling silly, albeit harmless, remarks. These scrawlings appear on pages covering a period of time between 1769 and 1784; most of them have been made by the same person using the same pen and ink, obviously upon the same occasion. They are invariably written at the tops or bottoms of pages, wherever there chanced to be an empty space. One suspects very strongly that a ringleader, with one or two companions, fetched this (at the time discarded) accounts book from a cupboard or drawer on a dull evening when there was nothing else to do and had a little fun with it.

It is in fact possible, by attentive examination of subsequent official entries, to identify the writer of the major scribbles with some certainty as young John Dungleson junior, or Dunglinson as he sometimes wrote it, for his very unmistakable handwriting (and spelling mistakes) reappear later in the second half of the book when, in 1809–12, he became the real road surveyor for Braithwaite.

Who his companions in the scribbling mischief were we shall never know. Their game seems to have come to a rather abrupt conclusion; conjecture should not play part in the serious study of old documents, but one can't resist the thought that perhaps the evening of light-hearted entertainment ended with a good box on the ears!

In 1791 the book was brought into official use again, without ceremony, apparently in the middle of a set of accounts, strongly indicative that records for 1784–91 had been kept in some other book and that, when the pages of that one became filled up, this old book, which still had plenty of empty room left in it, was resurrected for reasons of economy.

Some interesting developments had taken place during the intervening seven years; the collection of purveys had become established, for instance, seventy-five of these being collected annually between 1791–94, amounting on each occasion to £15 18s. 2¾d. Furthermore the period had arrived when, throughout the region, structural alterations were being made to the little old bridges. These had been designed for animals carrying protruding pack-loads and had therefore been built narrow, with very low parapets, or in some cases without parapets at all. Now that these bridges were being used by wheeled vehicles they had to be widened and their parapets raised as a safety precaution. Entries show Braithwaite busy with this problem. For example, this entry for 19 October 1791:

	£	s.	d.
For calling and Expences of Letting the Low Bridge at Braithwaite	0	3	6
Let to James Wilson to ad 4 foot to Low Side and to have 3 stones to set up at Each Corner to stand 2 foot above the top of the Bridge and the Ledges to be the same heyht and to be set with stones all on top of Ledges and to be dasht over and to be finisht to the satisfaction of Jacob Gibson Surveyor	2	16	0
James Wilson the undertaker for to Compleet the Same			

There is no real system to these final eighteenth-century entries; they speak of a still very rural community with little comprehension of the importance of official records or of civic organisation. They are casual, carefree, idiosyncratic, haphazardly written with no attempt to keep the writing proceeding on straight lines. There is an uphill-downdale appearance about the final pages for the seventeen-nineties which is symbolic of the countryside around Braithwaite and the figures in the columns of the right-hand margin eddy and whirl like the waters of a beck in full spate. John Crosthwaite, road surveyor for 1798, was 1s. 8d. short when he handed over to his successor, Robert Hogg, in October of that year.

Robert Hogg is worth quoting extensively because, apart from the fact that he is the last eighteenth-century personality to appear in the book, his phonetic spelling gives a most vivid idea of what Cumbrian speech then sounded like.

He listed seventeen persons as having performed statute labour in June and July 1799. These names include such phonetical delights as Rechert Whaite, Churstfaire Lonstaine, Charrfester Dexson, Isaik Wokere and Samuail Grave (Churstfaire and Charrfester are both variations upon the theme of Christopher). The spelling of "Dexson" is particularly interesting; Hogg without doubt pronounced it Deexon, which he spelled out D-E-X-S-O-N.

We do not know what Hogg was by occupation. He was plainly not the most scholarly inhabitant of Braithwaite, his handwriting being uneven and suggestive of one who did not readily take up his pen. However, once he did address himself to the task of wielding his pen he did so boldly, without actual physical difficulty; there are no blotchings, scrapings out or signs of painful hesitation in this department. His spelling, bordering as it did on the fantastic, was nonetheless spontaneous and unashamed; very occasionally he put in a small correction, but only very occasionally. With figures it was a different story; the agitated scrapings out and alterations amongst his pounds, shillings and pence and the errors involved indicate the trouble he had.

One gains the distinct impression of a most likeable and decent man who put on no airs, took everyone and everything as it came, had friends all over the district, was not impressed by officialdom as such. He had agreed good-naturedly to become road-surveyor in 1799 because James Wilson, Jacob Gibson, Adamson Fletcher and the rest declared that they had had enough of it, and thus, having agreed to shoulder the appointment, found that the duties involved were of a pleasurably sociable nature, although time-consuming. He .made several trips, on horseback, in pursuit of his official duties and his conviviality is clearly demonstrated by the fact that he unabashedly recorded solemnising the highways transactions with gin instead of ale; generous quantities of gin, too. He was chivalrous also, heading his list of persons liable for statute work with the name of the one female who qualified: "Mary Wokere, two days hand labour." Ladies first.

He didn't trouble himself with accounts until 19 July, when he wrote the above-mentioned list. For the rest of the summer he seems to have been too busy to attend to such matters. Suddenly, on 15 October, he realised that within two days he was due to go to Whitehaven to swear to accounts that were not even yet written.

So he sat down and in one fell swoop wrote up twelve months of highway activity in the form of a dialect running-commentary-cum-monologue which makes quite the most fascinating reading in the entire ninety years of records:

October	1799	£	s.	d.
15	Recevead 54 pervays	11	8	4
Pad to John Crostaite for Beldaing Lettele Brathwate he Bradge—		9	10	0
3 Bredges Reparain at Brathwate—		0	14	9
pad to John Lankestare for Repairainge mill Bradge at thronthwate and the medle Bradge at Brathwate		0	3	1
goaing to Cokrmouth at the Sesains about Lettele Braitehwait he Brarge for the hors & me Expence		0	2	6
2 caled at church the he Bradg at Lettele Brathwate & once at Kewaicke to Beld*		0	0	10

* This, translated, means that the building of High Bridge, Little Braithwaite, was publicised as an available job to let, being cried twice at Crosthwaite church and once at Keswick. The crier was paid 10d. It will be noticed that these entries are not in chronological order.

	£	s.	d.
to Isaik Mirtain for warain gowain to Mr Hoskains & comaile* to Setreaite for	o	3	6
the horse mesellf	o	2	6
to John Braisto for half a galaine of gaine† for Lataing the he Bradge at Lettel Brathwate to the Loais beder	o	3	o
to Robert Stenone for callain the Bradge to Lete Brathwate	o	2	6
	11	2	8

	£	s.	d.
gowaing to comele‡ Setrwate and Mr Hoskains for to Sertfaie for Braed at Lettl Brathweat and the Road for the hors and me Expence	o	2	6
Medele Braige Sandaing	o	1	o
paed to John Crostawate the Ballains the Last yeare	o	1	8
gowaine to Whaithaven for the hors & me Expences	o	3	o
	o	7	8
Brought overe	11	2	8
paed out	11	10	4
Ballains due to me	o	2	o

These accounts were duly sworn to and allowed by William Harrison and John Sarjiant at Whitehaven on 17 October 1799. Robert Hogg then added a postscript:

* ? cornmill.
† half a gallon of gin.
‡ ? cornmill.

for Brathwate meddele Bredge			
by the prvaye for Legaine*	o	3	4½
pad to Mr Hoais† for the order	o	2	0
Ballaince Due to me	o	7	4½

Hogg never served a second term of office as road surveyor!

Imperceptibly the nineteenth century brought changes; not only in the actual system of road administration, but in the attitudes too of the road surveyors and the inhabitants of Braithwaite. In every respect a new era emerged. The process was, of course, gradual, but for all that it was inexorable.

By 1811 the roadwork was 'let out' in lots; people were paid for the amount of work that they did on their respective lot. At the commencement of that year Braithwaite was being assessed at 1s. 6d. in the pound for the highways; by the end of the year 1811–12 the tax, or assessment, had gone down to 9d. in the pound and for the first time we read in these records that money collected was sent to London (£37 11s. 8d.), The entire expenditure for Braithwaite's roads for that year amounted to £10 5s. 2d., of which 4s. was for two gallons of ale. There was considerable defaulting in payment of road tax; an 1817 entry reveals that of twenty-six persons liable to pay, eleven were 'not workt up'. The total amount of tax owed that year came to £1 14s. 11½d. There is no indication of how individuals who defaulted were penalised, if penalised they were. Neither were the defaulters all members of the poorer section of the community.

The road rates fluctuated ceaselessly. In 1842 they stood at 4d. in the pound; the country allowed a rebate for bridges. In 1844 the rate dropped to 2d.; 51 Braithwaite inhabitants were listed that year as rate-payers. The following year it was decided to make Peat Lane into a highway and as a result of this new expenditure the rates rose by a penny. In 1848 they went up by another 3d., reaching 6d. in the pound. John Bowe, however, received a tax rebate; he had 4s. returned to him for "2 years overcharge . . .". But the rate never remained stable for long; by 1850 it was down to 2½d. Sums were now being deducted 'for

* ledging.
† Hogg's way of spelling Harrison.

the poor'; the entries concerning these are unfortunately too scanty to provide any real information.

By this time the road surveyor was receiving a salary (25 March 1839 is the first date in these records to mention the matter). It was at first £2 per annum, remaining at this figure until 1854 when it was increased to £3. By 1840 there was also a road rate collector, receiving 5s. a year.

By now the actual records themselves had assumed a much more sophisticated appearance; several of the surveyors ruled pencilled lines to ensure that their entries presented a neat, methodical look and steel nibs were being used (the last quill entry seems to be in 1835). The accounts were annually examined at ratepayers' meetings before being taken to the justices; from the year 1834 the accounts were sworn at Cockermouth instead of Whitehaven. The ratepayers' meetings originated as vestry meetings held regularly for the discussion of local affairs: the first mention in these records for such a meeting is dated 6 February 1829. The first meeting we find designated in these records as a *ratepayers'* meeting was on 30 March 1838.

A local inn was selected as the meeting place once these gatherings had moved into a secular sphere. On 1 April 1842 it was "at the House of John Stamper Innkeeper". On 29 March 1843 it was the house of "Isaac Fearon Innkeeper". On 18 March it was the Skinners Arms. No more meeting places were specifically named again until 27 March 1850 when once more it was the Skinners Arms. But in 1851 the meeting was held at the Royal Oak, Braithwaite; thereafter the meetings took place, with a nice eye for fair play, alternatively, year and year about, either at the Oak or the Skinners Arms (which in 1856 changed its name to the Crown Inn).

The actual road work itself still continued to be of much the same nature as it had been since the Turnpike Acts first came in. Hedges were shifted, gravel that had been 'washed down by flod' was 'showled' (shovelled), gutters cleared, the pinfold mended. For 5s. 'a sheep strank yat' was fixed across a three-road drain; a 'sheep strank yat' being one of those strong wooden barriers made of a pole with hurdling beneath, which one finds placed across becks to prevent sheep passing up or down stream, out of their grazing area into the next.

In 1836 George Watson had become road surveyor. He was to remain so for the next twenty-three years, until the book's end in 1859. He took up his post at a difficult moment. A mere £8 7s. 11d. had been

collected in statute money at Braithwaite that year. A vestry meeting
was held at which a resolution was passed that, "This sum being considered insufficient to cover the expenses likely to be incurred during
the year, at a meeting held on the 3rd March 1836, it was agreed that
an additional Late [collection] of 3d in the pound should be wrought or
paid for, to be wrought as might hereafter be determined."

This additional rate was necessitated in order that Braithwaite might
defray its share of the expense in defending a piece of indicted road in
the township of Portinscale. £8 3s. 2d. was brought in by it in 1836, in
1837 the rate was raised to fourpence and an extra £10 10s. 4¾d. collected thereby, after which this additional rate was dropped.

The statement of income and expenditure presented to the ratepayers' meeting of 30 March 1838 reads as follows:

Statement of the income and expenditure on the
Highways in the Township of Braithwaite Parish
of Crosthwaite from the 24th March 1837 to the
25th March 1838.

	Income.	£	s.	d.
1837 July 8th.	Rate collected in full	10	10	4¾
1838 Jany 13th.	Rate collected in full	15	18	1
	Amount carried forward	26	8	5¾

		Expenditure	£	s.	d.
1837					
Nov. 25		Pay'd to John Rennick on Acct for Contract in cleaning Water-courses and forming Roads	1	0	0
July 8	„	Magistrates Signature to rate		2	—
	„	Mr. Spedding as treasurer for Law expences for Portinscale road indict.	9	0	0
Sept. 13	„	Thomas Mitchel for repairing Braithwaite Bridge Ledging—		4	6
Dec 16th	„	Wm Winder on Acct for breaking Stones for road near Braithwaite	2	—	—

27th	„	Wm Winder for Balance of acct for collecting and breaking 31 yds 24 feet of Stones as above at 2/3 per yd	1	10	4½
1838					
January 13th		Magistrates Signature to rate		2	–
		Amount carried forward	13	18	10½
		Brought forward amount of Rate collected	26	8	5¾
		Collected in part of last rate		3	9	4
		Total	29	17	9¾

(Signed)   George Watson
                        Surveyor

This Acct Examined at a Public Meeting of Ratepayers
on the 30th Day of March 1838

(Signed)   Joseph Sim
                        Thomas Bowe
                        George Walker
                        John Bowe

By mid-century (when a John Stamper was collecting the rates, which fluctuated between 6d. and 3d. in the pound) we find increasing quantities of gravel being spread, obtained from the shilly-beds of Barrowside, still very much in use for the same purpose today. Progressive amounts of slate, too, were purchased from the Quey Foot Quarry Company (the now disused quarry near Grange in Borrowdale which in 1967 was converted into a landscaped car-park). The road-making was becoming considerably more professional in nature.

The final entries in the book (apart from some scribbled in pencil on the end pages and one interpolation for 1862 squeezed in between the accounts for 1837 and 1838) are for 1858–59. George Watson was ageing, his handwriting had grown shaky; William Nicholson was now collecting the rates, Isaac Bowe was chairman of the ratepayers' committee. In that year the rate stood at 4½d. in the pound. The meeting learned that Messrs Nicholson and Abbott had contracted for cleaning watercourses and scraping roads, including 10s. for bridge roads, at a total payment of £4. Daniel Tolson had received 5s. for cart work, Thomas Bell 5s. 10d. for a water grate. The magistrate had received 1s. for signing the accounts as correct and the surveyor had had his salary of £3. The accounts balanced out at £19 0s. 11½d.

Isaac Bowe signed these records in pencil because his ink supply ran out; one can see the point where it failed him, at the top of the down-stroke of his *I* for *Isaac*. John Bowe and John Walker added their signatures to his, also in pencil. Someone did a little inconsequential pencilled sum in the left-hand corner of the page.

With this the accounts end, the final two pages having been glued together; holding them up to the light reveals no writing on them. Upon the end-papers there is much scrawling in pencil in the same hand which made the 1862 interpolation mentioned above. This inter-polated entry was a simple list of roadwork performed by various persons, the end paper entries are of the same nature. It looks very much as if the 1862 road surveyor (I incline to think that he was a Bowe, for the old records book was by now in that family's possession), who was keeping his contemporary accounts elsewhere, ran out of paper and turned to this old book in the hope of finding a few spare pages on which to jot notes. These final informal pencilled entries tell of men, still from the same old local families, providing horses and carts to fetch stones, lime and sand, repairing Stonycroft bridge. At the bottom of the page are several contemplative sums of the addition and sub-traction variety. And here the voices of the road surveyors of the high-ways of the township of Braithwaite cease, so far as this old book is concerned, after almost a century of communication.

CHAPTER THREE

In Quest of Wadd

WADD, PLUMBAGO, GRAPHITE, black-cawke or black-lead (the several names apply to the same article, "wadd" being the traditional local nomenclature) as a very substance misleads and mystifies. It is almost invariably, but erroneously, referred to throughout its literature as a mineral; even John Postlethwaite, in his *Mines and Mining in the Lake District* (Whitehaven, 1877) makes this mistake. Clifton Ward, speaking of wadd, says that, "since it consists almost wholly of carbon . . . it must be derived either from vegetable or animal matter . . ." (Ward, John Clifton, "The Geology of the Northern Part of the English Lake District", *Mem. of the Geological Survey*, 1876, H.M.S.O., 1876). The Oxford Dictionary defines a mineral as an inorganic substance "not animal or vegetable, got from the earth by mining". Demonstrably, therefore, wadd is no mineral.

Postlethwaite, on wadd, relies upon (and extensively quotes, frequently word for word) Clifton Ward. Ward for the most part quotes Keswickian geologist Jonothan Otley's paper to the Manchester Literary and Scientific Society: "Account of the Black Lead Mine In Borrowdale" (*Manchester Mem.*, 2nd series, vol. iii, 1819). Reading up wadd one discovers that most of the authorities are merely repeating the words of a previous writer; thus one digs one's way downwards through a slag-heap of endless (and sometimes erroneous) repetition.

The wadd, according to legend, was discovered originally by shepherds, after a large ash-tree on the fellside (an alternative version of the tale gives it as an oak) had been uprooted by a gale. The date of the discovery is unknown. When first found the substance was simply used by the local people for marking their sheep (continues the legend). Fleming and Guptill in their book, *The Pencil Since 1565* (1936), give the discovery date as 1554, but no information upon which this date might be based. Collingwood did not think that the wadd holes were known until shortly after 1577. German experts prospected and worked the mines of this region (the Mines Royal Company was chartered in 1561 when indentures were made between Queen Elizabeth and Thomas Thurland, Master of the Savoy, and Daniel Hechstetter of Augsburg, for the discovery and working of minerals); the known Augsburg accounts and mining inventories, which are extremely detailed, end in 1577, making no mention of the wadd holes.[1] For this reason Collingwood[2] suggested that the wadd was not found until after that date (one of the old veins of the wadd mine is called *German's Vein* which may or may not be regarded as confirmation that the Germans did in fact work the wadd. The men who named the vein may have been surmising too!). Assuming (but bearing in mind that there is no real evidence whatever to support the assumption) that the Germans did work the wadd holes after 1577 it is perfectly possible, of course, that miners who were other than Germans wrought holes before that date.

It has been conjectured that the Furness monks may first have mined the wadd, since the manor of Borrowdale, in which the wadd holes lay, was in their possession. However *Valor Ecclesiasticus* of 1535 contains nothing to show that the monks of this region were concerned in mining of any kind.

A cache of plumbago moulds found at Nether Wasdale in 1865 has given rise, over the years, to some lively expert discussion. To quote from R. S. Ferguson's paper, "On Some Plumbago Coining Moulds Found at Nether Wasdale" (*Trans. Cumberland Association for the Advancement of Lit. and Science*, vol. i, 1875–76, p. 35),

A mould of plumbago, found in April 1865 in a small cairn of stones in a straggling oak coppice a little outside the village of Nether Wasdale, near the river Irt, composed of two blocks of pure Cumberland plumbago, one weighing 5 ozs 3 dr the other 5 ozs 7 dr. . . . This mould, when open, reveals the dies of the obverses and reverses of five coins. The largest is a groat either of Edward IV or Richard III. The second is the half-groat, exactly similar to, but smaller than, the groat. The other three are silver pennies of Henry VII. These moulds would seem to be the tools of some coiner, who worked in the early part of the reign of Henry VII. . . .

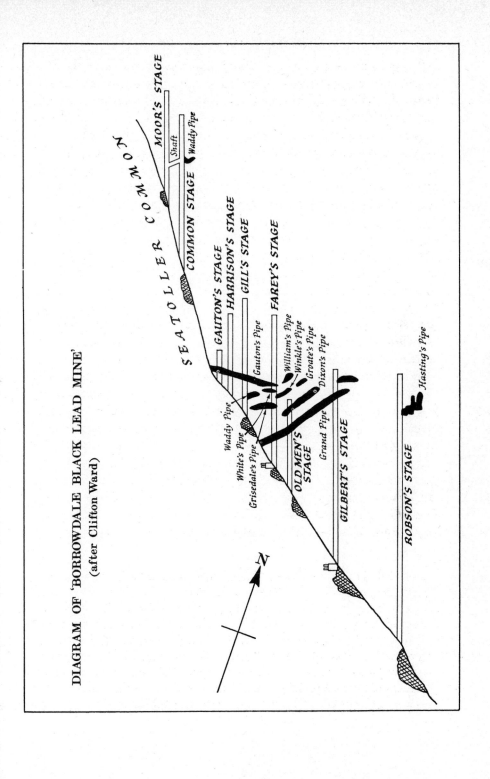

DIAGRAM OF 'BORROWDALE BLACK LEAD MINE'
(after Clifton Ward)

Later than Ferguson's paper are the observations of C. A. Parker in *The Gosforth District* (Kendal, 1904) in which he suggests that the counterfeiter might have been a Furness ecclesiastic, but Parker's arguments strike Professor G. P. Jones as thin. "It has . . . to be borne in mind," says the Professor, "that since there was importation of foreign coinage, possibly including counterfeits (C. Johnson, *The De Moneta of Nicholas Oresme* etc., pp. xxxl, xxxvll, 50, 321) plumbago blocks might have been imported. There was a lot of counterfeiting in Elizabeth's reign, e.g. in Berwick 1569 and in the Marches in 1590 and 1596."

D. L. W. Tough in his book, *The Last Years of a Frontier* (Oxford, 1928) provides more detail:

> . . . some of the best soldiers in Berwick garrison, men with wives and children, made a practice of counterfeiting Scots money, and were leniently treated by Hunsdon in 1569. . . . [There was] a fresh outbreak about 1575 when Scots money was again coined. . . . Coiners were at work in the English Middle Marches in 1590, and in 1596 one of the Grames [Grahams] of the English West March kept a 'coyner' at work in the top of his own house and "in Geordy marks sheyld in the myllers howse end."

Thus the Nether Wasdale find cannot be regarded as reliable evidence that Seathwaite plumbago was being mined early in the reign of Henry VII. If these moulds were from a counterfeiter in the reign of Elizabeth this would be in accordance with Collingwood's opinion that the wadd was not found before 1577.

The Seathwaite wadd holes were certainly being worked by the close of the sixteenth century and the wadd was being used for a species of crayon, being purchased for that purpose by merchants from Holland and the Low Countries. Camden, who in 1582 made his journey through the north of England into Scotland, for purposes of research, tells us in *Britannia* (1610 edition, translated P. Holland) that wadd was "a kind of earth or hardened glittering stone which painters use to draw their lines and make pictures of one colour in their first draughts. . . .".

The extent of the demand by painters of this period for Seathwaite graphite is unascertainable; it could not have been very extensive. There are no known records in existence of any kind of activity connected with the fashioning of these rudimentary crayons in Keswick itself at this time; even if one were to suppose that the wadd were sorted into sizes there (it required no processing, once fetched out of the ground, apart from washing and sorting according to size), it would be very premature to speak of a "Keswick pencil industry" in Elizabethan days. Nevertheless, legend has it that Keswick was "making pencils" during the reign of Elizabeth I: here, as upon Seathwaite Fell, one is moving in a very obscure landscape. Fleming and Guptill state that Konrad von Gesner, the Swiss scholar, in 1565 first described a writing article in which graphite was inserted in a wooden holder. Keswick claims, purely on hearsay handed down over 400 years, which cannot be either proved or disproved, that this writing article originated there.

The actual wadd holes still survive on Seatoller Fell; an exploratory visit involves a sharp pull of 1,100 feet up the fellside and is only worth making in winter or early spring as at all other times bracken effectively obliterates the ground. On no account should the mines be entered by the uninitiated, for like all the old mines of the region they are dangerous. They may be reached, on foot only, from either Seatoller or Seathwaite.

Seathwaite Farm would seem from early times to have provided lodging for the miners and for some of the Honister quarrymen too. The miners and quarrymen remained at Seathwaite during the week, dispersing on the Sabbath to visit their families and/or spend the greater part of their earnings on drink. Many are the old local tales of drinking and fighting Old Men.

In the final years of the mine the Old Men became markedly more respectable, their families lodging with them at Seathwaite. The late Mr Edmondson (father of Mr Stanley Edmondson, Senior, presently farming at Seathwaite) who was born at Seathwaite 115 years ago and had many youthful memories of the mine, which was then approaching closure, recalled that there were, at one time, eighteen children living at Seathwaite, members of mining families! How many men the mine then employed is not known. True to the mine's tradition of obscurity, the actual date of its closure seems never to have been definitely recorded and is already a matter for surmise. The late Mr Edmondson apparently put it round about 1865.

The old pony track from Seathwaite Farm to the mines may still be followed, its cobbled surface clearly discernible. The ancient bridge across the Derwent and the stepping-stones at the ford immediately below the bridge have been washed away by storms, for which the head of Borrowdale is famous (the three most notorious being those of 1884, when it is said that the stepping-stones went, 1898 and 1966). The stone steps of the original bridge still remain intact. The old mine road may be traced again on the other side of the ford, cart ruts still showing. This road leads to a ruined group of mine buildings, the largest of which, according to Seathwaite father-to-son hearsay, was the sorting and washing house. A sheep-fold here is very probably made with stones from this building.

Near these ruins lie two stones which replace two earlier stones (whose original position is not known), inscribed "John Bankes Esquier" and dated 1752, which were destroyed by vandals in 1887. The Bankes stones (three, possibly four, are known to have existed) are sometimes erroneously referred to as memorial stones; they were in fact erected to mark the mine as the property of Messrs John Banks and John Shepherd (or Shepard), joint proprietors of the mine from *circa* 1710 until 1759. 1752, the date inscribed upon all the existing stones, was a very important date for the wadd mine, for in that year an Act of Parliament was passed to protect it from thieves and pilferers.

A third stone stood, within living memory, on the top of the spoil heap of Robson's Stage (the lowest adit); this was thrown down by campers, replaced, thrown down again, broken, and is now lost. It is said to have borne an inscription, but what the words were nobody remembers.

The one surviving original "John Bankes" stone stands some 500 feet up the fellside; presumably in its true, undisturbed position. Finally, on the very summit of the open fell, beyond the enclosure wall (upon what was known in the old days as Seatoller Common), almost concealed now by heather, is a fifth and final marker-stone, inscribed "John Shepard Esq".

The mines, or wadd holes, are mainly situated between two gills, the gill on the left (as one faces the fell) being Wadd Hole Close, or Newhouse Gill. To the left of Wadd Hole Close and some 200 feet up the fellside is the now blocked adit of the lowest level or stage, Robson's Stage. Beneath the adit is a large spoil heap and over and immediately above the adit are the ruins of a small building. An attempt has been made to screen this adit and spoil heap with a planting of larch trees, which renders exploration extremely difficult.

A well contoured and zig-zagged sled-gate must once have commenced at the buildings on the beckside and have proceeded thereafter up the fell, from level to level, but today it is untraceable until it emerges from the planting to cross the gill; when once the bracken is up, this sled-gate is wholly obliterated. It leads from Robson's Stage in an ascent of 300 feet to Gilbert's Stage, where is another large spoil heap, a blocked adit and, over the adit, the ruins of the once celebrated 1800 security-house. Above Gilbert's Stage are to be found the further stages; the Old Men's, Farey's, Gill's and Harrison's, with Gauton's, Common Stage and Moor's Stage beyond the wall; virtually on the common, the moor (see diagram). Many of the adits are blocked. Some have small ruined buildings over them. The Grand Pipe yawns treacherously, albeit picturesquely, fringed with holly and rowan, between Farey's Stage and Gill's Stage; this mouth of the Grand Pipe is claimed to be the legendary spot where the wadd was first found beneath the uprooted ash.

The adits are confusing, for they do not rise successively and uncomplicatedly one above the other as the Clifton Ward diagram suggests. Immediately below the maw of the Grand Pipe is a small vaulted gallery cut through a rock outcrop; this gallery leads into the shaft of the Grand Pipe and on the other side of the shaft can be seen, continuing as a level, Farey's Stage. Presumably the shaft was formerly bridged to allow access from gallery to level. The Grand Pipe itself descends steeply for nearly fifty feet to the adit of the Old Men's Stage, the early working belonging to the first (?–?1678) phase of the wadd holes.

Gill's Stage lies on the right-hand side of Wadd Hole Close, just below the wall; it has some three adits, one of which is actually in the bed of the small beck which flows down the Close.

The wall enclosing the fellside with the major wadd holes is tall, strong and beautifully constructed, which suggests that it may well have been first erected with an eye to mine security. There is an aperture in it at the top of the Close which could have been a narrow and easily defended gateway (there is no gate now). Wall, ruined security houses over the main adits, marker-stones; all point to strong precautions against thieves.

On the flat summit of the fell (Seatoller Common), besides the three stages, Gauton's, Common and Moor's, are numerous ruined stone huts and a little quarry from which material for the mine buildings was obtained. There is also evidence of some open mining. According to Clifton Ward the mine, in its earliest phase, seems to have been worked at several places where wadd appeared at, or near, the surface.

Again to quote Clifton Ward (quoting Otley) the wadd was found in the mine in pipes, strings and sops, occurring:

> in close connection with a dyke of highly altered diorite lying between two other masses of intrusive blue trap (diabese) of a compact character. The diorite is much penetrated by quartz strings. . . . Although . . . plumbago does occur in this diorite . . . yet have all the principal pipes been found in connection with the very compact blue diabese. . . .

The editors of Hutchinson, writing some forty years earlier than Otley, gave a description of the wadd holes which, they acknowledged, was obtained first-hand (1792) from John Ladyman, Keswick's earliest discoverable pencil manufacturer, who obviously had a practical know-ledge of mining wadd as well as of manufacturing:

> There are two workings, the lower one is about 340 yards above the level of the sea, the upper one about 390; the perpendicular depth of the lower is about 105 yards, and of the upper between 20 and 30 yards. There are no certain marks on the surface to direct the miner to the mineral. . . . The miners generally work through a quantity of earth mixed with stones of various kinds, then a species of hard grey granite, and after that a dark blue stone of a softer nature, where they sometimes meet with it [wadd]. . . . The rock adjoining the mineral is sometimes tinged as black as the mineral itself, to the depth of 2 or 3 feet. . . .
>
> The mineral [lies] in the mine in form resembling a tree; it hath a body or root, and veins or branches fly from it in different directions: the root or body is the finest black-lead, and the branches at the extremities the worst, the further they fly. . . . It is sometimes found in sops or floats, in a body without branches . . . sometimes there is a wet sludge between the [blue] rock and the black-lead. The metal in the low mine lies in two veins, one crossing the other, where they cross is the main body, and the best black-lead; and these veins fall perpendicular for 60 fathoms in depth, the blue rock on each side; at the end of 60 fathoms they found the end of the cross vein, and a large sop of the mineral, which came out as if it had been in a wrought basin, the form of the black-lead and the rock were so equal.

After the Dissolution the manor of Borrowdale passed into the hands of the Crown, thereafter to be distributed, either by gift or sale, amongst various persons. Walter Graham, "goodman" of Netherby in 1600 and 1602, held lands in Braithwaite, Watendlath and Borrowdale; in 1606 the Graham clan was deported to Ireland for causing constant Border disturbances (Chapter One). On 12 March 1613 William Whitmore and Jonas Verdon received from James I a grant of the lands presumably forfeited (says Collingwood) by Walter Graham, including the manor of Borrowdale and the wadd holes within the "commons of Seatoller", these wadd holes being then in the tenure of one Roger Robinson at an annual rent of 15s. 4d.

Whitmore and Verdon, by a deed bearing the date of 24 November 1614 (and known thereafter as the Great Deed of Borrowdale) conveyed to Sir Wildred Lawson of Isel and thirty others therein named:

> . . . all the said manor of Borrowdale, with the appurtenances of what nature or kind soever, except all those wadd holes and wadd, commonly called black cawke, within the commons of Seatoller or elsewhere within the commons and wastes of the manor of Borrowdale aforesaid . . . one half of these belonging to Henry Banks, Esq., M.P. and the other half subdivided in several shares. . . .

Sir John Banks was certainly mining the wadd by 1622. But once this fact is stated, the scene remains obscure; we know next to nothing of this first definite wadd-mining phase, which might be termed the period of the Old Men. Otley tells us that, "On opening one of the old workings in 1759, it was found to have been carried to a great extent without the help of gunpowder." Before the employment of gunpowder, levels were cut through hard rock by the stope and feather method: "feathers" being two thin pieces of iron, about 6 inches long and $\frac{1}{2}$ inch broad, flat on one side and round on the other, while the "stope" was a thin tapering wedge of iron of the same length and width. A hole was first bored in the rock and the feathers were placed in it, with their flat sides together, and parallel with the cleavage of the rock; the point of the stope was then inserted between them and driven in with a hammer until the rock was rent. A laborious process.

The date of the cessation of this first phase of the mining is a matter of conjecture based upon Bishop Nicolson's observation, made in 1710, that there had then been no search for wadd during the previous thirty-two years. It is possible that the first phase of the wadd holes came to an end because the Old Men were unable to carry their mining operations further under the existing primitive conditions. Upon the other hand (again according to Otley, but other sources confirm this) it was the practice, in the eighteenth century, to work the wadd holes only at intervals and "when a sufficient quantity had been produced to answer the demand for a few years the mine was strongly closed up till the stock was reduced". This may in fact have been the practice of the Banks from their earliest days at Seathwaite, although thirty years seems to have been a long period over which to leave the wadd holes in abeyance.

Although the wadd holes were, at the turn of the seventeenth century, undergoing a long term of closure (if Bishop Nicolson's information is correct) Robinson, in his *Natural History of Westmorland and Cumberland* (1704) makes it clear that there was a demand for wadd and indicates that there were stocks of it available at that date:

> Its natural uses are both medicinal and mechanical. It is a present remedy for the colic; it easeth the pain of gravel, stone and strangury; and for these and the like uses, it is much bought up by apothecaries and physicians. The manner of the country people's using it is thus: first they beat it small into meal, and then take as much of it, in white wine or ale, as will lie upon a sixpence, or more, if the distemper require it. It operates by urine, sweat and vomiting. This account I had from those who frequently had used it in these distempers with good success. Besides these uses that are medicinal, it had many other uses which increase the value of it. At the first discovering it, the neighbourhood made no other use of it, but for marking their sheep; but it is now made use of to glaze and harden crucibles, and other vessels, made of earth or clay, that are to endure the hottest fire, and to that end it is wonderfully effectual. . . . By rubbing it upon iron arms, as guns, pistols, and the like, and tinging them with its colour, it preserves them from rusting. . . .

According to Robinson the wadd was "much bought at great prices by the Hollanders. . .".

William Nicolson, bishop of Carlisle from 1702 to 1718, an eminent scholar as well as a diligent and successful bishop, in a letter written to Dr Woodward on 5 August 1710, described his visit to the wadd holes:

From Keswick, we travelled up the valley of Borrowdale, along the banks of Derwentwater, six or seven miles or more, till we came to Seathwaite moor, where, ascending a high mountain, we at length reached the mine, and were courteously received by Mr Shepherd, one of the proprietors of the work, who was waiting for his co-partner, Mr. Banks. On the first opening of the old level in the latter end of June last, great discouragements appeared; for no search having been made in thirty-two years, they found that some pilfering interlopers had carried on the old work, till they had lost it in the rock. Upon the 3rd of July (the day before we got thither) a new belly was happily discovered before the forehead of the *Old Man* which proved so rich that in less than twenty-four hours they had filled several sacks with fine and clean-washed material. . . .

Under the partnership of Banks and Shepherd the wadd holes clearly proved highly profitable; by mid-century the wadd was "necessary for divers useful purposes . . . more particularly in the casting of bomb-shells, round shot and cannon-balls". What its price was on the market at this time we do not know; it was obviously well worth stealing. Furthermore, it was an easy substance for pilferers to handle, for it weighed but little and it was equally easy to dispose of to dealers since, once fetched from the ground, it merely required washing and sorting to be marketable. In 1751 there was an attack on the mine-steward's house by a gang, traditionally said to have been of local men, organised to steal wadd (to the value of £1,000 yearly). Further details of this attack are unfortunately not discoverable, but this threat to the wadd was taken seriously by the authorities and the aforementioned Act of Parliament (25 Geo. II c. 10) was passed in 1752, making it "felony to break into any mine or wadd-hole of wadd or black-cawke, commonly called black-lead, or to steal any from thence. . .". Messrs Banks and Shepherd simultaneously with this Act erected their name-inscribed stones upon the fellside.

There is a good deal of semi-legendary hearsay information about wadd-stealing and smuggling, but since none of the tales carry dates one cannot assign them to any particular period in the mine's history. Postlethwaite tells us that local lore had it that at the time of the Parliamentary Act an illicit trade in wadd was being carried on "between the eminent scholar as well as a diligent and successful bishop, in a letter written to Dr Woodward on 5 August 1710, described his visit to the wadd holes:

and by night during the periods when mining was in process. There are tales of persons at Seathwaite looking across at Seatoller Fell and seeing the flicker of lanterns carried by these surreptitious searchers: "A successful night's work could be more rewarding than a week's labouring in the nearby Honister Quarry or on the farms."[3]

Among the several tales of pilfering handed down, one at least seems to bear a vivid ring of authenticity:

> As the miners worked out near to the surface of the fellside they used to shove a bar up in front of them until it broke through to daylight. They then removed the bar and pushed a stick through, just protruding above the surface, and marked it. They then used to pack the end of the level with sorted wadd and block it off with waste material, telling the overseer that the wadd supply had run out. They then searched the fellside until they found the stick and went back at night, removed the topsoil and then dug down until they got to the cache of wadd; removed it, filled up the hole with boulders and replaced the top soil and got away with a fortune in wadd. . . . (See notes.)

The same source adds: "As to any that could be smuggled past the watchman, a mouthful was as good as a day's wage and a pocketful brought up to three guineas."

The mine is said to have been heavily guarded. An old blunderbuss found some forty years ago in an outbuilding of today's Rain Gauge Farm, Seathwaite, was thought to have been used by one of the guards at the mine.

Another legend claims that Hanging Stone, near the top of Sour Milk Gill, was used by members of a smugglers' ring as a hiding place for stolen wadd (search reveals no apparently suitable holes on the Stone itself, but near at hand are several borrans, or small caves, which would make excellent places of concealment). The leader of the ring is said to have collected the wadd until some 300 lb. or so had been amassed; this was then loaded on a mule and taken to Ravenglass. The profits from such a load would have been considerable.

The route used by such a smuggler would doubtless have been Moses' Trod, the old track running from Grey Knotts, near the summit of Seatoller Fell, via Brandreth and the foot of Gable Crag to descend to Burnthwaite by Beck Head. Since it is named Moses' Sledgate (trod is a more recent variation of the name) after Moses Rigg, a notorious smuggler who hovers on the borderline of the mythical, there is every indication that this remote, but skilfully contouring and most efficient route between Honister and Wasdale Head, may well have been a smugglers' way. One would like to think that Moses himself was the man with the mule, but this is carrying romantic surmise a little too far!

Any attempt at a sustained history of the wadd holes has to be pieced together from a somewhat hotch-potch variety of sources. At the time of the Great Exhibition of 1851 at the Crystal Palace, Kensington, where Seathwaite wadd was exhibited, an article about the wadd holes was featured by the *Cumberland Pacquet*. This stated:

... in 1759 the mines were the property of Mr Banks of Corfe Castle and Mr Shepherd of Boonwood, Cumberland. In that year Mr Shepherd let his half of the mine for 99 years to several gentlemen, chiefly resident in London. The first mining operation under this lease started in 1761, and again in 1765, but there is no record of plumbago being found on either of these occasions. The low mine was opened in 1769 when $18\frac{1}{2}$ casks of pure lead [wadd] were obtained. ...

It was this low mine, an old level, which Otley described as having been worked to a great extent by the Old Men without the help of gunpowder. In 1788 a deposit was therein found, says Postlethwaite, "which yielded 417 casks, 70 lbs each of the best graphite which at 30/- per lb, the price then current, would represent £43,785". Otley now takes up the tale:

... this vein, being pursued to the depth of a 100 yards and upwards, much inconvenience was experienced in working it, to obviate which, in the year 1789, an adit or level was begun in the side of the hill which, at the length of 200 yards, communicated with the bottom of the old workings. Through this level the water passes off, and the produce is brought out to be dressed, and on its mouth a house is built where, when the mine is open, the overseers dwell, and the workmen are undressed and examined as they pass to and from work. ...

This new level was known as Gilbert's Stage. The new security house received a good deal of publicity in the national press, for the mines had by this time won popularity as a gothic attraction with the ever-increasing tide of Picturesque Tourists. It seems that the wadd holes had come into vogue as the result of an article, signed G.S., which appeared in the *Gentlemen's Magazine* in 1751. This article set the tone for the romantic tales written about the Seathwaite mine over the next century, not infrequently by persons who had never actually visited it:

> I had long intended a journey to the wadd mines and . . . in the beginning of August 1749 I set out . . . in company with two or three friends. . . .

(Follows a description of a trying journey, with much bad weather on their arrival in the Lake Country. At last, however, the party found themselves penetrating the fastnesses of Borrowdale, each extension of the valley being more alarming than the last):

> We now entered another narrow valley, which winded through mountains which were totally barren and, in about an hour, we arrived at Seathwaite, which is just under the mines and, as near as I can compute, about ten miles from Keswick. The scene that now presented itself was the most frightful that can be conceived; we had a mountain to climb for above seven hundred yards, in a direction so nearly perpendicular that we were in doubt whether we should attempt it. However, recovering our resolution, we left our horses at a little house that stood by itself . . . and approached the mountain. . . . We had not ascended far before we perceived some persons at a great distance above us, who seemed to be very busy, though we could not distinguish what they were doing; as soon as they saw us, they hastily left their work, and were running away, but, by a signal made by our guide . . . they returned, to the number of eighteen. We came up to them after an hour of painful and laborious travelling, and perceived them to be digging with mattocks, and other instruments, in a great heap of clay and rubbish, where mines had been formerly wrought; but though they were now neglected by the proprietors, as affording nothing worth the search, yet these fellows could generally clear 6s to 8s a day, and sometimes more. . . . About an hundred and fifty yards above this rubbish is the miner's lodge, to which the ascent is very steep. . . . We had now reached the summit of the black-lead hill; but were astonished to perceive a large plain to the west, and from thence another craggy ascent of five hundred

yards, as near as I could guess. The whole mountain is called Unnesterre, or as I suppose, Finisterre, for such it appears to be.

The poet Thomas Gray, generally agreed upon as the first of the Lake Country tourists, made his famous pioneer visit in 1769; he is renowned for *not* having travelled up Borrowdale, "that ancient kingdom of the mountaineers, the reign of Chaos and Old Night" as he so splendidly described it; the local people had scared him off with horrible tales. This did not prevent him from writing about the wadd holes, his remarks being second-hand and not worth repeating here, except that he did give the price of the best wadd, at that date, as thirty shillings the pound.

Hatchett's account of a tour through the North in 1796 refers briefly to the wadd holes and is interesting:

> Mr Hy Banks M.P. for Corfe in Dorsetshire has one half of this Mine, the remaining half is divided into 8 shares of which Sir Jos. Banks has one. . . .

According to Hatchett the mine at that date employed seven men and the expenses of the enterprise were very little, but, "Great loss falls on the Proprietors by the pilfering of the men. . .". Hatchett concluded, "Borrowdale is very Romantic. . . ."[4]

His fleeting observation is the only information that we are ever given, at any time, about the numbers of men employed at the mine; visitors being more intent upon describing the romantic scenery rather than in giving prosaic details about mines and mining. W. T. McIntire in his short article "The Wadd Mine of Borrowdale" (1935) managed to discover (he does not say how) that for over 150 years members of the Dixon family held the position of manager at the wadd mine; it would seem confirmed by the fact that one of the main pipes of wadd was named "Dixon's Pipe".

With the opening up of Gilbert's Stage and the erection of the security house over its adit, Seathwaite wadd entered upon what was possibly its most energetic and lucrative period. The *Saturday Magazine* for 21 July 1832 contained a short, very inaccurate, article on the wadd mine, complete with a small sketch of the security house. Since this sketch definitely creates the impression that Derwent Water may be glimpsed beyond and behind the house it should not be relied upon as accurate in other details; for what it is worth, it depicts the house as two-storied, with windows each side of a central doorway and a lean-to shed at one end of the building. A tree, growing behind the house, tops the roof.

Examination of the ruined house today indicates that it had a fairly wide central doorway on the left-hand side of which (as one faces the building) was a small room which seems to have been reached by a short flight of stone steps just inside and to the left of the main entry. There seems probably to have been another room on the other side of the entry. The building was actually constructed over the adit and all wadd and spoil had to be fetched out through the building; the spoil was tipped on to a heap immediately below the house. The slates from the fallen roof lie amongst the rubble on the ground; one window remains, with a wooden lintel over it; a crude wooden beam projects from the disintegrated walls. Behind the house, above the now blocked adit and true to the sketch in the *Saturday Magazine*, are the roots of a largish tree. Everything about the building points to very tight security arrangements indeed.

The expense involved in opening the new level complete with security house quickly paid off; Postlethwaite tells us that a deposit found in 1803 (the *Cumberland Pacquet* gives it as a "sop" found in Dixon's Pipe), ". . . yielded $31\frac{1}{4}$ tons, which [at the price of 30s. per lb] would realise £105,000. During this year £3,795 was expended in working the mine and the net profit realised was £92,690. . . ."

The *Cumberland Pacquet* on the other hand gives the sum of £3,801 19s. 3d. as the total expense (including building the security house and driving Gilbert's Stage) of running the wadd mine for the years 1800–3; the *Pacquet* further states that "annual profits after deducting these expenses stood in the region of £27,000".

Postlethwaite concludes his account of the mine's history thus:

In 1812 Winkle's Pipe was discovered and 87 casks of the best quality, and 495 casks of inferior graphite were obtained from it. The 87 casks of the best quality alone realised £9,135.

After this date the search for the mineral was less successful and the price rapidly increased. The produce of a deposit found in 1829 sold at 35/– and one found in 1833 at 45/– per pound. About this time the pencil manufacturers discovered an inferior species of foreign graphite which when compressed could be utilised for their purpose; therefore the demand for Borrowdale graphite decreased, and the price again descended to 30/- per pound.

Since 1833 the mine has been worked at intervals by various parties; but although a considerable extent of ground has been explored, no deposit of value has been found.

The story of the wadd holes now merges and finally loses itself in the story of the Keswick pencil industry.

In its early days the pencil as we know it did not exist; it was, as we have seen, simply a species of crayon, wound in string, pushed into tubes and later held in the claws of metal holders called *porte-crayons*. For these crayons the Seathwaite graphite was used in its native condition, hence the name *crayons d'Angleterre*. However, the relative scarcity of the Seathwaite commodity stimulated Continental research into successful methods of binding graphite dust into usable shapes with gum, resin, glue and similar adhesives (Fleming and Guptill) and in 1662 the first graphite composition pencil was made at Nürnberg. Graphite shapes glued in fir or cedar were described by J. Pettus in 1683. In 1795 Napoleon issued a patent to Nicolas Jacques Conte for a pencil lead manufacturing process that was the forerunner of the modern pencil. In Vienna at about the same time Joseph Hardtmuth achieved the same results. In 1839 Johan von Faber of Nürnberg improved the Conte process by extruding paste through a die and introducing machinery that cut and grooved wooden slats that enclosed the leads to form a pencil.

The rudimentary crayon period seems to have been that of the early (Old Men) period of the wadd holes. After the reopening of the wadd holes in 1710 Messrs Banks and Shepherd found a home market which required wadd for a variety of purposes more lucrative than crayons: "the casting of bomb-shells, round-shot and cannon-balls" (although without doubt some of the top quality continued to be sold for *crayons d'Angleterre*). However, it was not until the turn of the eighteenth and nineteenth centuries that the pencil industry proper emerged. Lysons, writing of wadd in 1816, says:

... its chief use is now for making pencils: the coarser sort is employed in the composition of crucibles, and for giving a black polish to iron, etc. ... When the mine is opened, a sufficient quantity is procured to answer the demand for several years; the black lead of the best quality is packed in barrels and sent to London by the waggon, the proprietor of which is bound in a considerable sum for its safe delivery. It is then deposited in the cellars under the Unitarian Chapel in Essex Street; and on the first Monday in every month there is a sale of it in an upper room of a public-house in the neighbourhood. The pencil-makers attend, and selecting pieces of the best quality, purchase according to their respective wants. The coarser sort is afterwards sold for other purposes. About three thousand pounds worth of the black lead is sold in a year; the price of that of the finest quality is 35s per lb; of the coarser, 120 l. per ton. . . . (Lysons, D. and S. *Magna Britannia*, vol iv, Cumberland, London, 1816.)

The first edition (1798) of *Encyclopaedia Britannica* names the factory of George Rowney as the earliest British pencil mill; records of this factory, its exact date of opening, even its whereabouts, have been lost; it is known that it was certainly not at Keswick. The story of the Keswick pencil industry probably deserves 1792 as a tentative first date, since it was in that year that John Ladyman provided Hutchinson with information on Seathwaite wadd. Ladyman is identifiable as a Keswick manufacturer who in 1805 was connected with the Millbeck woollen enterprise. To quote Brigadier J. W. Kaye, ("The Millbeck Woollen Industry", *Cumberland and Westmorland Antiquarian and Archaeological Society's Transactions*, New Series, vol lvii):

In 1805 the partners of the old mill granted to John Grave and John Ladyman, manufacturers of Keswick, the right . . . to use the water of the already existing mill-race for the wheels of the fulling and new carding mills. . . .

In 1817, the Millbeck records tell us, John Ladyman left the woollen trade to devote himself to pencil manufacturing. That he was already engaged in this is made clear by an 1814 entry in the register of baptisms at Crosthwaite, Keswick, which states that George, son of John Ladyman, pencil-maker of Keswick, was baptised on 21 October 1814. Thus John Ladyman was definitely connected with Seathwaite wadd by 1792; he was a manufacturer of some unspecified commodity in Keswick by 1805, by 1814 he was certainly making pencils. The Crosthwaite register begins to describe persons as 'manufacturers' from about 1790 onwards, but does not in any instance specify the type of manufacture until some twelve years later. The first person therein designated as a pencil-maker was one John Foulk (23 April 1814), but we know of nothing to connect him with earlier manufacturing, or with wadd, as we do in the case of John Ladyman.

The earliest named pencil-makers in Crosthwaite registers are John Foulk, John Ladyman, Jacob Banks, John Gates, Charles Hewer Wright, John Scratchard, William Robinson, Christopher Harrington, William Atkinson, John Harrison, John Green, William Forster; these names alone appear until 1830.

There were several pencil mills in Keswick but since their records have disappeared and only scattered and fragmentary information concerning them has survived, it is extraordinarily difficult to construct a true picture of the Keswick pencil industry in the early nineteenth century. The old corn and grinding mill and forge on Greta-side, known as Forge Mill, may well have been the first of these pencil mills.

The firm of Banks and Co. was founded at Forge Mill in 1832, but we know that by March 1827 a Joseph Ladyman, pencil-maker, and his wife Isabella were living at Greta Lodge, part of the Greta Hall estate, upon which estate was also Forge Mill, and this suggests that quite possibly pencil-making was by that date taking place at Forge Mill. Where one Ladyman was making pencils one might reasonably expect to find another pencil-making member of the same family employed also. John Ladyman (not Joseph's father, but perhaps a brother) was making pencils in Keswick by 1814 at the latest and from this one might tentatively conclude that Forge Mill was a pencil mill by that date; perhaps as early as 1805, or even sooner.

The Greta Hall estate by 1831 belonged to Mrs Jane Richardson; upon her death Robert Richardson inherited it.[5] 'Banks and Co, Greta Pencil Works and Black Lead Mills' was thus established in Forge Mill in 1832; the company being also joint lessees of what was now called the 'Borrowdale Black Lead Mining Company'. Jacob Banks (whose wife was formerly Ann Robinson) was succeeded at the pencil mill by his sons Joseph (who also had a wife named Ann) and Thomas (who married Sarah, daughter of Daniel Dover of the Millbeck industry —see Chapter Five). The foreman of Banks and Co.'s pencil works was, by 1834, one Thomas Tate.

From 1830 onward the new names of men employed in the expanding Keswick pencil industry appear thick and fast in the Crosthwaite register. Abraham Wren had formed a company by 1837; the Fosters too had their own company. Robert Thwaite was pencil-making at Brigham. In 1842 Robert Gibson purchased the Greta Hall estate, including the pencil works, from Robert Richardson; but the name of Banks and Co. was officially retained at Forge Mill. Undoubtedly Banks and Co. was Keswick's leading pencil firm, gaining the prize medal in the Temple of Art and Industry at the International Exhibition at the Crystal Palace in Hyde Park in 1851. *The Illustrated Magazine of Art* in 1854 contained a highly informative article entitled "Pencil Making in Keswick" which in fact dealt exclusively with Messrs Banks and Co.:

> The factory itself consists of a house of several stories, in the premises connected with which the cedar logs are stored . . . amounting in the course of a year to no less than from five thousand to six thousand cubic feet and serving for the manufacture of some five or six million cedar pencils. . . . On entering the workshop . . . the eye is confused by the machinery in motion . . . the ear is filled with the hum of saws . . . and the nose is irritated by the flood of fine wood-dust which fills the room, and which . . . before long occasions annoyance, and even nausea, to one unaccustomed to it. . . .

It is interesting to note that between the years 1850 to 1900 the bulk of the Florida cedar wood used for the pencils came from the old U.S.A. railways which at that period were being redeveloped; the torn-up cedar-wood sleepers were sold in the U.S.A. to agents who thereafter in turn sold them to the pencil-makers.

The Keswick pencils had hitherto been hand-made with pure Borrowdale wadd and Florida cedar, the tools required being a small handsaw, handplane and an ordinary darning-needle. The graphite in these early pencils stopped an inch or so short of one end of the pencil. By 1851, although pure Borrowdale wadd was still being used, and continued to be used by Banks and Co. until at least 1906, the article in the *Magazine of Art* makes it clear that pencils were no longer hand-made by this firm.

The cedar logs, said the article, were sawed into lengths and then into thin planks. Each plank was then cut into thin oblong strips in a special machine and, while this was being done, the machine operator regulated with his feet the action of another circular saw (placed at right

angles to the one with which he cut the strips) which incised the grooves
for the insertion of the lead. One half of the pencil having thus been
prepared, a smaller oblong piece was also cut, which was fitted against
the first, completing the whole.

> The wood having been thus far prepared, it is given to a sorter, who selects
> it from those pieces which have irregular parts; these are put aside for
> firewood . . . a great deal [of which] is sold to the women of the neighbour-
> hood.

The lead (wadd) was then sawed into thin slices, or scantlings, and
carefully selected for the right degrees of hardness so that "when they
are made up it may not be found that a pencil is an HH at one end and a
BB at the other. For the hardest pencils the lead is prepared chemically
and for the softest an increased thickness of lead is inserted. . . ." The
'lead' was then fitted into the grooves in the strips of cedar and these
filled cedar rods were then passed to a 'fastener-up' who glued the
cedar covers, or slips, over the filled rods, which were next rounded.
"The machine by which this is accomplished . . . is only found in this
establishment. . . . [It will] round from 600 to 800 dozen of pencils a
day. . . ." The pencils, still in the form of long sticks, were then
smoothed with a plane and polished:

> To effect this, benches are provided, at each of which two boys are at
> work, who take up some five or six sticks in their hands, and then pull
> them up and down between a roller covered with leather and a leather
> board . . . by which means the pencils are made to present the appearance
> of nice smooth walking-sticks, some thousand dozen being polished each
> day by each boy.
> The fashion of varnishing pencils has come up very recently. It first
> began with inferior kinds, but is now adopted with the best, and many
> sorts of pencils will indeed hardly sell without it.

The polishing completed, the rods were cut into lengths; first by a
circular saw, then by a man using a gauge and a razor-blade fixed in a
wooden handle. The pencil heads were finished off by a guillotine
"used only by Messrs Banks. . .".

Finally the pencils had the name of the maker stamped upon them,
together with indication of their quality. An ingenious tool was used

for this which 'could letter 120–200 pencils in a minute'. Some pencils had gilt letters instead of mere impressions on the wood. The pencils were, as an ultimate step, fastened up in dozens and later in half grosses.

Some ledgers, day books and order books of Banks and Co., dating back to 1847, have survived (although the bulk of the firm's records unfortunately perished in an accidental fire), these are now in the County Archives Office at Carlisle. Details of their contents here would make this chapter far too long: suffice it to say that they reveal extensive sales all over the British Isles and a number of overseas orders. The London ledgers record as purchasers (among very many others) the Educational Supply Association; Faber's of Nürnberg; Deakin Stationers of Tottenham Court Road; Ordish and Co. of Hatton Garden; Army and Navy Co-operative Society; Rubber Stamp Co. of Holborn Viaduct; Central School Depot, Paternoster Row; Church Missionary Society (large and regular orders over a very long period); Straker's; Kelly's Directories; Crocker's Stationery Co.; Dean's Iron-mongers of Cowes, Isle of Wight; the Hardy Patent Pick Co.; Water-ton and Sons, Sealing Wax Makers of Ludgate Circus; Letts and Co.; the Mutual Co-operative Society; Mongers West Australian Stores; the Patent Plumbago and Crucible Co. of Battersea; G. Royle and Son of Lovell's Court, Paternoster Row; Pitman's; Harrington's Wholesale Stationers (very large regular orders); the School Board at Hockley; and in July 1895 and again in 1898, on each occasion for a small order only (of under five pounds), the "Independent Labour Party, per J. S. Rigby, Secy, Trading Dept., Club House, 578 Fulham Road".

Banks and Co. had it as their main advertising line that genuine "pure Borrowdale plumbago" was used in their pencils. In 1851 at the Great Exhibition and again in the exhibition of 1862 the company exhibited, on their prize-winning stands, what the *Cumberland Pacquet* proudly described as,

> ... their very splendid collection of pencils. The fire-proof pencil points manufactured by this firm are spoken of in the highest possible terms, their great recommendation being that they will stand heat, and consequently can be exported for use in any climate. ...

Also exhibited at these two exhibitions were "several specimens of very unusual size of the purest Borrowdale lead". One of these large lumps of wadd still survives in the possession of the Birkbeck family, complete with the original ebony stand on which it was displayed.

At the time of the 1862 exhibition a letter appeared in *The Times* inferring that the claim of Banks and Co. to be using pure Borrowdale plumbago in their pencils must be a false one, since the stock of that commodity was totally exhausted. In refutation of this Messrs Banks and Co. retorted that they had in their possession "eight or ten tons of the purest Borrowdale lead; stock which had never been out of the country".

By 1884 three Keswick pencil mills survived: Banks and Co., the largest and best known; A. Wren and Co. and the firm of Hogarth and Son at Greta Bridge. These three firms together (according to an article in *Chambers Journal*) employed "about a hundred work people, male and female. The men earn on an average about twenty-five shillings a week, the women about twelve." The article added that an eminent firm of toilet-soap makers bought all the cedar sawdust that was a by-product of these mills. The rejected cedar wood was increasingly used now for making tourist souvenirs; Thomas G. Newby of 34 Main Street and John Tangye of 115 Main Street, both described as cedar goods manufacturers, appear in the lists of Keswick trades people.

In 1886 the firm of Hogarth and Hayes took over the old firm of Abraham Wren and this change in the Keswick pencil world was followed by the establishment of a new company, Mrs Ann Banks & Co., in the former woollen mill by Greta Bridge. This new firm seems to have been in no way connected with Banks and Co., indeed it showed very distinct signs of rivalry. According to the *Carlisle Journal*, Mrs Ann Banks had, by the introduction of new machinery and methods, given "fresh stimulus to Keswick's pencil trade", and her firm had a monopoly upon "genuine Borrowdale black-lead. . . ." The firm of A. Banks, said the newspaper, had had the opportunity of purchasing a large consignment of Borrowdale lead from Professor Brockedon of London who was the "sole holder of the entire stock of this valuable material in England, which was afterwards bought by A. Banks of Keswick and ultimately came into the possession of this company. . .". This claim of course sublimely ignored Banks and Co., who still had their own stock of Borrowdale graphite.

It has been suggested that Ann Banks, wife of Joseph Banks of the original Banks and Co. purchased, or had purchased in her name, a stock of wadd when Gibson's took over Banks and Co. and that this stock was used to float the new company forty years later. This, however, would seem to be very much a matter of surmise.

In 1876 Robert Gibson had made a gift of conveyance of the Greta Pencil Works and adjacent properties to his daughter; it is said that he offered her the deeds, not specifying what they were, but asking her playfully if she would care to give him ten shillings for them, which she did. Miss Gibson made Banks and Co. a most successful proprietress, having as her factory manager Henry Birkbeck, who in 1906 himself became owner of the firm, to be succeeded by his son, Simon.

The story of wadd ended round about the year 1906, when pencils ceased to be made from it; the graphite used thenceforth coming from Ceylon, Mexico and Korea, to be employed not in its pure state but mixed with a special clay in order to produce the required leads, or strips as they are known in the trade. By 1910 the three surviving Keswick pencil firms were Hogarth and Hayes at Southey Hill, Banks and Co. (Birkbeck proprietors) at Forge Mill and the Cumberland Pencil Co. (C. Greenwood) in Ann Banks' former mill by Greta Bridge. Today the Cumberland Pencil Company's large and up-to-date factory adjoining the site of the old Hogarth and Hayes works (whose original mill still stands) greets the eye of all comers to Keswick from the west; the town thus still boasts a thriving and famous pencil industry. Simon Birkbeck retired from making pencils in 1921 and his old firm closed in 1928, when antiques took the place of pencils at Forge Mill. As for the pencil mill at Greta Bridge, these buildings have now been most successfully converted into premises for a flourishing youth club.

CHAPTER FOUR

Statesmen's Progress

THE GRAVE FAMILY of Skelgill, Newlands, of ancient yeoman farmer or statesmen (estatesmen) lineage, claims to have been at Skelgill since 1347 (the name, Skelgill, derives from the Norse *scale*, meaning a spreading of waters). The first discoverable deed relating to Skelgill is dated 1647—an unfortunately not very informative document, a large central portion having been eaten by mice. It records the transference of the tenancy of Skelgill by John Studdart and Garvin Baron of Crosthwaite to Robert Bell of Skelgill,[1] this being done with the licence and consent of the Earl of Egremont, lord of the manor of Braithwaite and Coledale.

This deed in no way invalidates the Grave family's claim to Skelgill tenancy since the fourteenth century; the Graves, as customary tenants, could have let to Studdart and Baron while they themselves farmed elsewhere during the early seventeenth-century period. It is very much more probable, however, that Graves were at Skelgill together with these other tenants, since it is more than possible that by 1647 there were two holdings at Skelgill (High Skelgill and Low Skelgill), as there certainly were a century later and still are today; the Grave family occupying Low Skelgill. It is likely that they, originally the sole tenants at Skelgill, might at an early date have leased part of their holding to another farmer, thereby creating the "two messuages or tenements or dwelling houses at Skelgill" which we find specified in later deeds.

The Lake Country statesmen-tenants held their tenements by customary tenant right which seems to have been tantamount to freehold. The customs upon which these ancient rights of northern tenure were based varied between different manors and lordships, but there were certain characteristics common to all.[2] The whole tenement normally descended to the eldest son, or failing male issue to the eldest daughter and in most instances seems not to have been divisible, though provision for the widow was generally required. The heir had to appear in the manor court to have his admittance entered on its roll and as evidence of his admittance he received a parchment strip, which in essence was a copy of the entry on the court roll.

Recorded instances of tenants of this kind exist for the early sixteenth century. As late as 1771 we find Reuben Grave (for clarity's sake here referred to as Reuben II), only son and heir of John Grave (I), deceased, appearing at the manor court of the Earl of Egremont to have his admittance entered on the court roll and thereafter to receive his numbered copy of the entry, which tells us that he took over tenancy of Skelgill at the customary annual rent of 13s. 10d.,

> to have and to hold the premises aforesaid during the life of the said Lord of Egremont and the said Reuben Grave rendering to the Lord yearly at the feasts of St Michael the Archangel and the Annunciation of the Blessed Virgin Mary the aforesaid rent. . . .

Grave, on his occasion of becoming heir, paid the rent of 13s. 10d. and he also paid a *gressum* or fine (fee would be the modern term) of £30, by which he was admitted tenant. He was entitled to let the premises, or any part of them (though not without licence of the lord or his officers) and tracing the history of Skelgill from 1647 onwards it transpires that the tenant was even entitled to sell, subject again to the licence of the lord of the manor or those acting for him. How general this right was throughout the region we do not know, but in the seventeenth century such transferences of land by deed, implying mortgage or sale or lease, were certainly not uncommon.

The tenant owed specified obligations to the lord of the manor and might forfeit his holding by failure to discharge them. Besides owing rent, he might also owe a number of days service in ploughing, shearing, reaping or carting; he owed a fine, or *gressum*, at any change of tenancy (Reuben Grave's £30 fine) whether by death or alienation, and at the death of the lord; he was bound to provide horse and armour for Border service, or to participate in the cost. To compensate for these obligations a tenant had certain perquisites, such as being entitled to timber for fuel and building purposes, to common grazing for his cattle, geese and pigs, and the right to cut peats from the common for the needs of his own household. The customs of Borrowdale, as declared in 1583, well illustrate both the obligations and benefits of tenants under the terms of customary tenure:

1. The customary tenants enjoy the ancient custom called tenant-right, namely "to have their messuages and tenements to them during their lives, and after their deceases, to the eldest issues of their bodies lawfully begotten. And for lack of such issue, the remainder thereof to the next persons of the same blood, paying yearly for the same the rents accustomed to the lord or lords of the said manor, at the feast days of St James the Apostle and St Wilfred, by even portions."

2. The tenants shall be ready at the bidding of the Lord Warden of the West Marches, to serve at their own costs, namely as horsemen in summer and footmen in winter.

3. The tenants shall pay on change of the lord I gods penny, and at their death or on change or alienation of their holdings 1 year's rent.

4. The tenants shall pay a fixed tithe-commutation.

5. They shall have all their fishings at the usual rents.

6. They shall have all underwood and top or lop (not being timber).

7. They shall have sufficient timber for the repair of their houses, hedges, and implements by view of the bailiff. (Duchy of Lancaster Surveys, 25 Elizabeth; Hall, H., *Society in the Elizabethan Age*. London, 1887).

The statesman was, of course, predominantly a sheep farmer; a flock went with his farm and had to go with his farm. As tenant or owner-occupier he might increase the size of his flock and this additional tally of sheep, the result of his own enterprise, was his to sell or to do what he liked with, but the basic flock had to be handed over by the outgoing tenant to the incoming tenant, an integral part of the farm: this system still prevails throughout the region. With the flock went grazing rights and the sheep-heath, or *heaf*, on the fell. The animals of each flock were, and indeed still are, marked in a manner traditional and peculiar to that flock alone. The identity marks are of two kinds, smit marks and ear marks; both methods of marking are used for each sheep. The smit marks, in red or dark dye, take the form of pops (blobs) and strokes, with occasionally the initial of the farmstead to which the flock belongs. The ear mark are various incisions; bitting, ritting and crop-pings.[3]

The rest of the farm stock in early times was scanty; cattle were few, most establishments kept a pig and most statesmen's wives had their hens, ducks and geese. Horses were numerous in the region as a result of the terms of Border service. Farm implements were crude: ploughs, sickles (although scythes were known, all corn was reaped by sickle) and flails for threshing. There was no machine for dressing the corn; this was done either on a suitable 'deetin' hill', where the corn was winnowed by throwing the grain up against the wind which scattered the light chaff, while the corn itself dropped down on to the 'deetin' cloath' or, when the weather was unsuitable for outdoor winnowing, the process was carried out in a barn with doors at opposite ends, the corn being tossed from one end of the barn to the other.

Carts were primitive and few; sledges, or sleds, were used in prefer-ence to wheeled vehicles on the high-country tracks. Those carts which were in use were 'tummel cars', the axles of which revolved with the wheels: there were no spoke wheels in use. The cart had no iron staps, or shoulder links, only 'hammer bands': the horse was yoked to willow or hazel rings sliding on the shafts which were retained in their place by a pin. There were no boards in the cart bottoms, ends, or sides; these were composed of 'fleeks' made of wands, or 'symes', straw ropes, wound among the straps. There were no breechings for the horses, to hold back the carts when descending hills. The horses' collars, 'braf-fams', were home-made of symes of hay and straw; some bridles were made of cord, but more usually of hemp, sometimes even of plaited 'seeves' (rushes). Leather harness was regarded as effeminate and further-more as a rather vulgar display of wealth; 'sonks' (green sods) girthed on with hay or straw bands were the common substitutes for saddles.[4]

There was a considerable degree of cultivation, since the fell farms had to be almost entirely self-supporting, but there was little variety in the actual crops grown. Oats, 'havers', and hay were the main crops; the staple diet of the dalesfolk being whey, oaten bread, porridge, thin oatcakes or 'clapbread', hard home-made cheese, and beans, which last were also fed to the animals. Fresh meat was almost unknown. Turnips and potatoes did not reach Cumberland until the mid-eighteenth century; the introduction of turnips meant that the annual slaughter of cattle, with resultant salting and smoking for winter eating, was no longer necessary since live-stock, turnip-fed, could now be maintained throughout the winter. Barley (called 'big' or 'biggins') was grown and malted for brewing. A little rye was also grown, but wheat was a great rarity. Some garden vegetables such as peas, onions and cabbages were grown in small quantities. Many farms grew a little flax and sometimes, too, small crops of hemp for plaiting twine.[4]

For labour the statesmen relied almost exclusively upon their own families, although on some of the larger farms, hands, or hinds, were employed; sometimes these were orphans or fatherless children on the parish, who were apprenticed out. The womenfolk assisted with the lighter farmwork, which included much of the peat-cutting; theirs, too, was the task of spinning, weaving and knitting, the making of clothes and other household necessities such as curtains and quilts, rugs and linen, rushlights and soap.

A remarkable set of dialect verses describing rural habits in Cumberland in "them oalden times, when George the Third was King", by William Dickinson of Thorncroft, Workington, and published in his *Cumbriana, or Fragments of Cumbrian Life* (1876), gives a vivid idea of a way of life which basically can have changed little between the late sixteenth and early nineteenth centuries. Dickinson describes the statesmen's progress month by month throughout the year. Christmas feasting was kept up well into January, on roast beef, raised goose pies, giblet pies, mince pies, and 'Lamplugh puddin''—a large bowl of hot ale, well spiced and with biscuits steeped in it. Acting on the principle that "It's a lang teyme till neist Christmas" everyone threw themselves with gusto into the celebrations,

> They kevvel and swing, and dance ledder-te-spetch,
> And royster and swatter like ought . . .

Mornings, not surprisingly, found them "outa fettle for work". But fuel had to be fetched in and certain basic chores performed. The days were short, snow-filled and dark; one rose by rushlight and went to bed by rushlight. For those who stayed out late, a lantern was hung on the fold-gate for guidance.

In February came barley-threshing time. A 'burying skin' (dried horse-skin) was thrown down on the barn floor and the threshing then done by flail. Later it was carried to the 'deetin' hill'. Of this barley some had to be "cree't for frummerty", by bruising it in a stone mortar at the barn door.

Candlemas, too, was the time when debts were paid and received; the master and mistress rode off on a pillion to the market town to settle this business.

The long evenings were spent at the fireside; the men making and mending farm implements, the womenfolk spinning, weaving and sewing. There was a lot of gossip and story-telling and (we know from other accounts) a lot of card-playing too, Cumbrians having a great passion for cards.

March brought ploughing-time. Dickinson is celebrated especially for his description of ploughing:

> Now out wid a heamm-meadd roan-tree plue,
>   Wid ironin' scanty eneuff;
> Lait up strea braff'ms—reapp traces enue,
>   And see 'at they're o' draft preuff.
>
> Next yoke in o' lang-horn't owsen two pair,
>   Two lang-tailed horses unshod;
> Co' t ' plue hodder, plue-co'ers—two or three mair,
>   Wi, speadd, and wi' pettle, and prod.
>
> Now t'bullocks nit yok 't sen plue-time last year,
>   His horses out'liggan, and lean,
> And kaim'tly—and t'trappins o' flimsily gear
>   And t'ley fur stark as t'town green. . . .

This, translated, means, fetch out the home-made rowan-tree plough (rowan-tree wood was greatly preferred for all farm implements; in addition to being very hard it was said to hold magic properties; this reason for its preference undoubtedly became lost and forgotten over the course of time, although the preference itself persisted). The plough, adds the verse, had little iron about it. After the plough, seek out horse collars and traces of straw and ensure that they are in strong condition for the work ahead. Next yoke two long-horned oxen and two unshod long-tailed horses, and call out the ploughman himself, and his assistants who will lead the animals, keep them going steady, and turn them in at the ends of the furrows; together with two or three more men armed with spades to break up the earth untouched by the plough-share, and others with goads for the animals. After which the fun: for the bullocks have not been yoked since plough-time last year and the horses, unstabled all winter, are lean, and frisky. The harness is flimsy, and the ground as hard as the village green. The result (which must be read in the original for the full flavour) is straining horses, distracted ploughman and assistants, roaring and swearing, "shockin' bad lan-guage" from all. ". . . t'oxen gits kysty and kevels about" and finally kick over the traces. The horses get out of control and pull the plough-man down by the neck (for it was the custom for him to wear the guiding cords in one piece, the centre being behind his neck, so that his hands might be free for holding the stilts of the plough—and hurling sods at his team when his impatience overreached his invective, which can sometimes happen even to a Cumbrian!). But at last dwindling light brought the battle to a temporary close at least and the plough-man and his helpers returned home to a reviving supper of cow't lword and rich broth.

Other March days were devoted to dyking and hedge-repairing:

> And now for pwok-mittens on dinnellan hands
>   And dykin-mittens, and swatch;
> To mend up some gaps round plewin' lands,
>   Adn waik-spots, and creep-whols to patch. . . .

('Pwok-mittens' being poke-mittens, that is gloves without finger-stalls; 'dinnellan' hands are tingling hands, while a 'swatch' is a bill hook).

In April, after the last frosts, oats were sewn and a little hemp; manure was spread on the far intakes, carried there in horse panniers. Potatoes were planted in trenches (this fixes the date as mid-eighteenth century or later); potato disease was unknown. It should be noted that peeling potatoes was regarded as scandalously wasteful and the 'prentice was set to scrape them, a tedious task:

> Than he wad git drowsy, and noddle and scrape,
>   As an unpaid 'prentice wad dee;
> His knife and his tatie wad seun get so slape
>   They wad rowl out o' hand off his knee . . .

The sleeper would be roused by a "clout ower t' lug, or a skelp".

In late April came lambing time, with work early and late. The following verse might well be a dalesman speaking today on the subject of his lambs:

> If yance they git milk and can wander about,
>   They care not for frost nor for snow;
> For it's plenty o' suckle 'at gars them git stout,
>   To skip, and to lowp, and to grow.

After the pasturage had been cropped bare in May by the ewes and their lambs (who were then let on to the open fell) there was little grass left for the cows and, to provide them with extra nourishment, tender ash-sprouts were spread out on the ground "to give to t'oald milkers a treat".

June was peat-cutting time; the top layers being removed with a flay-spade, the lower black peats with a long, special peat-spade. The peats, when cut, had to be spread out to dry, being turned from time to time; this task was allotted to the bairns.

In July came sheep-washing, followed by clipping-time. These activities were both noisy and lively:

> Sek bleatin' o' lambs, and sek barkin' o' dogs,
>   Sek jybin and jwokin' o' men;
> Sek clatt'rin o' lads in their oald cokert clogs,
>   Sek drinkin' o' whisky. Amen!

After the clipping came supper-feasts with sports, singing and dancing. Dickinson gives a very old clipping song, during the singing of which the guests had in turn to obey the commands of the second and third verses and if the glass was not emptied by the end of the refrain the penalty was enforced a second time. Doubtless little forcing was required:

> Here's a good health to the man o' this house,
> The man o' this house, the man o' this house,
> Here's a good health to the man o' this house,
>   For he is a right honest man.

And he that does this health deny,
Before his face I just defy;
Right in his face this glass shall fly,
So let this health go round.

Place the canny cup to your chin,
Open your mouth and let liquor run in;
The more you drink the fuller your skin,
So let this health go round.

After the celebrations everyone rolled home happy, to be up betimes
next morning for another day's clipping and another clipping-supper
at the close of it:

To help a good neighbour at his merry meetin',
A heall country side to employ;
In housin' and clippin' wi' much friendly greetin',
For clippins are meetin's o' joy.

August brought hay-time, with its early rising, its midday resting
and its late night working in the gloaming and moonrise:

Now mowers can't work through t'middle o' t' day,
For t'bitin' o' clegs, and for heat;
So they snoozle some hours on t' new gitten hay,
An' mak't up by workan at neet.

Till t'glowworm leets up, than to blanket they stakker,
To snatch a laal sleep, and then rise;
And at it (while white-throats in t' dykes cherr and chatter),
And whittle-t-whet their long scythes.

Then skalin' and turnin' wi' fork and wi' reakk,
And skewin't about to dry;
And cockin', and brekkin, for good hay to meakk,
And rake into plat forbye. . . .

Hay-time was followed by harvest-time in September; when all had
been safely gathered in came the kern supper, which in this region was

not, in fact, such a great occasion as a clipping-supper. Harvesting was succeeded by the steeping of hemp and lint and bleaching it on the grass, preparatory to storing it away for making twine (a commodity colloquially known in Cumberland as 'michael').

With October and the back-end came a lull in work, affording time for shepherds' meets and merry-neets, sales and toffee-pulls. Schooling commenced for the children, to be attended throughout winter; in summer the scholars could not be spared from their farm chores. It should be borne in mind that the statesmen as a class were far from being illiterate; popular education in the Lake Country, although often seasonally intermittent, dated back a long way before the introduction of state education in 1833 and by the seventeenth century there was a surprisingly high level of literacy in the region, although reading matter itself was very restricted.

Salving, or 'sarving', was the task which absorbed the menfolk towards the close of October. It is no longer practised and it is difficult today to find anyone who is able to describe the process in any detail.[5] It was an early substitute for dipping (which did not come into common usage in the fells until the close of the nineteenth century). The salve was made of stockholm-tar mixed with lard (cheap foreign butter was used in the nineteenth century). The wool of the sheep was pulled apart in clusters or sheddings, as they were called, and the salve applied to the sheep's skin. Before long the warmth of the animal's body would cause the salve to melt and run, thus spreading well over the skin surface.

The salvers themselves were professionals who travelled the region, from farm to farm, as an itinerant labour force; they were called 'scab doctors'. It would take a good man to salve as many as twenty sheep in one day; this was reckoned serious going.

Some of the old salving, or sarving houses still survive; examples may be seen at Gatesgarth farm and at Taw House.

With November the young folks went out to the sykes to collect rushes for making rush-lights by peeling them and then dipping them in grease:

> T' young fwoaks'll gang till a cannel-seave syke,
>   And pick a shaff strangans for leets!
> Then hotter to heamm, through bog and wet dyke,
>   To peel them and dip them at neets. . . .

The statesmen families grew up to farming, the oldest son usually becoming his father's right-hand man at an early age. The second son was, when the family could afford it, sent away to study a profession. The younger sons, at the age of fourteen, would seek employment upon other farms, hoping at the age of thirty or so to have the experience and financial resources to get a small farm of their own.

The hiring fairs were at Whitsun and Martinmas and the largest were those held at Cockermouth and Keswick. The boys, in brand new suits and vast neckties of green and red, given them by their parents, stood with straws in their mouths as a sign that they wished to be hired as 'lads'. At sixteen or seventeen they would be hired as 'men'. As men they received wages of twelve or fourteen pounds a year, living in, all found: wages considerably higher than those prevailing among agricultural workers in the midlands and the south.

In December the farmers dressed oats for meal, drying them in a kiln in the kiln-croft and afterwards taking them to the 'bond-sucken' mill —the manorial mill to which statesmen were frequently bound, by their terms of tenure, to convey their corn for grinding. Afterwards, the ground meal and refuse from the oats were carried back to the farm and 'sooins' were made as a delicacy by soaking the refuse in water for two days, straining off the liquid and eating the remaining jelly with a little salt and water. And then folks found themselves preparing for Christmas again; once more the twelvemonth cycle had completed itself.

Dickinson concludes his verses:

> And now you've a swatch o' them good oald days,
>   'At fwok brags on as hevvin' lang sen;
> And you know summat now o' their wark and their ways;
>   Wad y swap eb'm hands, good men?

Many of the farmsteads in which Dickinson's statesmen lived and worked still survive, not greatly changed in outward appearance, if considerably converted and modified within. The seventeenth-century farmstead which we see at Low Skelgill today must have been constructed very near the time of the 1647 deed; clearly upon the site of, and in part with material from, an earlier building. Medieval building patterns survived in the Lake Country without fundamental alteration until about 1650, when the development of mining and industry, the improvement of means of transport and the enclosure of fell-lands brought about a minor revolution in housing. Throughout the region the old-style buildings of clay, timber or, in cruck-construction, a combination of the two, were replaced by the stone edifices so typical of the Lake Country as we know it today. The beams of many of these mid-seventeenth-century farms are clearly timbers which were formerly part of the cruck-trusses of earlier buildings; such re-used crucks are in evidence at Low Skelgill.

The two major variations of the standard plan of mid-seventeenth-century statesmen's farmsteads were a single range of outbuildings and dwelling-house, or a dwelling-house and outbuildings grouped separately. Low Skelgill belongs to the single range pattern. A passage ran through the building range from front to back and, at the far end of this passage, opposing doors led to the kitchen on one hand and the byre on the other. A cross-wall, embracing the principal fireplace, separated the passageway from the kitchen; the dwelling-quarters consisted of kitchen and bower, divided one from the other by a wooden partition, the bower being sometimes further divided to form a buttery. Over these rooms was a loft used as a dormitory by the children and servants, master and mistress using the bower; this loft was gained by a ladder or, in later and superior houses, a stone staircase set in a projection. The farm buildings consisted of byre and barn with a wool-loft extending over the byre and cross-passage.

Although over the years Low Skelgill has inevitably undergone a considerable amount of alteration and conversion, it is still possible to trace the original plan of kitchen, bower and buttery, with a staircase ascending from the kitchen to sleeping-loft above. Alterations and improvements obviously proceeded along lines generally followed throughout the region. The principal bedroom (bower), formerly on the ground floor, was moved to upstairs and its place downstairs taken by the parlour. Increasing use of the first floor led to improvement of the staircase; by the early eighteenth century this, in the majority of statesmen's houses, occupied a deep projecting wing which was roofed by a continuation of the main roof slope to form 'an outshut'. Gradually other rooms, usually a scullery and a dairy, came to be added to this projecting staircase wing, thus forming a continuous range along the rear of the house. These rear rooms were either open to the roof or had a prism-shaped loft overhead in which the hinds, if any were employed, slept. In the early eighteenth century slate flags began to be used to replace the former thatched roofing; these early flags, of random sizes, were very thick and heavy and the roof trusses which supported them had to be correspondingly massive. Chimney stacks were single, wide and thoroughly idiosyncratic. Windows, small and square in shape with square mullions, had timber casements which flapped downwards and inwards. The main entrance of the house was sheltered by a solid stone porch, deeply recessed, usually containing two slate-seated, shelf-style benches. The heavy-oak door was metal studded; some porches had provision also for weather-boards.

Since few later innovations have been made to the exterior of Low Skelgill this farm still presents a reasonably authentic late seventeenth-century appearance. It compares very interestingly with its near neighbour, High Skelgill farm, the dwelling-house of which is late eighteenth century; this, placed on a slight elevation (the earlier houses were constructed with a shrewd eye to the lie of the land and the weather, being sited in sheltered positions under the fell and with a blind-end wall catching the prevailing south-westerly winds) is tall, symmetrical and single roof spanned, with grouped regular chimney stacks and large, rectangular, symmetrically disposed double-hung sash windows.

The Bell family remained in tenancy at Skelgill until 1723; either living in the seventeenth-century house surviving today, or, as seems more probable, in a neighbouring dwelling which has now disappeared, but which was very possibly on the site of the present eighteenth-century High Skelgill house. In 1728 we find Reuben Grave (Reuben I), described as being "of Skelgill", signing a deed of mortgage of Skelgill to William Topson of Stonethwaite in Borrowdale for £354 3s. 4d.

In 1733 we find a deed of transference of Skelgill, for £150, to John Smart of Chelsea Hospital, doctor in physics. In 1734 Dr Smart appointed Thomas Wholpdale, attorney of Penrith, to act for him when Susanna, widow of Brigadier Thomas Stanwix, claimed against John Smart and Edward Eyre, through Thomas Wholpdale, an arrear of dower amounting to £31 10s. in respect of Skelgill. Unfortunately, some documents in this collection are missing and therefore gaps and omissions occur in this highly complicated phase of the Skelgill history. Full details and final outcome of the lawsuit do not transpire, but it becomes increasingly clear that by this period, at all events, there were two holdings at Skelgill.

By 1745 Lawrence Washington and his wife Grace were owners of a property at Skelgill. Washington, a Whitehaven dyer, retained this property for several years but seems to have let it, himself living in Whitehaven; during his period of ownership we find a John Crosthwaite of Ormathwaite and a Mary Topson, spinster, appearing at the manor court to pay rents as Skelgill tenants.

Yet during this same period (in 1747) John Grave I, described as being "of Skelgill", entered into an agreement with Joseph Borough of Portinscale, whereby Borough "granted, bargained, sold, conveyed and confirmed meale tithe, tithes of corn, grane and sheaves and all other tithes due to be paid to Joseph Borough . . . arising and increasing upon the tenement and lands of Parkside in the tenour or occupation of John Crosthwaite of Ormathwaite and all sums of money for tithes from Gillbank now in the possession of John Fisher" for a seven-year period of time, during which John Grave, should he choose so to do, might take up the tithes for ever.

This John Grave, obviously a thrusting character, first appears as a name in the Skelgill documents in 1723, when, described as "John Grave son of Garven Grave of Broadstone, Crosthwaite" he placed himself as apprentice to Thomas Sanderson, carpenter, for a term of seven years. There is no documentary evidence to tell us when John Grave moved to Skelgill; his father, Garven Grave, may have succeeded upon the death of Reuben I. In 1748 we find John purchasing from Thomas Wholpdale, for £300, a Skelgill property which included that part formerly belonging to Dr Smart: with this property went a "fflock of sheep containing ffifty in number".

In 1749 John Grave bought Parkside from John Crosthwaite for £25 5s. 0d. Grave (described now as being "of Waterend") five years later purchased this Waterend property from "Daniel Fisher of Skelgill"; for Waterend, Grave paid £93 7s. 6d. to Fisher and to the Earl of Egremont "the yearly customary rent of five shillings and twopence and twopence free rent for Swinside common . . . and also paying one penny to the purvey. . . ."

A deed of 1759 shows us Lawrence Washington entering into a covenant of sale of his Skelgill property with one Willgoose of Brandelhowe. Washington died before this sale was effected (we do not know the date of his death) and by 1770 John Grave had purchased this Skelgill holding from Washington's widow, Grace. In this way Grave seems to have gained full possession of the entire Skelgill holdings with the exception of a Skelgill property still under the tenancy of Daniel Fisher.

A romanticist would say that in John Grave we see the portrait of a man who set out to restore his family's fortunes and gather together their scattered ancestral inheritance. However, John Grave was obviously no sentimentalist, for in 1770 he was raising further money by mortgaging the former Washington property to John Stainton of Underskiddaw, "with the licence and consent of the Earl of Egremont", the property being,

> all that his customary messuage and tenement . . . together with all and singular houses Edifices Buildings Barnes Byres and Stables Walls Hedges Ditches and fences Wayes Watters Watercourses Comons Comon pasture and Intaks Closes Lands Meadows pastures feedings Wastes Washground moors Mosses Sheap Heaths and Cattlegates. . . .

A year later John Grave was dead (his age must have been in the neighbourhood of sixty) and, as we have seen, his son Reuben II succeeded him. An official inventory of the late John was made, which reads as follows:

		£		
1.	Purse and Apparel, House and Furniture	15	–	–
2.	Goods within the bodystead of the House, Clock, Brass, Chairs etc	8	–	–
3.	in the Milk House & thro' Gate Vessel etc	–	15	–
4.	in the Back Kitchen Kettals etc	1	5	–
5.	in the Kitchen Chamber upstairs	1	10	–
6.	Parlour and Parlour Loft	1	10	–
7.	First room upstairs in the House, Ark, beding Wool etc	10	5	–
8.	Two more rooms upstairs in the House	4	00	0
9.	Corn Barn, Wood and Corn etc	5	15	0
10.	New Barn, Wood & Hay Coops and Carts	8	00	0

11.	Old Barn Hay etc	2 00	0
12.	The Shop Wreight Geer etc	4 10	0
13.	Latts etc	1 10	—
14.	More Wood, Cart Stangs etc	1 00	0
Chattles	One Mare	6 00	0
	Two Hoggs	6 00	0
Sheep 355 at 7s		124 5	0
Horned Chattles 13		45 00	0

Appraised by us   Total   246 05 0
(Signed) Daniel Fisher
       Joshua Grave

The numbers of statesmen who were holders by tenant right diminished from the mid-eighteenth century onwards for two main reasons: many customary tenants were enfranchised by agreement, while others became freeholders as a result of enclosures. Reuben Grave II was enfranchised in 1771: a deed for 20 May of that year tells us that "the Earl of Egremont did grant, bargain, sell, alien, remise, release, enfranchise, ratify and confirm unto Reuben Grave of Skelgill and his heirs all those two messuages or tenements or dwelling houses at Skelgill foresaid . . . " by payment of £232 and a further sum of £83 2s. 5d. as the price of timber and woods and a further £313 2s. 5d. and "the ancient yearly customary rent of £1 3s . . . to be ever after paid as a free rent . . . by the space of Twenty-one days next after any of the said several Feast Days of Times of Payment. . .". The earl retained the right to any ores and quarries which might be opened on the property.

Enfranchisement was expensive; it may have taken even prosperous statesmen families such as the Graves a considerable time to recover from such financial strain and it is clear that some statesmen never really recovered from the cost of being enfranchised. Reuben Grave, in 1772, leased part of the Skelgill property to the Topsons of Borrowdale but, since a lapse of forty years now occurs in the Skelgill papers, it is impossible to draw any conclusions as to what extent the price of enfranchisement embarrassed the Graves. In 1821 we find Reuben's sons (Reuben III and Simeon of Skelgill and John II of Coledale) entering a bond for £340 with John Harryman of Portinscale. This loan may have been taken up to provide capital during a period of expansion; for expanding

the Graves now were. How Coledale had come into the family's hands
we do not know (nor do we know the exact family relationship of
Peter Grave who was farming at Gatesgarth at the turn of the century).
Gillbank and Low Snab (both Newlands farms) were soon to come into
the family through marriage; Reuben Grave IV (born in 1809) first
saw his future wife, Grace Thwaite of Gillbank, as an infant at her
christening; he was then twenty-one and he made up his mind to wait
until she was grown up and then to marry her! This remarkable
decision he took in 1830; they were ultimately married on 25 June
1857. They went to live at Low Snab, which belonged to the bride's
family.

The way of life of the dalesman may be said to have proceeded,
since the mid-seventeenth century, without truly drastic change until
the advent of the motor-car. Simeon Grave (or, as he wrote it, Graves)
II of Gillbank kept random journals, one of which has survived to
demonstrate the basic similarity between the life of a mid-nineteenth-
century Lake Country farmer and flock-master and his statesmen
ancestors.

The first eleven pages of Simeon's notebook are devoted to details of
sheep sales; descriptions of lots, names of purchasers and the smit marks
of sheep purchased. For instance:

Lot		Lambs		£	s	d
1	Gimmers.	Pop near shoulder	20			
		Daniel Tolson	8/6	8	10	–
2.	„	Pop Far Shoulder	21			
		John Bell	8/–	8	8	–
3.	Weathers	Near Shoulder	12			
		Robt Parker	5/6	3	6	–
4.	„	Tail Head	10			
		Wilson Clark	5/6	2	15	–
5.	„	Pop on Shoulder	12			
		John Thwaite	6/–	3	12	–

And so on, lot by lot. As well as lambs, there were sold ewes varying
in price from 7s. 6d. to 12s. 6d. each, gimmer twinters at 10s. 3d. or
10s. 9d. each, wether twinters from 8s. 3d. to 16s. 6d., old wethers varying in price between 11s. 9d. and 16s. 9d. and tups, for which the
individual prices are not given.

The next series of entries relate to ewes put to tup:

```
1861   Nov 10 the White Faced Tup
         1 Wite face ewe Tupt 12 novem
         12 Ditto 13
         Fell ewes First Tupt 18 november
         4 next on the week after
The Fell Tup let louse on 28 nov
         86 ewes to it
1868 Herdwick Tup on 30 November
93 ewes first week Red Pop on the Near
Hook second week ewes on the far Hook. . . .
```

Like all farmers of the Lake Country Simeon displayed an almost obsessive interest in the dramatic vagaries of the region's climate:

1859
Dry season began April 5 and lasted till September except a thunder shower or two . . . the scarcity of hay and straw brought the cattle and sheep to Distress all Cumberland over the sheep died by hundreds.

1860
. . . a very hard winter . . . the snow storm came 29 December covered all the fences and lasted to the 20 of January 1861 another snow storm fell on the 9 of Feb and continue to April and then we had fine wether to Swithen day after that we had one flood or 2 every week to the 10 October we had a week or two fine wether and after that we had storms every week . . . On the 25 of November we had one of the largest floods that was ever remembered by mankind and another on the 12 of December simelar to the last.

1868 this year Begun with the greenest winter that we ever saw It begun to be dry in April but the last 10 Days in April was wet May was the finest Spring Month that we ever saw There was rain every night and Hot Days all through the Month. June begun with Cold and Dry for 10 Days then we Hot and Dry every day. . . . The land was Browned that you could not see a live Pile of grass the Corn was very short In general we commenced Harvest on the First of August we got part of our Corn in very Dry. . . . R. Folder finish Houseing His Corn on the 11th of Aug. . . . We Finish the Hay on 24 July. We clipped sheep in June. . . .

These dates are several weeks in advance of the usual times of clipping, hay and crop harvesting in the region. The Graves finished cutting their corn on 17 August and had all gathered up by 20 August. "Barley was as Dry as Hail shot". On 22 and 23 of the month there came very heavy rain and "On the 25 of Auts we had a large floud and continued to 26." September began "with a roasting sun and the weather remained fine . . . there was much grass". November set in wet.

1869 started off cold. March was cold and dry with thick snow; April was warm, May cold and dry. "June began to be fine to the 15 we had cold storm and covered all with snow down to the fences. We began to cut the lea grass on the 17 and Skiddaw was covered with snow half after that. . . ." This cold spell was succeeded by some "fine warm weather and an excellent hay time. . .". Hay was finished 10 August, reaping commenced on 19 August and finished on 28 August, corn was all housed by 3 September.

Sept began as fine as ever the first week and then we had storm after storm every day for three week flood after flood to the end of the year. 1870 Begun with dry and frosty and the four first months was winter. May Begun to be Spring and we had plenty of showers. June was likewise fine growing. July Begun very dark for hay Harvest and about the middle it broke out roasting hot. . . .

In between these weather entries (which have drawn from a modern Newlands farmer the comment, "Weather in those days seems to have been much as it is now, uncertain like") there appears, scribbled hastily in pencil and then carefully copied opposite in ink, the verse,

> Time like an ever rolling stream
> Bears all its sons away
> They fly forgotten as a dream
> Dies at the opening Day
> Watch for you Know not what hour your Lord doth
> come

The final two entries in the book are veterinary. The first is a recipe for "Red Water Drink" (sub-titled, upside down, "James Thronthwaite receip") and bears all the signs of having been scrawled during the course of a conversation at some shepherds' meet or similar convivial occasion:

    1 ounce Glober Salts
    1 oz of cream of Tartar
    1 oz of Salt Peter
    1 oz of grounded ginger
      Half a Pound of Treakel
    2 quarts of Boiling warter

Put the The warter in and Let it Desolve and give it about new milk warm give it about gill of cold water

Finally comes a "Cure for the renderpest":

Take equal portions of small red pickling onions not the green & garlick peel them and pound them together so that they are reduced to a fine pulp add to this about one third of their weight of ground ginger then take Assafoetida to about two thirds of the weight of the ginger. Pour sufficient water over it to cover it thoroughly, and allow it to boil stirring it all the time so that little or no sediment remains. Pour the liquid which should be of a milky appearance over the pulp and mix it thoroughly; boil some rice in water till it is thoroughly soft and add the rice water to the mixture so that the former may be one and a half times in excess of the latter and mix thoroughly and allow the whole to cool.

Dose. To a full grown animal a good Pint, to a Heifer, a good half pint; to a calf rather less. The medicin should be given the moment the animals breath is the least tainted. . . . If the mouth be sore wash the gums with a pulp made with the rind of Seville oranges boiled Diet. Two hours after the . . .

Unfortunately here it stops, since the last few pages of the book are missing.

By the second half of the nineteenth century the fast expanding industry of tourism was bringing new sources of wealth to the Lake Country farms; there was flourishing summertime trade in teas and accommodation. In some instances former statesmen even ventured into the hotel business proper, running hotel and farm simultaneously. Buttermere's Fish Inn was popular with venturesome visitors by the close of the eighteenth century, the proprietors being Robinsons, of ancient statesmen descent. Their daughter, Mary, rated as a beauty, brought notoriety to Buttermere when, in 1802, she was abducted by the forger, John Hadfield, who was executed at Carlisle in 1803. Mary's family sensibly refused to be abashed by this unhappy incident and used their daughter as a very successful tourist attraction. She finally married a Caldbeck farmer and was able to sink into fat and tranquil obscurity.

Successors to the Robinsons at the Fish were the Clarks. Daniel Gate, schoolmaster of Newlands, persuaded Mrs Clark to advertise in the first issue of the shepherd's guide which he produced in 1879 as rival to the long-established guide edited by William Hodgson. The number of tourists reading *Gate's Shepherd's Guide* must have been infinitesimal but Mrs Clark took a full-page advertisement which reads:

Fish Hotel, Buttermere,

(The Oldest-established Hotel in the Village, and formerly the residence of Mary Robinson, the celebrated beauty of Buttermere.)

J. A. Clark, Proprietress.

The above Hotel has been recently enlarged, and contains large and commodious Coffee Room, spacious Sitting Rooms, Smoking Rooms and well-ventilated Bed Rooms & being fitted up and replete with every modern improvement appertaining to a first-class Hotel, enables the Proprietress to offer to Tourists and Visitors to the Lake District every comfort, combined with moderate charges.

The FISH HOTEL is situated amongst the most charming Scenery and pure air, and its proximity to the Lakes of Crummock and Buttermere, makes it a most desirable residence for parties fond of Angling, which may be enjoyed to repletion, the Lakes and Streams abounding with Trout and Char. Fishing Parties may confidently rely upon meeting with every attention, the promotion of whose comfort will ever be the study of the Proprietress.

Luncheon ready every day from 1 till 5 o'clock.

PRIVATE DINNERS AT ANY HOUR.

Special arrangements made with parties for Board and Residence by week or month.

CONVEYANCES, POST HORSES, MOUNTAIN PONIES,

AND GUIDES.

BOATS KEPT AT THE FISH ONLY.

This last was a dig at the rival establishment, the Victoria Hotel, run by Edmondsons, cousins of the Clarks. The Victoria Hotel (today the Bridge Hotel) had formerly been a cornmill; the millpond and race may still be seen in the wood above the bridge by the hotel. Mrs Edmondson, too, inserted a full-page advertisement in *Gate's Shepherd's Guide*; the main body of this advertisement reading word for word like that for the Fish, except that for "Fish" the name "Victoria" was substituted. Mrs Edmondson, of course, could not boast of Mary Robinson.

During the summer months increasing numbers of people appeared in the district; horse-drawn brakes travelled the popular Buttermere Round as it was called (Keswick, Borrowdale, Honister Pass, Buttermere, Newlands Pass, Portinscale, Keswick). A considerable part of the tour was performed by the passengers on their own feet, on account of the steepness of the roads which horses could not possibly negotiate with a full load of trippers!

The region was undergoing rapid change, yet there was still much remaining which seemed never to alter. On 6 February 1907 John Grave of Skelgill held a sale of miscellaneous household goods and farm stock, recorded in an accounts book supplied by Mumberson & Son, auctioneers and valuers of Keswick, which makes interesting comparison with the inventory of John Grave of Skelgill in 1771:

The cattle sold by John Grave of 1907 consisted of three bullocks, nine heifers, seven cows and one bull, the last selling for $16\frac{1}{2}$ guineas. The heifers sold at prices ranging between £6 15s. and £12 10s., the cows between £15 5s. and £22. A bay cob mare went for $14\frac{1}{2}$ guineas, a cur dog for one guinea. Fifteen hens were sold at prices between 1s. 6d. and 5s. 2d. each.

A pan and toast rack went as one lot for a penny, some old iron for the same price, some tins for twopence, a straw mattress and a bedstead for 3d., a cupboard for 6s., a tip-up cart for £1 5s. A set of harness fetched £3, a bridle and collar 3s. 3d., a pair of oil carriage lamps 17s., three milk bowls, together with other implements and sundries, 1s. 4d. Simeon Grave III bought a stack of meadow hay for £3 5s.; another stack, on Low Moor, went for £5 15s. Bedding (for stock) went for 14s.

Advertising for this sale cost £1 17s. 6d. Auctioneer's commission, at $2\frac{1}{2}$%, came to 7s. 3d.; the sum realised for cattle amounted to £241 19s., for mare, dog and hens £18 7s. 8d., for sundries £17 7s. 1d., for crop £9 14s. The grand total (plus a guinea put in for the dog) amounted to £286 6s. 9d.

Today the Grave family is still at Skelgill. The present owner, Mr Thomas Grave (son of Simeon III), has had electricity and the telephone installed; thus the story of an ancient home of Cumbrian statesmen is brought fully up to date.

CHAPTER FIVE

The Woollen Industry of Millbeck

THE MILLBECK LEDGER for the years 1823–56 and the day book for 1830–41 have survived to give us a detailed and fascinatingly unexpected story of a thrusting woollen textiles industry in the recesses of a small gill on the southern flanks of Skiddaw.[1]

Wool for these mills was purchased from all over the Lake Country and in addition special imported wools were also bought. Apart from the basic raw material of wool, other items obtained for the day-to-day running of the mills included machinery from Carlisle; oil from Liverpool, Whitehaven, Rochdale and London; soap from Carlisle and Whitehaven; teazles from Rochdale, London and Paris (12,000 teazles in a case); paper from Egremont and Carlisle; cards from Kendal, Cleckheaton and Halifax; yarn from Whitehaven and Halifax; twine from Cockermouth; wrappers (for baling) from Kendal workhouse; brimstone from Liverpool; sulphur and fuller's earth from sources unspecified. Goods travelled from all directions to Millbeck and, as a result, there flowed from Millbeck exports that travelled over the world.

The company's shippers and agents were Bowe and Bushby (later changing to Bushby Son and Foster) of Liverpool. While most goods for export were shipped from Liverpool some were sent from Whitehaven, Workington and Maryport. The ships recorded in the ledger have names strongly evocative of the period: *Hercules, Adventure, Carraboo, Ambassador, Superb,* contrasting with homely ones such as *Eliza Ann, David Maffit, Mary Jones.*

In the first twenty-four years from the opening of the ledger in 1823 goods were exported regularly to New Orleans, New York, Baltimore,

Philadelphia, Quebec, Montreal, Jamaica, the islands of St Thomas and
St Croix and the Cape of Good Hope. There was a substantial demand
for caps (selling at 7s. the dozen wholesale) in the island of St Thomas
and to a lesser extent in St Croix. From North America and Jamaica
came a steady demand for blankets and pennistones (a cheap coarse
woollen cloth 1¾ yards in width, made in lengths of 600 to 800 yards, in
blue and indigo); this material and the blankets were highly popular
with slave owners. One typical order for this period reveals that in
June 1832 fifty-six bales of blankets were sent to New Orleans, each
bale containing one hundred blankets at 6s. each blanket. Blankets,
brown or fawn in colour, were of various qualities and sold from 2s. to
9s. each. 'Fine' blankets were 10s. 6d., 'heavy' (9 ft by 4 ft) were 12s.
each. 'Imitation French', introduced in 1836, were sold for 11s. 6d. The
military, as well as the slave markets, took large quantities of the coarser
variety of blanket.

Millbeck trade on the home market was no less impressive. Blankets,
pennistones, kerseys, checks, sheetings and caps sold as readily in the
British Isles as they did abroad, while flannels of various qualities,
'brattling' (small check effects produced by warping both ends of the
cloth two white, two coloured, and checking in the same manner),
'sagathie' (a coarse mixed weave), serge (ordinary, saddler's pannel and
seat), linsey, house cloth, white 'fearnought' (fearnought being a stout
thick woollen cloth used for seamen's coats, scarves and jackets and also
as covering for portholes and the doors of powder magazines), 'bratts'
(various overgarments of coarse cloth), 'happins' (wrapping cloth),
plaiding, blue duffle, jersey cloth, blue flax, 'thrums' (odd lengths of
yarn, marketed by the pound and used for making into rugs), horse
blankets and sheeting, rugging, carpet weave and carpeting, drugget,
mats, canvas, bagging, cart covers, collar cloth, show cloth, common
flocks, bandages, 'crankie' (a linen cloth used as table-linen, woven in
small squares and broad widths, also used for bed ticking) and bonnets
(at 1s. 8d. each) sold to drapers, upholsterers, charities, work-houses,
farmers, saddlers, coachmakers and whip-makers, ironmongers,
colliers, ship-builders, public-houses.[2]

Charities which the ledger names as regular customers include the
Carlisle Blanket Society, which each autumn, from 1830–55, made
purchases at an average expenditure of about £125. This charity was
assisted at the Millbeck end by means of a special discount as well as by

a subscription from the company. The Female Visiting Society of Carlisle also bought blankets or blanketing annually; these goods had to be marked FVS before they left the mills. The trustees of the Sir John Bankes Charity in Keswick bought blankets and blue flannel, while for many years John Hodgson, manager of Keswick poorhouse, bought blankets, blue duffle and stocking-yarn.

Many of the company's overseas customers paid in kind; rum, sugar and coffee from the West Indies, casks of wine from the Cape of Good Hope. Local customers not infrequently followed a similar procedure; one £5 bill was settled with a ten-gallon cask of gin (double-strength); a £10 15s. account was paid in the shape of a cow. Other 'payments' included a 24½ lb. ham valued at 16s., a firkin of butter at 47s., a quarter of mutton at 1s. 1½d. per lb. Potatoes seem to have been a favoured currency; at all events the management always had quantities of them in hand to sell to mill workers.

In 1829 Daniel Dover, managing director of the Millbeck industry, felt sufficiently prosperous to build a Sunday-school attached to the mills. Until the Factory Acts of 1833 liberated the children of the poor from daily labour, Sunday was the only day on which they could receive any form of education and the rudiments of the three R's, as well as the catechism, were taught therefore at Sunday-school. The Sunday-school movement was very strong in this region; the South West of Cumberland Sunday-School Society, which was founded in 1818, by 1821 had no fewer than thirty-three Sunday-schools in the ward of Allerdale above Derwent, with 4,220 pupils on the registers and 442 unsalaried teachers giving their services.

Thus Millbeck flourished. For many years the clerk who kept the books was a particularly vigilant and loyal employee, as transpires from the nature of his entries. Alongside a payment made by Messrs Bright, Martin & Co of Birmingham in 1828, he wrote, "they have deducted 25/- shillings, and this we cannot allow". There are no further records of transactions with Messrs Bright and Martin. Again, in an entry in the day-book in May 1836 he noted, of a purchase of 105 stone 9 lb. of wool from William Martin of Patterdale, "wett, to be weighed again when dry".

As the name Millbeck implies, there had been a mill there since time out of mind; it can be traced at least as far back as 1260 and was originally a corn-mill. At first, like all the small, water-powered mills of ancient origin with which the Cumbrian valleys once abounded, it would have been built of timber, to be reconstructed in stonework during the late seventeenth or early eighteenth century. The majority of these little corn-mills remained operating as such until the latter half of the eighteenth century, when corn grinding was gradually canalised to large mills near the new industrial centres. As a result small local mills up and down the country fell into disuse; though it is true that in the more remote dales of the Lake Counties several did survive well into the nineteenth century (the mill at Stair, for instance, worked as a flour-mill until about 1885 while the crusher, which rolled oats, operated until 1918). Nonetheless, by mid-eighteenth century many water-wheels in this region had ceased to turn and it is legitimate to assume, from what we know, that Millbeck was one of them.

The earliest major industry of the Lake Country, wool production and the fabrication of woollen textiles, saw Kendal early established as textile centre for the entire region. It was famous in medieval and Tudor times for the production of long-wearing cloths; harden, frieze and Kendal green, kerseys, 'cogware, coarse Cottons and Carptmeals'. The toughness and durability of these northern textiles derived from the characteristic fleeces of the mountain sheep, clothed by nature to withstand rough weather and icy blasts; cloaks of Kendal green and jerkins of kersey kept the poorer classes of men similarly warm in winter. Much of the wool that went to the Kendal fulling-mills was spun and woven in the homes of local people; in Westmorland and Furness and to a lesser degree in Cumberland these cottage industries became a valuable source of additional income to the families of the farmers and agricultural workers.

Between the close of the sixteenth century and the mid-seventeenth century there occurred a long period of depression in the woollen industry, further deepened in the Lake Country by outbreaks of plague and the dislocations of Civil War. After these years of recession Kendal gradually established a large trade, both for home and overseas, in 'cottons', linsey wolsey and knitted wares, these last mainly stockings, the bulk of which were knitted in the cottages and farmhouses (by the close of the eighteenth century Kendal was handling nearly 30,000 dozen stockings a year). The century from 1770 onwards convoluted with warfare, resulting in an incessant demand for coarse, strong textiles with which to clothe and blanket the troops, while the expanding colonies opened up unlimited export markets for British manufacturers. The invention of water-powered textile-manufacturing machinery made possible mass-production to keep pace with this explosion in demand and, quite suddenly, speculators were searching the Lakeland valleys for forgotten water-mills in which to set up spinning frames and start business.

By 1796 a carding-mill was established at Millbeck and had been there for some time, although it would not appear to have been in existence as early as 1760. This carding-mill was in operation under the management of six partners; Joseph Hodgson of Brigham, a flax-spinner; Jonathan Younghusband of Millbeck; Joseph Younghusband of Little Crosthwaite; Robert Hodgson of Dancing Gate, yeoman; Benjamin Sealby of Keswick, shopkeeper, and John Gibson of Millbeck Hall, yeoman. By a deed of 2 August 1797 Joseph Hodgson sold for £170 to Daniel Dover, a manufacturer of Underskiddaw, his one-sixth share in "the trade of business of Buying, Carding, Spinning and Selling of wool which hath for some time been established and carried on at Millbeck aforesaid in the Carding Mill".

Daniel Dover was the youngest son of Joseph Dover, woollen manufacturer of Keswick, who died in 1810 at the age of eighty-five and was buried close to the main south door of Crosthwaite church under an impressive tombstone on which were recorded the names of his nine offspring; it is still there. The carding-mill, which was of course the converted corn-mill, stood in the lower portion of a close named Low Rudding, above which lay the close of High Rudding. The mill race, taken off the beck by a sluice, cut through these two closes. Some time shortly before 1805 a fulling-mill, weaving rooms, warehouse and press-room were built in High Rudding. In 1805 a pay-office was built on the far side of the beck and was connected with the fulling-mill by a flying bridge. A new carding-mill was built in Low Rudding. A row of old cottages in Low Rudding was demolished and five plain cottages built in their stead, to house mill-hands. The face of Millbeck thus underwent drastic change, with the result that there ensued one of those celebrated Lakeland controversies (Chapter Seven).

The old, picturesque Low Rudding cottages were known as 'Catherine Dixon's houses' (Catherine Dixon had died in 1782 at the age of ninety-seven) and were a favourite tourist attraction, enchanting, amongst others, Dorothy and William Wordsworth and Coleridge, who had taken Robert Southey to view the cottages when Southey had first come to Keswick. Southey, outraged at the destruction of the poetic cottages and the erection of the complex of new buildings, which became known as Millbeck Village, wrote of this act of philistinism (so he and the Wordsworths regarded it) in his *Colloquies on Society*, to demonstrate the disfiguration of the countryside by buildings of "unqualified deformity".

"Time will not mellow them, nature will neither clothe nor conceal them; and they will remain always as offensive to the eye as to the mind." Thus Southey on behalf of the preservationists. To which Macaulay replied, for the progressives: "Here is wisdom! . . . Mortality and cottages with weather stains rather than health and long life with edifices which time cannot mellow."

We do not know if Catherine Dixon had lived out her ninety-seven years in one of these weather-stained cottages which Macaulay had spoken against; if so she had not done badly. Nor shall we ever know if time might not have mellowed the new buildings of "unqualified deformity", for these were pulled down in 1903. However, since time has very comfortably mellowed the mill buildings which remain in High Rudding, one suspects that Southey would have been proved wrong, too.

Old Joseph Dover was behind this development at Millbeck; the earliest agreements concerning the fulling and new carding-mills were in his name. Daniel Dover was in on the new carding-mill by 1810 (the year of the old man's death) and the fulling-mill by 1817; from thenceforth, until his death in 1842, Daniel was managing director of the Millbeck industry (a deed of 1834 gives the name of the company as Dover, Younghusband and Co.). Daniel, who lived at Skiddaw Bank (Millbeck Place) just above the mill, was assisted by his nephew, Joseph Dover, of Low Grove. John Dover, Daniel's brother, did all the dyeing for the firm at the Forge, Keswick; dyeing bills not infrequently amounted to as much as £500 or £600 per annum when the company was at its height of production and prosperity. The peak year of Millbeck's export trade was 1834. The mill was then employing over a hundred workers.

During the following twelve years this export trade dramatically declined. In 1842, when Daniel Dover died, to be succeeded by his son

Arthur, the Millbeck industry was clearly flagging; from then on the way led inexorably downhill.

Steam was the new power in the land. The little mills, mostly family concerns on the banks of our northern becks, had not the resources to readjust to this new era. The weight and vibration of the new machinery necessitated specially constructed buildings and such steam-powered factories, when built, were not scattered far and wide as the old mills had been but were placed near the coal-fields. The water-powered mills thus found themselves in every sense stranded on the periphery of the industrial future. Millbeck was particularly handi-capped by isolation, since the railway did not reach Keswick until 1865. Those goods which were not collected by their purchasers were trans-ported away by carriers, of whom the company employed five: Robert Deans of Ireby, Thomas Walker of Keswick, John Simonds of Wigton, John Robinson of Ambleside and John Robinson of Applethwaite.

On 9 June 1855 the following notice of sale appeared on the front page of the *Kendal Mercury*:[3]

All those Carding Mills, with the Ware and Wool Rooms, Weaving Shops, Fulling Mill and Tenter Ground, with 13 Cottage Houses all of which are situate at Millbeck and now in the possession of Messrs Dover, Younghusband & Co.

Lot 1.   A Mill, known by the name of the Old Mill, area 28' × 52', being three Stories high, and containing the following Machinery which is nearly new, viz:

Two Carding Engines, One Scribbler, One Cockspur Teazer, Three Spin-ning Billies and two Warping Mills. A new Cast Iron Water Wheel, 19 feet in diameter and 3½ feet in width and other machinery the whole of which is nearly new and in good working order. Also three Ware and two Wool Rooms, with Two Weaving Shops, containing Twelve Broad and Eight Narrow Looms, with Press House adjoining Also Six Cottage Houses and a good Garden.

Lot 2.   The New Mill, Area 36' × 48', Two Stories high, containing Two Carding Engines, One Teazer, and Two 76-Spindle Billies, with Five Cottage houses adjoining. This property is convertible to many other purposes.

Lot 3.   The Fulling Mill, area 24' × 45', having a new Cast Iron Water Wheel, 22 ft in diameter and 3½ ft width, Two Milling Stocks, One Raise Mill, and a Brushing Mill, with Brimstone Stove

Sheep clipping. About the same date as No. 8 but a different farm. (*George Fisher collection*)

Thomas Hodgson, Little Town. Upper key bitted near ear, cropped far, a pop on the fillets and one at the tail head, N on the near side.

Daniel Thwaite, Little Town. Cropped near ear, upper halved far, a short stroke over the fillets.

Simeon Graves, Skell-gill. Cropped and ritted both ears, a stroke over the fillets and across rather below the middle of both buttocks, SG on the near side.

Page from Hodgson's *Shepherd's Guide*, 1849. (*By courtesy of Mr J. Edmondson*)

Watendlath. Earliest known photograph of this typical sheep-farming settlement in remote valley above Borrowdale. Note single-range type building on left, additional barns and outbuildings on right. Picture thought to have been taken *circa* 1880. Watendlath, out of tourist season, remains little changed. (*George Fisher collection*)

Woollen mills, Millbeck, from a painting by Josh Flintoft, 1831 (*By courtesy of Brigadier J. W. Kaye*)

Early tourism: market square, Keswick. Note Riggs Royal Mail and coach offices on right (*Abrahams picture—George Fisher collection*)

Fish Inn, Buttermere, *circa* 1885. This is Buttermere village still very much as Wordsworth and Coleridge must have seen it. Note the Victoria Hotel (today's Bridge Hotel) on the far left; the former mill. Buttermere glimpsed on the far right. (*George Fisher collection*)

Carlisle Castle. (*Carlisle Public Library*)

Execution of rebels at Carlisle—a nineteenth-century print (*Carlisle Public Library*)

Carlisle Canal: steps into the dock basin. (*Photo: Michael Finlay*)

Carlisle Navigation Canal today; the canal has been drained and converted into railway track (see text) and this in its turn has been taken up. Note the former lock-gates, converted into a railway bridge. (*Photo: Michael Finlay*)

Carlisle Navigation Canal; outlet to the sea as it is today; derelict and silted. (*Photo: Michael Finlay*)

& Wet House, and Two cottage Houses with Gardens attached. Also an extensive Drying Ground and Nine Good Tenters.

The Mills are supplied with Water from Skiddaw, with Two Large Resevoirs, and the whole of the Property is Freehold. Millbeck is two miles distant from the Market Town of Keswick, and the above manufactory has been carried on for many years by the present Proprietors. Further particulars from Dover, Younghusband & Co or Arthur Dover, Skiddaw Bank, nr Keswick, or Mr Ansell, Solicitor.

Kendal, 4 June 1855.

There were, it would seem, no eager buyers: finally, in 1856, Sarah Younghusband and other partners sold to Arthur Dover himself their shares and interests in the fulling, new and old carding-mills. No ledgers survive for the period after 1856 and if there took place at Millbeck any further production subsequent to that date it must have been of very little consequence. According to local tradition Millbeck produced army blankets for the Crimean War, although there are no known records of this. The wheels are said to have turned for the last time in 1886. Arthur Dover had died in 1874; his widow Jane thereafter continuing in the ownership of the mills. She died in 1892 and the by then derelict mills passed to her grandson, John Daniel Banks.

In 1894 Skiddaw Bank, Rock Cottage (where the last works manager had lived), the three mills with water-wheels, pulling stocks and shafting, and twelve workers' cottages were put up for sale. As a result the fulling and new carding-mills and the workers' cottages (Millbeck Village) were demolished. The old carding-mill and its adjoining pair of cottages were not sold and in 1903 John Daniel Banks decided to convert this mill into a dwelling house. He favoured the notion of a Swiss chalet (fancifully romantic buildings enjoyed a great vogue in the Lakes) but on technical grounds this scheme proved impracticable and a less complicated conversion was embarked upon, resulting in today's 'pepperpot house' which structurally involved few serious alterations. The present owner of this house tells us that, "The wheel-house at one end of the mill and an annexe at the other end were removed; the front corners of the buildings were taken down and the two 'pepperpot' turrets built into them. . . . The north-west corner was pared off to give an angle window on each of the three floors; a staircase replaced the steep steps with their hand-ropes and rooms were partitioned off.

These were the only structural alterations that were made. The oak beams, twenty-eight feet in length, that carried the machinery still support the two upper floors. The turret caps, on which the weather-cocks are mounted, were fashioned out of blocks of lead by one then known in Keswick as Tinman Tom. The mill bell . . . now hangs under its canopy on the site of the mill-wheel."

In addition to the old carding-mill, in its guise of 'pepperpot house', there remain the warehouse, the weaving-rooms and the pay-office, its basement room, cut out of rock, stained a deep yellow from the storage of sulphur. All these buildings are in use as private residences. In their gardens are the two mill-dams and the mill-race, the lower walls and the wheel-trough of the fulling-mill and the grass terraces of the tenter-ground. The Sunday-school, nearby on the Terrace Road, is still in use as the Underskiddaw church room.

The higher reaches of the beck are now sacred to Keswick water-works. Millbeck is so utterly peaceful, drowsy even, that it is exceed-ingly difficult to believe that it was once the scene of a busy export industry. Only the carefully preserved ledger and day-book, solidly bound volumes, their paper of a quality seldom seen today, the entries beautifully and meticulously written, with much used fragments of blotting paper still lying between some of the pages, survive to tell a tale of enterprise, hard work, success, inescapable decline and fall.

CHAPTER SIX

The First of the Fellwalkers

SAMUEL TAYLOR COLERIDGE is, or should be, the patron saint of fellwalkers.[1] He first visited the Lake Country in November 1799, when he and William Wordsworth set out for what Coleridge gaily called "a pikteresk Toor" on foot. Picturesque tours of the Lake Country were at that time all the rage with fashionable people; S.T.C. was taking a mild dig at them. The picturesque tourists, like tourists today, concentrated on the lakes rather than the fells, although the ascent of Skiddaw was already a must and Helvellyn was fast becoming so. These mountain expeditions were never undertaken without guides. The touring about the valleys, from lake to lake, was done by carriage. We delude ourselves if we think that all Lakeland tourists of earlier times performed their sight-seeing on foot. They did not, unless they were eccentric or determinedly *avant-garde*. Coleridge and Wordsworth had the reputation of being both.

The first Lakeland pedestrian tourist of real note was Joseph Budworth, who visited the district in 1792 and again in 1799 and wrote accounts of these tours under the pseudonym of The Rambler. Although he made not only the usual ascents of Skiddaw and Helvellyn, but also climbed Coniston Old Man, Helm Crag and the Langdale Pikes, he was essentially a sight-seer and not a fellwalker. For all his ascents he employed guides and the dizzy heights and perilous paths so unnerved him that when things became too frightening he bandaged the eye on the side nearest the offending steep in order that he might not view the dangers that beset him, while his guide led him by the hand and helped him place his feet.

This, until Coleridge arrived, was the accepted, and indeed expected, attitude towards mountains. It is significant that even Wordsworth, as far as we know, although born and bred in the Lake Country, never ventured alone upon the highest tops.

The introductory tour of the Lakes upon which Wordsworth conducted S.T.C. in 1799 was confined to valleys and passes, with the exception of an ascent up Helvellyn from Grasmere (which the two poets reached via Bampton, Hawes Water and Hawkshead). Helvellyn, ascended from the south-west, is nothing but a long, tedious slog and the day was, weather-wise, a poor one. Coleridge's notes for this occasion reveal nothing of the excitement that was to grip him when subsequently he reclimbed the mountain some ten months later, alone. Indeed, apart from one or two flashes of stimulation (the description of light on Bassenthwaite Lake, the account of morning mist and light upon Ullswater) Coleridge's notes for this introductory tour are rather subdued and his comments reveal him as deeply under the influence of Wordsworth; the denunciation of white houses, for instance, the description of the scenery of the Vale of St John as "savage and hopeless sans-culottism". Later we find Coleridge changing his mind about white houses and becoming increasingly stimulated by wild scenery (Wordsworth was undoubtedly depressed by it). During this novice excursion Coleridge marched obediently alongside his guide looking where he was directed to look and saying what he was expected to say. Certainly, within his limitations, there could not have been a better introductory guide to the district than Wordsworth; neither could there have been a more receptive newcomer than Coleridge.

Sympathetic as they still were to one another at this stage of their friendship, each poet had a totally different way of *seeing*. Wordsworth had the eye of a camera, Coleridge the eye of a painter. Wordsworth counted forty cattle feeding as one, Coleridge saw a herd as, "Gleams of the white Cows streaming behind the Trees . . . on the Marge of the Lake." Wordsworth, scanning a fellside, noted with exactitude every boulder, every crag, every pasture in the dale, each bird in the sky. Coleridge saw "The Hill like a Dolphin so beautiful in the lines of Snow. . .".

The itinerary of their tour was comprehensive; from Grasmere over Dunmail Raise to Keswick and thereafter to Embleton, Lorton and Buttermere, from thence to Ennerdale by Floutern. In Ennerdale they indulged in conversation with local personalities, so Coleridge recorded:

Two years ago one friendly farmer saw Eagles—One took off a full-fed Harvest Goose, bore it away, whelped when weary, & a second came & relieved it—A little beyond Scale Force a man, named Jerome Bowman, slipped, broke his leg, & crawled on his hands & knees up & down Hill 3 miles to that cottage in Sycamores where we met the dirty old Woman with the two Teeth— All this in the night— he died soon after, his wounds festering—

This man's son broke his neck before this by falling off a Crag—supposed to have layed down & slept—but walked in his sleep, & so came to this crag, & fell off—This was at Proud Knot on the mountain called Pillar up Ennerdale—his Pike staff stuck midway & stayed there till it rotted away—.

Readers will recognise this last incident as that used by Wordsworth in his narrative poem "The Brothers".

From Ennerdale the two went to Wasdale Head and next day they crossed Sty Head Pass to Borrowdale. They then proceeded across Threlkeld and Matterdale commons to Ullswater, pausing between Keswick and Threlkeld to inspect Castlerigg stone circle. They found the famous stones defaced with white paint. Lakeland vandalism occurred, evidently, long before the twentieth century! Their final destination was Eusemere and the house of Thomas Clarkson, the abolitionist. Here, on Monday, 18 November, Coleridge left Wordsworth. His notes for the tour close on a scene traditional to this kind of holiday: "Wednesday, November 20th, Scotch Corner, Where I was obliged for the swelling of my left foot to use a very warm Foot-bath. . . ."

The Wordsworths moved into Dove Cottage a few weeks after the finish of the 'pikteresk Toor'. Coleridge, completely captivated by the Lakes, arrived to stay with William and Dorothy on 6 April 1800, remaining until 4 May. Later that summer he returned with his wife and child to make his home at Greta Hall, Keswick. Several of his friends, including Charles Lamb and the Wedgwoods, strenuously advised against this removal to the Lake Country because they feared (correctly, as it subsequently transpired) that Coleridge's infatuation for the Wordsworths would prove injurious to his own literary career and to his marriage. It was also pointed out to him that the northern climate could scarcely be expected to suit his health; he was a chronic sufferer from the effects of rheumatic fever. But Coleridge refused to listen to advice; he transferred himself to Keswick.

A month was spent at Grasmere waiting for Greta Hall to be ready for occupancy. On 24 July the actual move took place. Coleridge was immensely excited; on the very day of the removal he wrote to Josiah Wedgwood, describing the Newlands Fells as seen from the study window, ". . . a great Camp of Mountains—Giants seem to have pitched their tents there. . . ." For the next two days he sat writing exuberant letters to his friends describing the delights of his new home, while Mrs Coleridge, seven months pregnant, coped with the myriad problems of settling in.

Coleridge's enthusiasm for the district increased daily. A letter sent to Francis Wrangham vividly depicts his mood: ". . . my Glass being opposite the Window, I seldom shave without cutting myself. Some Mountain or Peak is rising out of the Mist, or some slanting Column of misty Sunlight is sailing across me / so that I offer up soap & blood daily, as an Eye-servant of the Goddess Nature."

Coleridge had a genius for rapidly grasping the essence of a place. He was not in the Lake Country long before discovering the ridiculous discrepancy between the exaggerated awe with which the picturesque tourists treated the fells and the confident manner in which the dalesfolk lived and worked in these reputedly hair-raising regions. Shepherds gathered their sheep upon the highest and roughest ground, as had their fathers for centuries before them. They relaxed themselves with fox-hunting over the same terrain during their hours of leisure. All the tops, crags, gills and gullies were intimately known to them by their indivi-dual, ancient names. Except in the very worst of weather the high passes were regularly crossed at all seasons of the year. For the dalesman, securely at home in the land of his forefathers, the region held few of the terrors which kept tourists agog.

At the end of August 1800 (we do not know the exact date) Coleridge felt sufficiently at home in the region to set off alone to explore Saddle-back. Starting by Windy Brow he climbed Blease Fell, at some point lying down on his face the better to appreciate the view up St John's in the Vale. He then jotted an account of the view in his notebook and having done this he climbed up to Knowe Crags from whence he skirted round and above the great amphitheatre of precipices and ridges which makes this walk so exciting and rewarding. Over the tops of Gategill, Hallsfell and Doddick he went, then dropped down north-wards to Scales tarn, ". . . a round bason of vast depth, the west arc an almost perpendic precipice of naked shelving crags (each crag a precipice with a small shelf)—no noise but that of the loose stones rolling away from the feet of the Sheep, that move slowly along these perilous ledges—"

He noted not only the big, dramatic strokes, ". . . the shadow of the Northern wall of the Bason, Green with huge scars of bare blue stone dust, & whiter stones . . . ", but also the details, ". . . North west between a narrow chasm a little sike wound down . . . at every fall the water fell off in little liquid Icicles, from the points of Moss Jelly bags—"

The joy of fellwalking, and he was insistent in stressing the word "joy", lay for him not only in the physical satisfaction of leaping, bounding and flashing over the tops (these again are the words he used to describe his progress) but also in the stimulation which he received, as an artist, from the landscape. His notes increasingly became exercises in an experimental technique of writing which would simultaneously and exactly record impressions of scenery and natural objects as they greeted his eye. He was training himself, in the course of working out this technique, to see shapes, lights, textures and to put down what he saw, "how to make things true, writing them, and put them rightly and not describe", as Hemingway was, over a century later, to explain the process.[2] Coleridge roamed daily and incessantly upon the fells, analys-ing sunsets, mists and storm-clouds, lights viewed over the lake, asking himself questions which later were to obsess the painters Corot and Monet: "What is it that makes the silent *bright* of the Morning vale so different from that other silence & bright gleams of late evening? Is it the mind or is there any physical cause?" As Kathleen Coburn remarks in her general notes to the Coleridge notebooks (Notebook $5\frac{1}{2}$, BM Add. MS. 47, 502), "The frequent conjunction of more than one kind of sensory awareness in moments of acute experience is striking; it involved him in heroic efforts to find new words to describe these apperceptions, with results that sometimes suggest a much later development in the history of painting and poetry".

Obviously a companion of any kind would have been a distraction to S.T.C. in the fells. "I *must* be alone," he wrote, "if either my Imagina-tion or Heart are to be enriched."

29 August found him on Saddleback again, exploring the beck spilling out of the tarn, struggling to put in words what he discovered with his eyes. ". . . what a view of that half-moon crag before me, and the inverted crescent on its right hand—ran along & in a half furlong another beck joined my fellow-traveller. I looked up into a magnificent embracement of cliff, an embracement two thirds of an oval / another tarn! I cried—I ran, & ran, as I approached, Psha! said I— . . . when I came up there was no Tarn. . . ."

It is considered a matter of some topographical confusion as to where exactly Coleridge was when he supposed that he had found another tarn; however his writing is so explicit that there need be no puzzle. If one follows the beck out of and down from Scales tarn, as he did, the problem resolves itself: the beck that joined his fellow-traveller was obviously the Glenderamackin. The two becks unite close to an old sheep-fold, beyond and above which the fell does indeed scoop out into an oval-shaped basin which, when approached from below, conveys a very strong impression that another tarn will be found there. The fell-side curves round in an embracement above, exactly as described.

S.T.C. stayed a night in Mungrisedale, then continued his exploration with Bannerdale Crags, Bowscale, Mosedale, Drycomb Beck and Bowscale Tarn. The day following his return from Mungrisedale he was off again; his objective, this time, Dove Cottage, via Helvellyn:

> . . . crossed the Greta, passed Window brow, went on thro' the wood by Westcote and kept the road till it joins the great Turnpike a little above Threlkeld, then got into a field, crossed the Glenderatara, then scaling stone fences wound up along the stony knot at the foot of the green fells/ under the Whitepike, a hot cloudy Day—Ascended, straight up, for at least an hour—and O! how glad I was to see the blue sky on the other side/ walked by a more leisurely ascent to the very summit of Whitepike.

From Whitepike he took the now classical route southward over the tops; Calfhow Pike, Great Dod, Stybarrow Dod, Raise and thus to Helvellyn. This part of the district was quite new to him; he jotted in his notebook a running commentary to the walk. "What are the names of the ridges? . . . What is the name of that high round hill?" (When he reached Dove Cottage he repeated the questions to Wordsworth, who was able to identify the ridges, hills, dales, and distant tarns that

S.T.C. had wondered about as they had successively presented themselves.) The explorer's enthusiasm heightened with every fresh view: "O Joy for me!" he exclaimed when, arrived on Stybarrow Dod, he saw Patterdale and Ullswater. The summit of Raise evoked another burst of enthusiasm and spate of notes.

S.T.C. had started out late and night was now falling, but it was a clear night and the moon was almost at the full. His notes reveal that by this time he was in a state of near intoxication from the excitement and beauty of the walk; in spite of the poor light he bounded along, above and past Keppel Cove tarn until he was standing with Brown Cove behind him, Lower Man to his right, Swirrel Edge to his left and Red Tarn, "quite round, a sweet pond", at his feet. The twilit, utterly solitudinous scene made a thrilling and tremendous impression upon him; his notes for this occasion are very different from those he made on his first ascent. Above all he was overawed by Striding Edge, "that prodigious Precipice of grey stone with deep Wrinkles facing me / ". He climbed the final slope to the summit of Helvellyn and stood there for a long time staring silently about him, then once more succumbed to the fascination of Striding Edge "sharp as a (jagged) knife, level so long, and then ascending boldly . . ."

The moon was now above Fairfield. Coleridge made a perilous descent by Nethermost Pike (perilous because of the poor light and the bad ground) and a slanting downward route, it would seem, across Birk Side and Seat Sandal, "a Hill of stones all dark, & darkling, I climbed stone after stone down a half dry Torrent & came out at the Raise Gap / and O! my God! how *did* that opposite precipice look—in the moonshine—its name Stile Crags." (Steel Fell)

He jogged down Dunmail Raise and reached Dove Cottage at eleven. William and John Wordsworth had gone to bed but Dorothy was browsing about the garden, enjoying the moonshine. She broiled Coleridge a chop and William emerged in his dressing-gown and they sat talking about the mountains and Helvellyn in particular and Coleridge read them a draft of the second part of his poem "Christabel", which he had brought with him in his pocket.

This solitary moonlight expedition over Helvellyn from a direction entirely new to him seems to me to have been, both in concept and daring, quite as remarkable as his subsequent ascent of Scafell. It is doubtful whether anyone had ever done it before.

On Tuesday, 9 September, Coleridge, back at Keswick, struck out for the Coledale fells. He explored Stoneycroft Gill, High Moss and Coledale, climbed Grisedale Pike and from there made the grand horse-shoe tour of Eel Crags, Crag Hill, Sail, Scar Crags and Causey Pike; a ridge walk which today is rated one of the classics. S.T.C. must have been one of the first, if not the first, to do it purely as a walk and not as part of a sheep-gathering routine or a fox-hunt. Within a decade of his treading it the excursion had become a popular one with tourists, although they were advised never to try it without a guide (Coleridge had loped along it in the carefree style of a twentieth-century Youth Hosteller). It is perhaps worth noting that Robert Southey, doubtless on the recommendation of S.T.C., became very fond of Causey Pike, often climbing it with his children; for these family expeditions they certainly never used guides! But when Ruskin and his bride honey-mooned at Keswick some forty years later they made heavy weather of a guided trip up Causey with ponies.

Coleridge's splendid Grisedale-Causey day was followed by a slack period, so far as fellwalking was concerned; his second surviving son, Derwent, was born on 14 September and this domestic excitement was probably the reason why fellwalking ceased for a while. On 10 October Coleridge made a sortie into the fells "back o' Skidda"; he describes the falls of the White Water Dash, ". . . more completely atomized & white than any I have ever seen . . . the fall assumes a variety & com-plexity—parts rushing in wheels, other parts perpendicular, some in white horse-tails . . . they are the finest Water furies I ever beheld." The fells of Skiddaw Forest and Caldbeck clearly fascinated him; he returned there frequently, exploring the Howk, the Caldew, Carrock. But ill-health put a stop to these happy roamings. Greta Hall, that winter, was distressingly cold, damp and draughty. S.T.C. spent from November to March largely confined to his room, first with one affliction, then with another.

Spring returned and summer, but sickness dogged him, making real walking impossible. In November 1801 Coleridge went to London for six months to write for the *Morning Post*. He returned in the spring of 1802, but was still in no state for serious fellwalking. His notebook contains jottings of a solitary stroll over Walla Crag on Good Friday, a scramble with William and Dorothy a little later in the month amongst the rocks of Nab Scar, looking for picturesque bowers which Dorothy sportively planned to plant with mosses, primroses and foxgloves; in spite of these diversions Coleridge was basically in a wretched state; physically distressed, opium reliant, emotionally distraught, involved in an endless succession of quarrels with his wife, Sara. Sometime late in May a quarrel occurred of such violence that S.T.C. fell acutely ill afterwards and believed that he was dying. Poor Mrs Coleridge was horribly frightened, though her husband mused darkly that it was the dread of becoming a widow that distressed her rather than the thought of losing *him*. Finally she threw herself upon him "and made a solemn promise of amendment". She would do her best to cherish sympathetic feelings for him and his friends (meaning the Wordsworths) while he "promised to be more attentive to her feelings of Pride, and to try to correct habits of impetuous and bitter censure". (Letter to Robert Southey, 29 July 1802.)

This pact agreed upon they contrived to keep an uneasy peace for several weeks, which so improved Coleridge's health that by mid-June he was planning an exploration of the highest and most inaccessible parts of the Lake Country.

He drew up a tentative itinerary, with rough calculations of mileage:

From Egremont to Wastdale Foot	14 miles
From Wastdale Foot to Coniston	18
From Coniston up thro' Eskdale	20
From Eskdale to Borrodale	12
From Styhead to Keswick	12
	76

He prepared himself for the expedition by making notes from William Hutchinson's *History of the County of Cumberland* which, having been published in 1794, was for Coleridge an up-to-date reference and guide. He relied heavily upon the map which Hutchinson included in the book, carefully copying the parts of this depicting the Scafell area. One can vividly appreciate the difficulties besetting a fellwalker of that period when one sees this Hutchinson map.

Coleridge's account of his celebrated Scafell tour was first jotted in his notebook as he travelled (now known as Notebook 2—BM Add.

MS. 47, 497). Entries are mainly in ink; Coleridge carried a portable inkhorn. His final itinerary was as follows:

> Sunday 1 August, Keswick to Ennerdale; Monday 2, St. Bees; Tuesday 3, Egremont; Wednesday 4, Wastdale; Thursday 5, Eskdale; Friday 6, Ulpha Kirk; Saturday 7, Coniston; Sunday 8, Brathay; Monday 9, back to Keswick.

The tour was of course performed entirely on foot. The notebook tells us that S.T.C. left Greta Hall on Sunday, 1 August, and proceeded to Newlands by Portinscale and Swinside. The weather was fine; he had grand views. He found Moss Force at the top of Newlands Hause the customary dry-weather disappointment; he referred to it as "Akern cataract", doubtless confusing the slopes of Buttermere Moss and Robinson on his left with those of Aiken Knott and Knott Rigg on his right. From Buttermere he walked to Scale Force; he was now retracing the route of that introductory 'pikteresk Toor'. He crossed "the pretty beck that goes to Loweswater" (Mosedale Beck) and sat down in a ruined sheep-fold to write some notes, ". . . a wild green view, bleating of Sheep & noise of waters. . .". He then continued past Floutern to Ennerdale, pausing repeatedly to describe the effects of the evening light and to list the names of the fells around him.

In Ennerdale he stayed the night with one John Ponsonby, an old man who talked with his visitor far into the evening and well through part of the next day. Cumbrians, although slow to start, once they do get going are amongst the world's most fluent conversationalists. Coleridge, himself an immense man for talking, could also be an attentive, indeed an avid listener when he had someone worth listening to; from Mr Ponsonby, a statesman and flock-master and also a great hunting enthusiast, S.T.C. got a mass of fascinating local information.

> Next to Ravelyn Angling Stone / Barter Crag—under Barter Crag the famous Bield of Foxes, 5 cubs—80 Lambs, Geese, Hares, Mice, Moles, Frogs, dogs— / Iron Crag—back of this the wild Cat fell into the water, four Hounds & a Terrier with it—when they came up, they were all of a mat, each hold of the Cat—the Cat of all of them / 5 minutes under the water . . .
>
> 38 hours without food by the Fox's Bield . . . because the 2 Foxes would

have taken away their young ... Fox (last killed) just in Bowness tumbled off the Crags, & broke his hind back—Old Man, in the house, bedrid, heard the hounds—& got up & out—fox trailing his back, & fighting—old man got him before the hunters—.

Bowness was Bowness Knot under Brown How, "the finest piece of savage rock-work I ever saw", jotted Coleridge when he viewed it. He was to see finer when he gained Scafell; he never set eyes on Pillar Rock.

He kept doggedly to his planned itinerary; at St Bees he had much difficulty in finding a bed and finally slept in his clothes at a miserable pot-house where his bill for a glass of gin and water, bed and breakfast, came to a total of elevenpence. Egremont he found greatly preferable to St Bees in every respect, including a good night's sleep in a good bed. On Wednesday, 4 August, he walked as planned to Wasdale Head, taking a rest at Strands, Nether Wasdale, where he sat down outside an inn to enjoy tea and to begin a long journal-letter to Sara Hutchinson, which he wrote in instalments:

Wednesday Afternoon, ½ past 3, August 4, 1802. Wastdale, a mile and a half below the foot of the Lake, at an Alehouse without a sign, 20 strides from the Door, under the shade of a huge Sycamore tree, without my coat—but that I will now put on, in prudence—yes, here I am, and have been for something more than an hour, and have *enjoyed* a good dish of tea (I carried my tea and sugar with me) under this delightful tree. In the house there are only an old feeble woman and a "Tallyear" Lad upon the table—all the rest of the Wastdale world is a hay-making, rejoicing and thanking God for the first downright Summer Day that we have had since the beginning of May.

He then went on to describe how he had set out from Greta Hall on Sunday at half past twelve, equipped with

a shirt, crevat, 2 pairs of stockings, a little paper and half a dozen pens, *a German book* (Voss' Poems), and a little tea and sugar, with my night cap, packed up in my natty green oil-skin, neatly squared and put into my *net* knapsack, and the knapsack on my back and the Besom stick in my hand...

The besom stick he had seized, at departure, from under the nose of the protesting Mrs Coleridge, leaving the besom part of the broom scattered over the kitchen floor.

Having written the letter up to the point where he was sitting under the sycamore tree writing the letter he concluded "here I am, and now I must go and see the lake . . ." and then he apparently put his writing things in his knapsack and, leaving the old woman and the tailor lad to the drowsy silence of the lonely inn on a hot afternoon, resumed his journey up Wasdale, into the "huge enormous mountains . . . all bare and iron-red—and on them a forest of cloud shadows, all motionless. . .".

Scribbling notes and diagrams of Wastwater and the Screes, Coleridge proceeded to Wasdale Head, where he spent the night with Thomas Tyson, at whose house S.T.C. and Wordsworth had stayed on their tour. Tyson now gave S.T.C. much valuable first-hand information about the Scafells and an address to stay at when he arrived in Eskdale. The weather still held fine for Thursday, 5 August, when he set out on his most ambitious project as a fellwalker: the first known ascent of Scafell by one other than a local dalesman. This exploit of Coleridge's has been several times described and need not be repeated in detail here; in any case, the best account is still his own. It was between two and three in the afternoon when he gained the top of Scafell from Broad Tongue and found himself standing on "a great mountain of stones", a breathtaking place "believed by the shepherds here to be higher than either Helvellyn or Skiddaw—". In his notebook he entered a description of the view, getting his 'lefts' and 'rights' confused in his excitement, while the extreme unreliability of the Hutchinson map resulted in his wrong identification of several mountains; in particular, he supposed Scafell Pike to be Bowfell. After listing, to the best of his knowledge, all the tops he saw, he made his way to Scafell Pinnacle, where he wrote yet more notes. The bright, hot day was thickening and darkening, "The clouds come on fast—& yet I long to ascend Bowfell . . ." (meaning, of course, Scafell Pike). He wrote another instalment of his letter to Sara Hutchinson, "surely the first letter ever written from the top of Scafell . . .", then decided, as so many have since, to proceed to Scafell Pike (his Bowfell). He walked until he stood above Mickledore, finding beneath him "a ridge of hill low down" as he put it, which joined, like a hyphen, the mountain on which he stood and its fierce yet irresistible neighbour. He decided to scramble down to this ridge, direct. He confessed to Sara Hutchinson:

> There is one sort of gambling to which I am much addicted, and that is not the least criminal kind for a man who has children and a concern. It is this. When I find it convenient to descend from a mountain I am too confident and too indolent to look round about and wind about till I find a track or other symptom of safety; but I wander on, and where it is first *possible* to descend, there I go—relying upon fortune for how far down this possibility will continue. So it was yesterday afternoon.

The gamble paid off, just. Coleridge arrived at the bottom of Broad Stand (for such it was) all in one piece, though his legs were shaking and the excitement and exertion had brought up, he wrote, large heat bumps all over his chest (he had a passion for giving his friends accounts of his physical symptoms). The clouds were now massing and lowering, so he decided to postpone his ascent of Bowfell and made, instinctively, the classical descent into Upper Eskdale by Cam Spout, sheltering in a sheep-fold from the heavy thunderstorm which soon broke. The rain fell in sheets, the thunder raged, a very strenuous day lay behind him and a good walk still loomed ahead of him and he was hungry, but his response to the situation was the real and true thing: "Oh how I wished for health and strength that I might wander about for a month together in the stormiest month of the year among these places, so lonely and savage and full of sounds!"

He spent that night at Taw House Farm (now National Trust property), the ancestral home of a family of statesmen named Towers. John Vicar Towers, a relative of Thomas Tyson, put his guest right on a number of topographical details, including the identity of the summit which Coleridge had supposed to be Bowfell. This, explained Towers, was Doe Crag (the pre-tourist name for Scafell Pike). Even after these conversations with Towers, Coleridge continued to get some names wrong; the difficulties of dialect perhaps caused misunderstandings, Bowfell he heard as Lowfell, Adam a' Cove as Adam a' Crag, while Esk Hause he heard as Esk Cause, an error which he handed on to Dorothy Wordsworth and which she repeated when she wrote her account of the ascent of Scafell Pike which she and William made with a guide several years later.

On Friday, 6 August, Towers took Coleridge on a tour of Upper Eskdale. They ascended the vale by 'a higher road', gained by the zig-zag track from Taws. Various crags and landmarks were pointed out to S.T.C. The most fascinating item on this sight-seeing tour was the Four Foot Stone, which Hutchinson in his *History* made much of as a remarkable natural phenomenon but which subsequently sank into oblivion.

According to Coleridge it lay at the base of Buck Crag. It was not a large stone; its interest lay in four marks on its surface, which apparently resembled the footprint of a beast (species not detailed, probably a cow), a large dog's paw (natural size), a boy's shoe in the mire and a child's shoe. Coleridge examined the marks carefully, much impressed by them; he measured them by making notches on his broom-handle walking-stick. These he records:

Child Shoe, first notch, 4 Inches
Beast's Foot, second notch, $5\frac{3}{4}$
Boy's Shoe in the mire, third notch, $9\frac{1}{2}$
The Breadth of the whole Stone 3 feet
The Breadth of the part which contains the marks is 1' $8\frac{1}{2}$
The Length is 2' $8\frac{1}{2}$

Coleridge noticed that the shepherd girl who accompanied them measured her foot in the mark of the boy's shoe to see how much she had grown since she last had visited the stone.

After a busy morning of sight-seeing S.T.C. dined with his host, leaving Taws at half-past one. He made his way down Eskdale, walked across Birker Moor, past Devoke Water, and regained civilisation at Ulpha, where he spent that night. Next day he walked to Coniston, by Broughton Mills and Torver: ". . . a day of sun & Clouds, with a thousand shadows on the Hills." On the morrow, Sunday, he continued to Brathay, where he spent the night with his friend, Charles Lloyd (he could not stay at Grasmere with the Wordsworths, they were in France). On Monday he returned home to Keswick. He had a hot bath and wrote an exuberant letter to Robert Southey: "Of all earthly things which I have beheld, the view of Scafell and from Scafell (both views from its summit) is the most heart-exciting."

After this triumphant expedition he had ambitious plans for a Wedgwood-financed Alpine tour and began giving considerable serious thoughts to boots. He planned to have two lasts made exactly to the natural shape of his feet; the boot soles to be "at least half-an-inch thick, the uppers three-quarters galocked". These were to be nailed in tempered steel to his careful instructions (see Notebook 1273 8.22 and Notebook 1358 8.93. 'Galock', incidentally, was the term then used for galosh).

However, as events turned out, he did little real walking for the next twelve months, spending but small part of that period in the Lake District. The Alpine tour never materialised. On 15 August 1803, Dorothy and William Wordsworth and Coleridge set off on a tour of the Scottish Highlands; this to be performed not on foot, but by jaunting-car.

What with one thing and another the Highland holiday did not turn out to be a success. The three friends discovered that they were not getting on so well together as they had in the happy past; they journeyed together as far as Arrochar, there S.T.C. parted from the Wordsworths and completed a solo tour of the Highlands on foot; Glen Coe, Loch Ness, Aviemore, Kingussie, Loch Tummel, Kenmore, Perth and so to Edinburgh. Throughout, he compared the Highlands unfavourably with his beloved Lakes, and as he travelled from Edinburgh back to Keswick, he began planning a Lakeland walking tour with Southey; Saddleback, Bowscale, White Water Dash, Caldbeck Fells, Uldale, Cockermouth, Mockerkin, Mosser, Loweswater, Mosedale, Scale Force, Bleaberry Tarn (he called it Blebba Tarn, the local pronunciation), High Stile, Scarf Gap, Hay Stacks, with a possible Pillar, Steeple, Haycock coda. He detailed this projected tour in his notebook; roaming in his fancy over the fells like the true veteran he had now become.

This dream of a homesick fellwalker materialised, or rather, half-materialised. On the morning of 29 September 1803, S.T.C. and Robert Southey started out at 10 a.m. from Greta Hall, S.T.C. a most enthusiastic guide. They walked to Threlkeld, climbed Saddleback, visited Scales tarn and Sharp Edge (Coleridge noting the breeze-race across the surface of the tarn, "blowing a rich blue like the Peacock's neck"). From Scales tarn they walked to Bowscale tarn, reaching Caldbeck via Heskett Newmarket. At Caldbeck they spent the night. Next day they closely inspected Caldbeck Howk; the Caldew was so low that they were able to see the whole "anatomy of the place", as Coleridge put it. Perhaps he spent too long exploring the anatomy of the waterfalls, perhaps Southey had found Saddleback, Sharp Edge, Bowscale Fell and Caldbeck too strenuous a first day; whatever the reason the classical situation arose where one fellwalker was not nearly so keen as the other. Coleridge described the process: "On our return from Caldbeck it seemed to threaten rain, one shower came, Southey was weary & already homesick / so we turned off at the 5th milestone. . . ." Southey was now showing that most unmistakable symptom of the non-enthusiast; he kept wanting to stop for refreshment. Coleridge who would, when alone, go all day without food, now found himself dining at one statesman's house and stopping later, at a quarter-past-three, at another farm for tea. They got home to Greta Hall at five o'clock. Poor Coleridge, he had planned a three, possibly four-day tour of vintage fell-pounding from Saddleback to Steeple and had instead ended up with a brief thirty-hour stint to Caldbeck and back.

Colds and the company of visitors (Southey and Hazlitt) prevented fellwalking for the next few weeks and a very wet autumn soon had Coleridge seriously ill again. On 11 November he wrote: "The Barometer for the last 3 days and more portentously low, & I not only frenzied with rheumatic tortures, now in the right jaws, teeth, face, eye, & forehead, & now in the left; but wandering about, unable to sit, or lie —& miserable when in motion—from a stifling asthmatic flatulence—". No climate could have been worse for a sufferer from chronic rheumatic disease. He decided to flee south, to Malta.

On 20 December 1803 he left Keswick. He stayed at Grasmere, very ill, until 14 January 1804. On that day he was fit enough to walk to Kendal to catch the stagecoach which bore him south. Four years elapsed before he returned to live in the Lakes, by which time he was a chronically sick man, devoting all his remaining strength and energy to serious professional writing. He occasionally made journeys about the Lake Country on foot, but these were merely performed to get from one place to another; for true fellwalking he no longer had either the vigour or the leisure. In 1812 he departed from the Lakes for ever, but in his subsequent poems, notes and literature are found repeated allusions to the Lake Country. Although his career as a fell-walker was of comparatively short duration, his exploits on the hills were wholly remarkable, his attitude to high places revolutionary and his notebooks covering the period remain unrivalled as prose writing about the Lake District.

CHAPTER SEVEN

The Chancellor, the Curate, and the '45

CARLISLE IN 1745 was still a walled city with a population not exceeding 4,000, all living within the walls with the exception of the inhabitants of a few cottages set just outside and about the city gates. The castle and walls, built in the reign of Henry I, and the Citadel, the work of Henry VIII's engineer, Stefan the Almain, stood with every appearance of their original strength, although in fact they were seriously neglected, while the castle was kept by a non-resident governor whose garrison was composed of elderly veterans technically known as Invalids, a nomenclature which unhappily in this case was also largely adjectival.

The city gates were closed every evening, as they had been throughout the centuries, to the sound of a gun fired from the castle ramparts and the citizens, thereby reassured of their traditional, albeit now false, security, retired to their beds and slept peacefully:

> And the gates of Carleil shall be shutte,
> No man shall come in therat.

All the warfare that these good citizens had seen had been of the bloodless kind. Carlisle of 1745 was, to quote Mounsey,[1] ". . . much divided in political feeling. . . . The principal people in the city were the members of the ecclesiastical body, the Dean and Chapter, and those who composed the Corporation; between whom not the best understanding appears to have subsisted. In short, Carlisle, in 1745, in regard to its condition to sustain a siege, differed from the Carlisle of Border history when a Dacre or a Scrope lay in it, as widely as it is possible to conceive."

The Dean of Carlisle was Dr Bolton. However, the most active and influential member of the ecclesiastical community was undoubtedly Dr John Waugh, D.C.L., Chancellor of the Diocese (a highly lucrative appointment in those days), a prebendary of Carlisle, vicar of Stanwix and rector of Caldbeck. He was the son of the former bishop and had married advantageously to Isabella Tullie, daughter of Thomas Tullie, Dean of Carlisle 1716–1726. The Tullies were an ancient and rich Carlisle family who in 1689 had built themselves the fine and famous Tullie House which still stands today as the nucleus of Carlisle's cultural centre. Tullie House was eventually, through marriage, to come into the hands of Chancellor Waugh; there is little doubt that he had his ambitious eyes set also on Rose Castle, palace of the bishop of Carlisle, who in 1745 was the seventy-eight year old and ailing Sir George Fleming, Baronet, of Rydal Hall, Westmorland. Enquiries about his lordship's health came solicitously and endlessly from Dr and Mrs John Waugh, being mostly asked of Mr and Mrs Joseph Nicolson of Hawksdale, near Rose Castle, who were close friends of the Waughs. Nicholson, himself nephew of Bishop Nicholson, Bishop Waugh's predecessor, was secretary, manorial steward, auditor and confidential adviser to Bishop Fleming.

On the secular side of local society, Lord Lonsdale was Lord-Lieutenant of the county and a Carlisle City alderman; at that date however the Earl of Carlisle still exerted the main parliamentary influence. His son, Major-General Sir Charles Howard, represented Carlisle in Parliament, together with John Hylton, Esquire. During the course of the '45 Rebellion General Howard was to be placed in military command of Carlisle but the citizens perplexed and annoyed him much by refusing to take his military role very seriously, instead plying him with civilian constituency matters.

The Mayor of Carlisle in 1745 was young Mr Henry Aglionby of Nunnery, who lived in the country and never came anywhere near Carlisle. His duties therefore were carried out by his deputy, the previous mayor, Thomas Pattinson, landlord of the Bush Inn. For some reason which is not now altogether clear, Mr Pattinson and Dr Waugh detested one another. The ecclesiastic never lost any opportunity to slander the innkeeper. James Walter Brown, in his nine-volume collection of reprinted pieces, *Round Carlisle Cross*,[2] has attempted to make amends for Dr Waugh's portrait of Pattinson as villain of the capitulation by depicting him instead as something of a hero. What manner of man Pattinson truly was we shall never know now. The Jacobites, in a contemporary ballad, were certainly not complimentary to him, but may well have hit the nail on the head: "O front of brass, and brain of ass, With heart of hare compounded!"

When Aglionby's term of office as mayor expired in Michaelmas of 1745 Pattinson's son-in-law, Joseph Backhouse, more familiarly known as 'Pedlar' Backhouse, became mayor. The outgoing mayor usually became deputy, but since Aglionby had never been seen in Carlisle while he was mayor, Pattinson retained office as deputy. According to Dr Waugh, Backhouse was no more than a titular official and Pattinson continued to play the active role.

Thus stood the Corporation. The City's military establishment in 1745 consisted of Lieutenant-General Foliot, non-resident Governor of the castle, who had not been seen in Carlisle for seven years past and Captain Gilpin, who was local and well connected and who held the command of the two companies of Invalids forming the garrison. Mr John Stephenson of Penrith was Master-Gunner, with three quarter-gunners under him; this represented the artillery force. In the event of emergency the Militia, drawn from volunteers of the two counties of Cumberland and Westmorland, could, theoretically at least, be called upon.

Relations between the Corporation and the military seem to have been cordial; the two parties understood one another. No secret was made of the bad feeling existing between the Corporation and the cathedral. The Carlisle ecclesiastics were staunchly, in Dr Waugh's case enthusiastically, Whig: they had everything to gain by supporting the Hanoverian regime and everything to lose if that regime were to fall. The citizens of Carlisle, indeed the people of Cumberland and Westmorland in general, were without doubt Jacobite in their loyalties and sympathy. To quote Mounsey again:

The people of Cumberland and Westmorland are of a race whose courage has been proved during centuries of warfare both regular and predatory. In antient times they bore the brunt of many a fierce inroad, and were never loath to return the compliment. . . . The people of the border counties had, through the accession of James the First to the English throne, obtained immense benefits. Hence in the Civil War they were found steadily adhering to Charles the First. Hence Carlisle, in 1664-5, withstood a siege and blockade of many months by the Parliamentary forces; and in 1648 Sir Marmaduke Langdale was enabled to head a body of 3,000 foot and 700 horse, raised in the Counties of Cumberland and Westmorland for the King. This shows the affections of the people to have been strongly interwoven with the ancient Monarchy; and it need scarcely be remarked that such feelings are not easily eradicated. In the revolution of 1688 the country people had little share. Lord Lonsdale, by his activity at that period, secured Carlisle for King William; and all remained quiet, whilst the change of dynasty was perfected elsewhere: but when in 1715 Lord Lonsdale, with Bishop Nicholson, mustered the *posse comitatus* of the two counties, and attempted, with 12,000 or 13,000 men, to face "the handful of Northumberland fox-hunters", as Sir Walter Scott termed them, who under Forster and Lord Derwentwater, had risen and proclaimed James the Eighth, they found themselves unable to bring a single man to measure swords with the insurgents: the whole body broke up and dispersed to their homes.

The old loyalties were still present, unvoiced but unwavering, as Bishop Fleming and Dr Waugh were, in their turn, to discover.

Prince Charles Edward Stuart landed on the Scots mainland, on the shore of an inlet, Loch nan Uamh, between Moidart and Arisaig, on 25 July 1745. The welcome which the Highland clans at first gave him was cool. The Prince, however, was resolute in his determination to regain the British throne for his father and on 19 August he set up his standard at Glenfinnan and from thereon his cause gathered strength. The English at the start were inclined to riducle him, certainly to underestimate him; although they were not in the position, in any case, easily to send a strong force against him, for they were deeply engaged in Continental war. Indeed the deepest tragedy of Prince Charles lay in the fact that he, sincere and passionate in his belief in the Stuart cause, was nothing more, in brutal political terms, than a decoy of the French to divert the attention of the British away from the main battle-front. The French use of the Prince was wholly cynical.

On the first news of the insurrection Sir John Cope was ordered into the Highlands with 1,400 infantry. It was hoped that this small force would be sufficient to suppress the Highlanders before they could gain support and impetus.

Chancellor Waugh did not underestimate the impending danger. He arranged a correspondence with Mr John Goldie, an intelligent and active magistrate of Dumfries, and with others in Scotland, who thus kept him informed about the progress of the Rebellion and this information Dr Waugh passed on to the Duke of Newcastle, then a Minister of the Crown, and also to Dr Bettesworth, Dean of the Arches, in London.

The Highlanders remained for some time very much of an enigma to the Lowland Scots and the English. Mr Goldie, on 15 September, wrote to Dr Waugh that, "We are uncertain as to the real strength and designs of the Highlanders. Our best accounts say, they have 2,000 fine fellows and desperate; and upwards of 1,000 more, who are very indifferent, and by us termed Waliedragles, but whether with these they will venture into our country, and so to England, we'll soon know."

The victory of the Highlanders at Prestonpans on 21 September and Prince Charles' occupation of Edinburgh rapidly dispelled doubts about the seriousness of the Rebellion. On 11 October Colonel Durand arrived in Carlisle to command there in the absence of the Governor. By 4 November the Highlanders were at Peebles and Carlisle clearly was in great danger. Dr Waugh sent the Bishop of London a brief letter:

My Lord,—

We are in great hurry and confusion here on the receipt of the inclosed letters, which came in the night, and this morning we have sent an express to M. Wade with copies, and I have sent the Duke of Newcastle copies likewise; we are all preparing for the defence of this place, though we have no garrison but the Militia of the two countys, the Townsmen, and two Company's of Invalids. Your Lordship will pardon my writing in some confusion as I have been up most part of the night. . . . I am, my Lord, begging your Lordship's prayers for our deliverance in this time of danger, Your Lordship's most dutiful and obedient humble servant,

(signed)   JOHN WAUGH.

Carlisle, Nov. 4th, 1745.

The letters enclosed were from the Duke of Buccleugh's Chief Steward at Langholm; from the Provost of Annan; from the Postmaster of Dumfries; from the Provost of Dumfries; and from a merchant of that same town.

The next day, 5 November, the following alarming letter arrived for Dr Waugh from the Provost of Dumfries:

> Dumfries, 5th November, 1745, 8 at Night.
> This moment I have advice, by an express from Moffat, that a Quarter-master belonging to the Highlanders came there about one of the clock this day to secure quarters for 4,000 Foot and 600 horse, and the messr. says he saw them within half a mile of the town before he came away. We expect them or a part of them this way tomorrow. I beg you will dispatch expresses to Penrith, Kendall, Lancaster, and Whitehaven; and am most respectfully your most obedient servant,
>
> (initialled) G. B.
>
> The messr. says this party is commanded by the Duke of Perth, Lord Geo. Murray, and Lord Kilmarnock.
>
> To the Rev. Dr John Waugh,
> Chancellor of Carlisle.

The next communication is very brief indeed, yet speaks volumes. It is from Dr Waugh to the Dean of the Arches:

> (No date).
> The clergyman mentioned sends word they advance this way very fast. Send no letters.

Six weeks had elapsed since the defeat of General Cope at Prestonpans yet nothing had been done by the Government to aid the defence of Carlisle. According to evidence placed by Dr Waugh before Colonel Durand's subsequent court-martial, when Colonel Durand applied through General Foliot for 500 men of Sinclair's and Battereau's Regiments to be sent him as they came from Ireland the Secretary-at-War replied that Carlisle was not, or could not be, of consequence enough to put the Government to the expense of sending an express on purpose!

Carlisle's moment of truth was now at hand. An account of what happened is best derived from the official report which Dr Waugh later wrote and the evidence which Colonel Durand produced at his court martial.

According to Colonel Durand, immediately upon arriving in Carlisle from London:

I went and viewed both the town and Castle, which I found in a very weak and defenceless condition; having no ditch, no out-works of any kind, no cover'd way—the walls very thin in most places, and without proper flanks; but agreed with Captn. Gilpin, who was the only person with me at that time, not to mention our opinion of the weakness of the place for fear of discouraging the Militia and the inhabitants; but on the contrary to speak of it as a strong place and very teneable. . . .

Examined the Garrison, and found it to consist of two companys of Invalids, making about eighty men, very old and infirm; two companys of Militia, about one hundred and fifty men; one troop of Militia Horse, about seventy; and the town's people, whom the Deputy-Mayor informed me he had divided into nine companys of about thirty men each; but whether they consisted of that number or not, I cannot tell—as I could never see them out, tho' often asked, in order to examine how they were armed, and to teach them a little discipline; but was always answered, that as most of them were poor labouring people, who served without pay, it would be taking them from their work, by which their familys would starve; but they would be forthcoming whenever His Majesty's service required it.

Captain Gilpin had also appointed eighty town's-men as gunners, for the service of the artillery in the Castle.

These appearing to me to be too weak a garrison for town and Castle (especially as they were only Militia) and being informed there were five companys more of Militia, disposed in the open towns and villages, I sent that night an express to Lord Lonsdale, . . . who was then in Yorkshire, to represent to his Lordship, that I thought it would be more for His Majesty's service for those companys to march into Carlisle, and reinforce the garrison, than remain where they were; and accordingly his Lordship sent a letter to the Deputy Lieutenants who brought them all in.

But some few days later, the month for which the Militia were raised being expired, many were for returning home, as there was no more money to pay them; and some of the men did go away, but were brought back by a detachment of Militia Horse, who were sent after them; upon which Sir John Pennington, the Chancellor (Dr Waugh), and myself and several other gentlemen proposed a meeting of all the gentlemen of the county, to think of some method for keeping up and paying the Militia for some time longer.

Accordingly a meeting was held at Carlisle, at which the Bishop and several other gentlemen attended. The Bishop said everything he could to engage them to keep up the Militia, and had great influence upon them. I offered to subscribe fifty guineas, or more, towards paying the Militia;

but the gentlemen would not allow it, and came to a resolution to order the Clerk of the Peace to advance the money, and they would be answerable to him for it.

According to Dr Waugh, when the Militia expressed the intention of returning home, some of the deputy lieutenants of the county wrote to Lord Lonsdale for directions, but it appeared from his lordship's answer that he did not care directly to give any. From this it would seem probable that his lordship, at least, had absorbed the lesson of Cumberland and the '15 Rebellion.

Colonel Durand now went ahead with full preparations against possible attack. He had cannon mounted upon the city walls, ammunition collected, the ramparts repaired; he laid in provisions sufficient to last the city for a siege of two months or more, checked the water supply, instigated security measures against possible spies, had all the ladders in the surrounding countryside brought into the city to prevent the enemy securing them as an aid to scaling the walls, ordered the local constables to make an exact inventory of all the spades, pick-axes and other digging tools in the hands of the local farmers, had a large number of sandbags made and filled; he took down a quick-set hedge close to the castle walls that might have afforded cover to a large body of rebels; after a struggle with the magistrates got some small houses and sheds, that were also dangerously close to the castle, at least partly dismantled (the magistrates objected to the destruction of these buildings on the grounds that they were private property). Colonel Durand had further trouble with the magistrates when he proposed that the Scotch and Irish gates should be walled up, leaving only the English Gate open; the magistrates objected to Colonel Durand that this would be "an infinite prejudice to the city; and as I might depend upon having two or three days' notice of the approach of the Rebels, I should always have enough time to do it".

If the Militia and townspeople proved uncooperative, the clergy exerted themselves to the utmost to be of assistance to the Colonel. Dr Waugh gives a very nice account of the activities of the church militant:

> ... as there had been some disputes between some of the townspeople and some of the Militia officers, it was necessary that persons of credit and some influence should be appointed to act in the capacity of Aid de Con's to the

Commanding Officers, especially as Col. Durand was lame with the gout, and would not move so nimbly as he otherwise would have done. The clergy on my proposing it to them undertook this part, and all executed it with a coolness and resolution yt. became them. Mr Wardale, Mr Bennet the Dissenting Minister, and myself attended Col. Durand in that capacity. Mr Wilson, Mr Brown, and Mr Farish attended Capt. Gilpin. Col. Durand likewise desiring two men might be placed in the day time on the Cathedral Church Tower with a large spying glass to make observations on the motions of the Rebels, the clergy undertook this duty,—that is, such of them as were able to go up, which I was not. . . .

Colonel Durand now resumes his tale:

When I had received certain advice that the Rebells were within a day's march of Carlisle, which was on the 8th of November, I desired the whole garrison might be divided into three reliefs, with a picquet, and one relief only to be upon duty at a time; and had made disposition accordingly . . . but the militia would not consent to it, and would be every night upon the walls, all of them or none; and also insisted upon the townspeople doing the same duty, tho' I often represented it was quite unnecessary, and that many and great inconvenincys would attend it; but all to no purpose. . . .

As they said they were volunteers, and would not allow I had the command over them, I could do no more than endeavour to persuade them to act as I thought most for his Majesty's service. . . .

On 9 November, about one o'clock in the afternoon, according to Colonel Durand:

a [rebel] party appeared above Stanwix Bank, and sent in a country fellow with a verbal message to the mayor, to provide quarters that night for thirteen thousand foot and three thousand horse, or the town should be reduced to ashes, to which no answer was returned; and the whole garrison appeared in the highest spirits, and seem'd resolved to defend the town to the last; and the cannon from the Castle firing upon the Rebells partys, they retired.

That night we sent an express to Marshal Wade, to acquaint him with the Rebells approach to Carlisle.

On Sunday 10 November, continues the Colonel:

About three o'clock in the afternoon, a country fellow, who said he was forced, brought the mayor a letter . . . which he shewed to me, the officers of the Militia, and chief inhabitants of the town, who were then assembled at the Bush; all treated it with the contempt it deserved, and unanimously agreed not to return any answer, and to detain the fellow who brought it.

This letter was a message in writing from Prince Charles in the following words:

Charles Prince of Wales, Regent of the Kingdoms of England, Scotland, France, and Ireland, and the Dominions thereunto belonging.

Being come to recover the King our Father's just Rights, for which we are arrived with all his Authority, we are sorry to find that you should prepare to obstruct our Passage: We therefore, to avoid the Effusion of English Blood, hereby require you to open your Gates, and let us enter, as we desire, in a peaceable Manner; which if you do, we shall take Care to preserve you from any Insult, and set an Example to all England of the Exactness with which we intend to fulfil the King our Father's Declarations and our own: But if you shall refuse us Entrance, we are fully resolved to force it by such Means as Providence has put into our Hands, and then it will not perhaps be in our Power to prevent the dreadful Consequences which usually attend a Town's being taken by Assault. Consider seriously of this, and let me have your answer within the Space of two Hours, for we shall take any farther Delay as a peremptory Refusal and take our Measures accordingly.

November the 10th, 1745.

Two in the Afternoon.

For the Mayor of Carlisle.

On Monday 11 November, says the Colonel:

... About Noon, a party of the Rebells appeared at Stanwix, but the Castle firing upon them they soon retreated; we were informed afterwards by some people of the village, that upon our firing upon them, they had retired towards Brampton, and that we had killed one of the Rebell's principal officers.

This movement of the Highlanders deceived both Carlisle and Marshal Wade: the latter seemed to think that the Prince was about to attack him, and so remained where he was instead of advancing to the relief of Carlisle, while Carlisle happily supposed that the Highlanders had departed, driven off by the city's gunfire and staunch behaviour.

Deputy Mayor Pattinson at once sent a dispatch to Lord Lonsdale and this promptly appeared in the *Gazette*:

Whitehall, November 15.

A Letter dated the 12 Instant, from Mr Thomas Pattinson, Mayor of Carlisle, brings Advice, that on Saturday Night, the 9th Instant, that City was surrounded by about 9,000 Highlanders; that at Three o'clock that Afternoon, he the Mayor had received a Message from them, to provide Billets for 13,000 Men, and to be ready that Night; which he refused. That the next Day, at Three in the Afternoon, he received a Message in Writing from the Person stiling himself Prince Charles, and subscribed *Charles P.R.*, in the following Words: . . .

(Here followed the Prince's message to the Mayor, already quoted.)

That he the Mayor had returned no Answer thereto but by firing the Cannon upon them: That the said Pretended Prince, the Duke of Perth, with several other Gentlemen, lay within a Mile or two of the City; but that their whole Army was, at the Time of the dispatching the above Advice, marched for Brampton, seven Miles on the high Road to New-castle.

This announcement of victory was premature. On the afternoon of Wednesday, 13 November, messages arrived at Carlisle with the information that the Highlanders were cutting down tall fir trees at Corby Castle and Warwick Hall and making scaling ladders with them. At four or five o'clock that afternoon, while Colonel Durand was at dinner at the King's Arms with several Militia officers, there arrived a letter from Marshal Wade in reply to the express message that the Colonel had sent him. In this letter Wade made it clear that he was not coming to the assistance of Carlisle, he no longer deemed this necessary, but hoped to meet the Highlanders and give them battle in Lancashire.

The Militia officers (who were clearly seeking any excuse that might allow them to repeat the story of the '15 and disperse without exchanging blows with the Jacobite forces) at once declared that since they could no longer count upon Marshal Wade's assistance they were not pre-pared to expose their men to further danger. They asked to have the English Gate opened for them that night. This request Colonel Durand indignantly refused; he thought that his anger and eloquence had pre-vailed upon them to stay, for he heard no more from them that night and they all went to their posts as usual. The next afternoon the rebels returned and surrounded the town. No message to this effect could be got through to Wade since the rebels had all the lines of communication blocked. The Militia officers assembled at the King's Arms and when Colonel Durand and Dr Waugh joined them there the Colonel was handed the following communication:

The Militia of the countys of Cumberland and Westmoreland having come voluntarily into the city of Carlisle for the defence of the said city, and having for six days and six night successively been upon duty, in expectation of relief from his Majesty's forces, but it appearing that no such relief is now to be had, and ourselves not able to do duty or hold out any longer, are determined to capitulate, and so certify that Col Durand, Capt. Gilpin and the rest of the officers have well and faithfully done their duty.

Given under our hands this 14th day of Nov., 1745.

(signed)	J. PENNINGTON	H. SENHOUSE
	M. FARRER	J. DALSTON
	Jos. DACRE	J. HOPPER
		Ed. WILSON
		Geo. CRAWLE
		Fle. FLEMING
		Jno. PONSONBY
		Jos. CRACKENTHORP
		Richd. COOK
		Giles MOORE

Dr Waugh was told by Captain Senhouse (and others) that, "They had all agreed, had shaken hands upon it, and would do it; if some spoke more than others, they were all of one mind and resolved, so it signified nothing to talk or argue about it."

It is worth nothing that the above list of names contained some of the oldest and most distinguished in the two counties. These were men who had reasons for capitulation well removed from cowardice.

Many of the Militia now suited action to the word and left their posts on the walls and downed arms. A meeting of the townspeople was held in the Town Hall to decide what to do; we are told that the confusion was indescribable. Deputy Mayor Pattinson took the chair; he said that the question facing the people of Carlisle was, "Whether we should open the gates to the Rebels, or not open the gates?" To this Colonel Durand, Mr Tullie the Recorder, the ecclesiastics and others replied that that was not the question; they had come to the Town Hall to decide what should be done in the present situation to defend the city, since the Militia would do no more. The Deputy Mayor asked Colonel Durand direct what he proposed to do: the Colonel replied emphatically that he would never capitulate with rebels, but would defend both town and castle as long as he could. Finally the Colonel, Invalids, clergy, several gentlemen of the town and their ladies and a group of Militia officers who appeared to have changed their minds, together with four hundred of their men, returned to the castle, there to make a spirited last stand against the enemy while the Deputy Mayor and the towns-people remained in the Town Hall wrangling amongst themselves. Finally, these decided to hang out the white flag and ask Prince Charles for terms of surrender for the city, not including the castle.

The castle, according to Dr Waugh, "was pretty well supplied with stores of provisions etc. . . . and all the beginning of the night we were bringing in wine, coals, and every thing we thought might be of use. . . . I went to the Castle, where my wife had been some time, and from whence I never expected to come out unless taken by force, which we did not fear, as we hoped we should be able to defend it till it could be relieved."

Colonel Durand was confident that, with his Invalids, the principal Militia officers who had joined him, and their men, together with the gentry volunteers, including the clergy, he had a sufficient garrison to make a good defence. Accordingly a messenger was sent out in an attempt to reach Marshal Wade with a dispatch expressing "complete resolution".

Towards evening the Mayor ('Pedlar' Backhouse, not Deputy Pattinson), together with Aldermen Graham and Davinson and Dr Douglass, a physician, came to demand the keys of the town in order to hand them over to Prince Charles as soon as terms of surrender had been arranged. Dr Waugh continues:

About the time they went out, Col. Durand sent the engineer to spike the guns on the Town Walls and the Cittadell. One of those on the Cittadell had been levelled in the morning at the hedge where the Highland trench was making and going off now by accident (or fired by Mr Dobinson) in the nailing, shot the engineer who was at work in the enemy's works in the trench, and killed him on the spot; they said he was the best they had.

This was to be the last real gesture of defiance from Carlisle.

Spirits at the castle remained high until about four o'clock the next morning when (to quote Waugh again),

... in the guard room, where we were, we had an account that some of the Militia officers ... began to talk as if they had come that night into the Castle for their security, for fear the town should be stormed in the night, there being now no guard on the town walls, and that many of their men were now, but not before, run away over the walls; that if they could have terms they would go out in the morning with their men—that they had sent out a power to treat in their names, and if they afterwards stayed in the castle they might be hanged by the rules of warr—that they had done enough, &c. I was sent for out of the guard room and told this, as was Mr [Prebendary] Wilson; we immediately acquainted Col. Durand with it, and that we found, upon enquiry, that it was too true; soon after this many of the Militia men came down, and would force their way out of the Castle; which was, by this means, by break of day abandoned by all except the garrison of Invalids and some few gentlemen, who then saw it was to no purpose to stay there ... as it was, in the opinion of all, absolutely unteneable. ...

About ten o'clock the messengers who had been sent out by the Militia and the Mayor being returned, said that the [white] flags had been sent to the Pretender's son at Brampton, and that the answer was—*That he would grant no terms to the Town, nor treat about it at all unless the Castle was surrendered; likewise if that was done all should have honourable terms; the inhabitants should be protected in their persons and estates, and every one be at liberty to go where they pleased.* These were the words as near as I can remember. ... No mention of any parole or any other terms. None of the Militia or townspeople were now in arms; all were looking after their affairs; and all thoughts of fighting over with them. I was gone to my own house, and was burning some papers, for which I was to be searched, when I received a message from Col. Durand to desire I would come to the Castle. I met as I went into the guard room most of the Officers of the Militia, and several of the principal inhabitants coming out; and was told by Col. Durand that they had acquainted him what the answer was from the Rebels; and that they had begged he would take it into consideration, that the Garrison was to be at liberty to march out with all military honours, and both officers and soldiers to be at liberty to go where they pleased; that he had called a Council of War, at which I might be present; the result of which was that the Castle was not to be held.

Sir J. Pennington, Colonel of the Militia, J. Dacre Esq., Colonel of the Light Horse, and the Mayor, Joseph Backhouse, then went out to settle the treaty. The Duke of Perth immediately entered Carlisle and took possession. Next day, 16 November, the Duke proclaimed King James III; the ceremony was attended by the Mayor and Corporation in their robes, with their city sword and mace. Later the keys of Carlisle were presented to Prince Charles at Brampton by Mayor Backhouse and the Corporation on their knees, and on Monday, 18 November, Charles Edward Stuart made his entry into Carlisle seated on a white charger and preceded by not less than a hundred pipers.

Deputy Mayor Pattinson did not play any active part in these final scenes of capitulation, although he certainly seems to have been eager enough to play a leading role earlier on. He was careful not to be too prominent during the actual moments of capitulation; this prudence at least saved him from being subsequently marched off to London as a prisoner, the fate which overtook Mayor Backhouse and his aldermen. Nobody, in the final count, could definitely prove that Pattinson had displayed Jacobite sympathies. The Jacobites themselves dismissed him thus:

> O Pattinson! Ohon! ohon!
> 　　Thou wonder of a Mayor!
> Thou blest they lot thou wert no Scot,
> 　　And bluster'd like a player—
> What has thou done with sword or gun
> 　　To baffle the Pretender?
> Of mouldy cheese and bacon grease
> 　　Thou much more fit defender!
> O front of brass, and brain of ass,
> 　　With heart of hare compounded!
> How are they boasts repaid with costs,
> 　　And all thy pride confounded!
> Thou need'st not rave, lest Scotland crave
> 　　Thy kindred or thy favour;
> Thy wretched race can give no grace,
> 　　No glory thy behaviour.

Colonel Durand was subsequently court-martialled for having surrendered the city and castle of Carlisle to the rebels "before he ought
to have done". The court unanimously acquitted him of the charge,
finding it "impracticable for him to make any longer a defence than
what he did".

Dr Waugh and his family, together with the Tullies of Tullie House,
left Carlisle on the evening of Sunday, 17 November, for Bernard
Castle, near Penrith. The Waughs subsequently found refuge in
York, where the Earl of Carlisle kindly put a house at their disposal.
Dr Waugh left his curate, Robert Wardale, to look after his house and
affairs in Carlisle.

Prince Charles made his headquarters in Carlisle at the house of Mr
Highmore, attorney-in-law, in English Street. This large, white-
fronted house near the centre of the city was also afterwards used as
headquarters by the Duke of Cumberland. Mr Highmore received
twenty guineas from the Prince for use of this house for four days,
though, as Mounsey tells us, "Highmore furnished nothing—not so
much as coal or candle: neither did it affect his appetite, for we are also
informed that, besides this liberal payment, he had two dishes of meat
at dinner, and as many at supper for himself and his wife, at the Prince's
charges."

The terms of the capitulation were honourably fulfilled; no mention
is to be found of any serious plunder, violence or licence on the part
of the Highlanders (although Hutchinson states that Carlisle raised
£2,000 to save the houses from being plundered there is no evidence to
support this). The effects that had been taken into the castle for safety
were allowed to be removed. Captain John Hamilton was made
governor of the castle, with a garrison of about a hundred. Sir John
Arbuthnot, an officer in the service of the French, was appointed
governor of Carlisle; he occupied Tullie House. He would seem to
have ingratiated himself with the townspeople; Mr Birket, a cathedral
prebendary, became so friendly with him, indeed, that he subsequently
came under the suspicions of the Duke of Cumberland as a result, while
Mr Wardale clearly looked to Sir John as a protector rather than an
enemy.

On the morning of 22 November, Prince Charles, dressed in full
Highland costume, marched out of Carlisle on foot at the head of his

troops, full of optimism. Although the country people around Carlisle had fled at the first approach of the Highlanders, they had quickly returned, finding that the Scots offered no violence. Curiosity was now the prevailing sensation, rather than fear. As Prince Charles marched south at the head of his men the people, we are told, came out on all sides to see him pass. He had given a strict command that "all respect should be paid to the female sex", and this command had been as strictly obeyed. Says Mounsey, "The Highlanders are remembered as having 'never used so much as a single woman in the whole country with indecency'—hence the women as well as the men did not scruple to indulge their prevailing impulse [of curiosity]. And in after times many an old matron could tell how, in her young days, she had mounted her pony and hastened to Barrock Fell to witness the march of Bonnie Prince Charlie and his gallant band."

After the Prince's departure Mr Wardale sent a letter to Mr Nicolson to acquaint him with how things went in Carlisle:

Dear Sir,

. . . As to Mr Chancellor's house . . . they have drunk about two dozen and a half of wine, two or three bottles of brandy, and eat a good deal of victuals; but done no harm to anything in the house; nor taken any thing out of it except a large map of England for the Prince's service (in their tearms). As to his hay, they have not I think committed much waste in the stable in town; and as to his stable at the garden, and hay stack at the Close, they are untouched: so that his loss that way I think is but trifling. I find they have attempted the wine vault, but by good luck the door and lock have proved too strong for them, for it continues still locked, but the lock so bent that the key will not open it, and I have clap'd two more padlocks on the outside; so I am satisfied all is safe within. I have been at Mr Tullie's to enquire how all things were there, and I find no harm done; and Sir John Arbuthnot, who lodges there, and is left Deputy Governor of the Castle, has promised me to take all possible care that no harm shall be done to any thing in the house; as he has done also for Mr Chancellor's, upon Col. Stuart's recommendation. . . .

I am, dear Sir,

Your most obedient humble Servant,

(initialled) R.W.

P.S. I hope Mrs Tullie, and Mr Chancellor need not be apprehensive of any future danger to their houses, at least no diligence or care shall be wanting in me to preserve anything.

Among the valuables taken to the castle for protection at the time of the advance of the rebels it would seem that there were several trunks of plate belonging to local notables. Chancellor Waugh had kindly made himself responsible for the plate of some of his more esteemed neighbours and had had it taken to the castle with his own. Under the scrupulously honoured terms of capitulation these things were retrieved from the castle by their owners. Thus on 28 November we find one of the Waughs' friends and neighbours, Lady Annandale, writing thus to Mrs Waugh:

Madam,—

    I have felt in the most sensible manner what you and the good Chancellor have gone through since I last had the pleasure to dine with you, and sincerely wish you may have found as few ill consequences from such an unhappy affair as the nature of it can admit. . . . I thank God I have escaped a visit from these dreaded gentlemen, tho' most of my neighbours of four miles distant from me had one, and some of them lost their horses. I must now return my thanks for the friendly care the good Chancellor and you have taken of my trunk of plate, which I shall among other obligations retain a grateful sense of; and if it's convenient, and the Chancellor and you think it safe to send it back by my servant, Adam Beckton, and Hewert's the carryers, when they come for it, I desire the trunk of plate may be delivered to them. I got a letter today by a private hand from Dicky, who tells he and Charles are very well, but desire to come home, as the scholars does nothing after this week, most of them being gone for fear of the Highlanders. I am at a loss what to doe till I know if it's safe for them and horses to pass through Carlisle, or if it's necessary to get a protection from the new Governor of Carlisle Castle. The Chancellor's and your opinion of this will add to the obligations of, Madam,

Your most sincere humble Servant,
(signed) C. ANNANDALE.

The problem of her ladyship's trunk of plate was handed to Mr Wardale to deal with. Trunks rather became Mr Wardale's speciality during the Occupation; here he is writing to Dr Waugh:

Carlisle, Dec. 2, 1745.

Rev. Sir,

    I have sent on the other leaf a catalogue of your goods in the two trunks, which I hope will come safe to you, as I hear of no parties now in the road.

I shall be very uneasy till I hear of their arrival. A line by the post I believe will come safe. We are much in the same situation as when I wrote last, very little disturbance. . . . Sir John is still at Mr Tullie's and is very civil and obliging, and still desires his service to Mr Tullie, and assures him of great safety, if he please to return home. Lady Annandale sent for her trunk today. . . . I think I have nothing more worth your hearing that I care to write. I beg my compliments to all friends with you, and shall always be glad to receive yours or their commands in anything in my power.

> I am, Rev. Sir,
> Your most dutiful and obliged
> humble servant,
> (initialled) R. W.

1st Trunk:—A cloth gown cassock, &c., a hat, 2 pr. of shoes, 1 pr. of slippers, a bedgown, a pr. of pink shoes, 12 bands, 1 doz. $\frac{1}{2}$ doz. of shirts, a pr. of breeches, a cloth waistcoat, blew back'd book, 4 fine shifts, 1 lawn, 3 cambrick, 1 muslin apron, 3 pr. of gloves, 1 pr. of clogs, a fan, 1 pr. of pink stockings, 2 pr. of cotton, a combing cloth, a pink handkerchief, 2 pr. of black stockings, 2 pr. of thread, 1 pr. of yarn, a bundle of lawn cambrick, &c.

2nd Trunk:—8 shifts, 4 coarse aprons, 6 night caps, 10 handkerchiefs, 10 neckcloths, 2 muslin handkerchiefs, 2 cambrick do., 3 white hoods, a bundle for Mrs Tullie, a flowered silk night gown, capuchin, stays, a yellow silk nightgown, a white quilted pettycoat, a white under pettycoat, a bed gown, necklaces, silk hat; in the box lid 2 canrs. of tea, lipsalve, pins, powder, brushes, razors, strop, a pr. of gloves, nail cutters, cased bottle, wigs, little bl. prayer book.

No wonder that Mr Nicolson assured Dr Waugh that, "Mr W. takes most extraordinary care of your affairs at Carlisle; they could hardly have been in so good hands."

By mid-December Dr Waugh was thinking of going down to London to ensure that his services to the Government were properly known and appreciated. Mr Nicolson suggested that during his absence Mrs Waugh and her children might be just as safe and happy at Caldbeck as at York. This suggestion was not taken up; the family remained at York.

A letter to Dr Waugh from the Bishop of London makes it clear why the Chancellor was anxious to get to London:

White Hall, Dec. 6th, 1745.

Good Sir,—

It is some time since I waited on ye Duke of Newcastle, to recommend you to his Grace; which I did in such a manner as I hope will be for your service, upon a proper occasion, if it please God to deliver us from our enemies, and restore us to a regular administration. Then it will be natural for our Governours to look back, and consider how to reward the persons who have distinguished themselves at such a critical juncture; among whom you are justly entitled to stand in the first rank. If the Earl of Carlisle be in town, I doubt not but he has been acquainted by the Duke with what I said to him concerning you and your character: for, as to your behaviour on this particular occasion, I found he was fully apprised of it before, and was sufficiently sensible of it. . . . The rebels were expected at Nottingham yesterday, having altered their scheme for Chester and North Wales. It does not appear to us here, whether they will bend their course to London or Yorkshire.

I am, Sir,
Your assured friend and brother,
(signed) EDWD. LONDON

It seems, however, that not all parties had spoken so well of Dr Waugh. Here is part of a letter to him from Lord Carlisle:

Sir,

I suppose by your letter I had last night that the Militia Officers, and so my Lord Lonsdale, have done ye some ill offices, tho' I am quite a stranger to it, having never heard anything of it. I am satisfied that your behaviour was perfectly right, and what your profession might justly have excused you from. I am sorry to hear that you have been such a sufferer. It ought, I am sure, and I hope it will be made up to you. I am glad to hear that you are coming to town . . . if you have been misrepresented, it is absolutely necessary to set that in a true light now, which, perhaps, may be very difficult to do some time hence. . . The King, I hear, is very well satisfied with Coll. Durand's conduct. . . .

I am, Sir, your most faithful humble
servant,
(signed) CARLISLE

The interest and sympathy shown by various people in high places seem to have inspired Dr Waugh with great private optimism of appointments to come and we find reports about the Bishop of Carlisle's health coming thick and fast from Mr Nicolson:

> Hond. Sir,
> The Bp. is got home, but not better than when he went away, for he is now in a pretty great cold, which he thinks was contracted at Allonby chapel, where he preached last Sunday. His lop. enquires much after you, and desires to be named when I write. . . .
>
> > Yours, &c,
> > (initialled)   J.N.

And again, showing how well Dr Waugh kept in touch:

> Last night I had the pleasure of your's, but how conveyed I cannot imagine, for Jack got it at the smith's shop, they said from Wigton. Having had several letters already seized by the rebels at Carlisle, I dare not send any more, but will dispatch my nephew to talk with Mr W[ardale] and get your directions performed to the utmost of our power. If you thought your horses safe here I have hay and corn at your service; but truly I cannot tell what to think, not only from our accounts from Scotland . . . but also from what I have just received from Mr Dobson, who saies that they had advice at Penrith yesterday from Kendal that the Rebels are certainly marching back again. . . . I shall acquaint my lord with your compliments sometimes today, and am yours &c, Dec. 11th, 1745.
>
> > Dec. 16th, 1745.

On the evening of Wednesday, 4 December, the Prince entered Derby. His victorious Highlanders had reached that far without a check; but now the courage of his leading officers evaporated. Before the Highlanders were arrayed three armies, each of which would have to be fought in turn: Wade's army at Wetherby, Cumberland's army of Flanders veterans, 12,000 strong, at Lichfield, and an army of 30,000 gathered upon Finchley Common to defend London. Furthermore, the English and Welsh Jacobites showed no sign of rising to aid the Prince and the French seemed more than unwilling to send assistance of any real calibre. Superficially, the advice to retreat which Lord George Murray and the Highland chiefs gave to Prince Charles seemed soundly prudent; viewed now, after a long period of time during which other evidence has become available, there is little doubt that had the Prince's advice been taken that the Highlanders should press on to London in the face of all obstacles they might well have won the throne for his father. The situation was all in favour of the Prince and audacity. The Highland army was in top form, its morale splendid among the fighting ranks. The forces ranged against it, on the other hand, were decidedly shaky. The great army waiting at Finchley was nothing more than a drunken rabble that would quickly have switched loyalties to the Stuarts had the Stuarts appeared the winning side; the Government was having to bribe men £6 apiece to get them to enlist. The Flanders veterans were not so solidly behind the King as might have appeared; a soldier in Sinclair's Regiment had received a thousand lashes at Ponte-fract on 26 October for drinking the Prince's health and declaring that half the regiment would join him. The spirit in Wade's army was known to be not good. The Duke of Norfolk was on the eve of declaring for the Prince in the name of English Jacobites and only two days after the Highlanders left Derby an envoy arrived from Sir Watkin Williams-Wynn to announce that the Welsh Jacobites would rise immediately. Once the British Jacobites were fully recruited for the Prince, the French, doubtless, would have been interested in sending real assistance. Indeed, the whole face of history might have been changed had the decision of the Highland Council of War at Derby been in favour of continued advance instead of retreat.

The retreat was not as orderly as the advance had been. The Highlanders, no longer borne up by confidence, were less amenable to discipline. They were closely followed by the Duke of Cumberland, who encouraged the country people to cut off and destroy stragglers. As Cumberland wrote to the Duke of Newcastle, "they have so many of our prisoners on their hands I did not care to put them to death, but I have encouraged the country people to do it".

The retreat, ably handled by Lord George Murray, took the Highlanders back to Carlisle. Cumberland's cavalry, which had been joined by Wade's cavalry under General Oglethorpe, were in pursuit and in a skirmish near Penrith they attacked the Highland rearguard, which beat them off in a brilliant little action. Meanwhile, Chancellor Waugh was once more in correspondence with Mr Nicolson about his personal property, which once again seemed in danger. The Highland occupiers of Carlisle had now become a little more stringent than hitherto. Nicolson wrote:

Dec. 16th, 1745.

Revd. Sir,

I was extremely glad to find by your's of the 14th inst. . . . that you are so agreeably settled at York, and hope that all will yet turn out well. . . . This day the whole country for ten or 15 miles round are up, with such sort of arms as they can procure . . . the Duke of Cumberland has sent expresses all about to desire the country to rise and take care of straglers, and he'll take care of the main body. These accounts I dispatched last night to Wigton, Annan, Netherby and Canonby; and this morning got a good many people up at Dalston . . . I was also, this afternoon, at Seburgham Bridge . . . in short, I have had a day something like one of your's at Carlisle, and indeed, if I was but capable of executing the office I might be allowed to be your successor in intelligence both as to trouble and expense.

I have got two of your packing boxes here as I told you before, filled I suppose with linnen, and have since got your iron chest and one other large chest, it looks like the upper part of that in your study; but no more can be done at present, nor dare I send one of your letters into town, for everybody is most exactly searched, and no one thing now suffered to come out of town, and the gates only open a very little in the middle of the day. . . .

To what extent the Cumbrians would have followed the Duke's orders and harried and butchered stragglers from the Highland army is a matter for speculation only, since they were not put to the test.

The Prince reached Carlisle on 20 December and found letters there from Lord Strathallan with an encouraging account of the army at Perth and from Lord John Drummond to say that he had brought over sufficient men and artillery to reduce the Scottish fortresses and that the French were shortly sending over a strong force. Thus encouraged, the Prince left the Manchester regiment, under its commander Colonel Townley, to garrison Carlisle castle pending his promised return with fresh forces; the Highlanders then marched back into Scotland, crossing the Esk at Longtown. On the morning of 21 December the Duke of Cumberland's army marched for Carlisle from Penrith. The castle was as impossible for the Jacobite garrison to hold against artillery as it would have been for Colonel Durand; the Duke of Cumberland, on first viewing it, termed it, "an old hen-coop". Bombardment of the castle commenced on 28 January; it surrendered on the 30th. On 10 February the prisoners were sent south, the officers placed on horseback, their legs tied under the bellies of the horses, their arms pinioned so that they could barely hold the bridle. Each horse was tied to the tail of the one before it. The privates marched on foot, their arms bound, fastened to a rope ranging between them. The fate of this garrison is too well known to need detailing here; some were subsequently brought back to Carlisle for trial and the hanging, drawing and quartering that was the sentence upon traitors; the others were tried in the south, meeting their deaths on Kennington Common. Their heads were dispatched back to Carlisle, there to be placed above the city gateways to rot, for the edification of the citizens.

The Duke of Cumberland not only sent the garrison prisoners south on that fateful February day; 'Pedlar' Backhouse, and the Town Clerk, Mr Pearson, were also taken in custody to London. They were not executed, but together with some of the aldermen and other suspect citizens, were kept in custody for a considerable time and then released without trial or any opportunity of explaining themselves. Colonel Durand, as we have seen, was able to state his case at a court-martial, which acquitted him; Dr Waugh and the other clergy were able to clear themselves effectively of all suspicion of failure to defend their city against the enemy, while the Militia officers escaped all enquiry into their conduct. The citizens of Carlisle, however, their side of the story given no hearing whatsoever, were apportioned all the blame. Their bad name clung to them for a long time.

During these events Dr Waugh and his family remained quietly at York. Dr Waugh was not only concerned now about his personal property but also about his invaluable curate. As he wrote to his friend, the Dean of the Arches:

Good Mr Dean,
    . . . The brave Duke of Cumberland saved our country. Penrith has suffered much by robbery and plunder . . . what will come of Carlisle we know not. I am in great pain for a worthy gentleman who has been my curate, and lived with me ever since I came into the country, and staid in my house with two of my women servants to protect my effects, and has managed so well that when I last heard from him, not only little loss, except in provisions, had fallen on me, but he had contrived to get out the most valuable part of my papers, and the best of my house linen, and my wife and family's clothes, linen, and what they thought most valuable that could be brought off. I have yet a great deal in the town to loose, but my

family are all safe; and if I could hear those I have persuaded to stay on my account were so I sho'd be pretty easie, and submit to the loss of the rest with less regret. . . .

Good Mr Dean,
Your most obedient servant,
(Signed) JOHN WAUGH.

York, Dec. 27, 1745.

Dr Waugh now travelled to London, for as the Earl of Carlisle advised him:

. . . I have been considering what may best be for your service, and I really think the sooner you come to town the better, for I would not let the Duke of Newcastle cool too long upon it, not that I think a few days either one way or other can signify anything. . . .

Good news now came from Mr Wardale, the curate:

Revd. Sir,

I have just time to tell you that you have suffered a good deal; but considering circumstances not so much, I believe, as you . . . might expect. I have luckily preserved your vault; the cellar in the house was plundered; the bed and bolster which were taken out of Mrs Waugh's dressing room, I shall recover, as I have found out where they are. A pair of coarse sheets, some blankets, and some coarse napkins are lost, I can scarce tell what; you shall have a further account soon. We have had but a dismal time this last seige, and very few people left in town, which made it more so; but thank God the good Duke of Cumberland has set us free at last. We have six officers and servants quartered here, who are gentlemen which behave with the greatest civility and goodness, and I daresay you'll sustain as little damage as can be imagined from them. . .

(signed) R. WARDALE.

General Howard now took over the command of Carlisle and it seems that Thomas Pattinson, the Deputy Mayor, tried to throw odium upon the name of Dr Waugh and his behaviour at the time of the capitulation, but this carried little weight. Little more is heard of Pattinson, and shortly after this he died a natural death. As for General Howard, he did not at all enjoy his command of Carlisle; here is a brief letter to Dr Waugh:

Sir,

I have only just time to tell you I am going into your house this moment to relieve Mr Tullie, who is come to town; I live the most miserable life yts. possible as you may easily imagine, and declare I had rather gone to Scotland than stay here; such is our fate: I wish you was at home, I am perswaded it would have contributed to my assistance much, but since that is not the case I wish you all success, and ye sooner I see you the better, and am

Dear Sir, most faithfully your's,
(signed) CHA. HOWARD

Carlisle, Jan. ye. 9th.

Although nobody in Carlisle cared to say as much in words, the forces of the Duke of Cumberland proved considerably less gentlemanly as occupiers than the Highlanders; there was, for example, the incident of the cathedral bells; here described to Dr Waugh by Prebendary Wilson:

Revd. Sir,

. . . A demand made by Major Balfour, in the Duke's name, of the bells of our Cathedral, as a perquisite to the train of artillery, was a surprise upon the member of the Chapter here, and very ill relished by them. Mr Birket, Mr Head, and myself waited on the Duke to desire his protection, alleging that the bells were the property of the Dean and Chapter, and given to them in their Charter; that the Chapter was not conscious of any behaviour in themselves but such as became dutiful and loyal subjects; and that the town had not any right in them. The answer given us was that the Duke would not interfere in it: that if it was a perquisite to a train we could say nothing against it. A moderate composition, I believe, would pacify the claimant; but I'm firmly resolved at present, as are my two brethren, not to submit to any. Is this the reward for our toil? If the Major takes them down, which he still threatens, I doubt not the Lord Chief Justice will oblige him to replace them. The Dean has been wrote to. . . . The Chapter here wod. be glad to have your sentiments in this affair,

I am, Rev'd. Sir,
Your most obedient, faithful, humble servant,
(signed) THOS. WILSON

General Howard now decided to billet himself at Dr Waugh's house, which greatly relieved Mr Wardale, who removed himself to the country for a much-needed, if brief, holiday. Before he left he wrote letters to the Waughs, the first to Mrs Waugh:

Madam,

As Mr Chancellor, I imagine, by this time is gone to London, and you must be desirous to know how affairs go at your house, I thought it my duty to give you this short and indeed imperfect account of the situation. . . General Howard has made your house his lodgings, which I am very glad of . . . because while he is here we need fear no burden from other billets . . .

One thing happened since our people got possession of the town which gave me much uneasiness and still does. A dragoon, who lodged in the servts. rooms, had forced open the closet door over the pantry and stole all the china out of a small box, which was corded up there, and which I knew nothing of, or else I would, I think, have had it remov'd or better secured. I found out the fellow, and had him severely whipped and drumm'd out of the regiment. But what satisfaction is that? We have recovd. most part of the new set of china and coffee kans, except the teapot and some old ones, and perhaps we may recover something more. I wish I knew what was in it; but that, to be sure, you cannot recollect

. . . The Genl's coming to the house has made me, I think, pretty useless in it; and therefore I believe I shall go over to-morrow to stay 4 or 5 days with Mr and Mrs Nicolson, at Netherby, to get a little fresh air, which I much wanted, having lost most of the little flesh I had during our troubles. This town is still very unsettled and uneasy. . . . I heartily wish you and your family the compliments of the season, and am, madam,

Your most obedient humble servant,
(signed) ROBT. WARDALE.

Carlisle, Jan. 12th, 1745–6

The letter to Dr Waugh repeats much the same; it mentions the curate's further attempts to track down the contents of the stolen box:

. . . we had the misfortune to have all the china stole out of the little corded box since our own people got the town; but I think now we have recover'd the most part of it, at least the new set of china, with coffee kans, is pretty compleat, unless the teapot was in that box: as to other things we can yet discover nothing more missing than what I mentioned before. . . .

Now comes a letter from Dr Waugh to Prebendary Wilson, concerning the bells:

Revd. Sir,—

Yr favour of last night's post surprised me not a little; I had heard of the demand of the bells, but would not believe it was so much in earnest; it surprises every person I have mentioned it to, and am fully persuaded no law of this land, nor any military law will justify Mr Balfeur's demand; and I most heartily and readily join in the resolution of not paying one farthing for a composition. I dined this day in company, with an old Liet-Gen. of great reputation (and others in that way of great consideration) who was out of patience at the mention of it. I shall take all opportunities of enquiring further about it, and let you know what I learn. To-night I have not time to say more than that,

I am, to you and your brethren,
An affectionate brother,
And faithful servant,

(signed) JOHN WAUGH

Chancery Lane, Jan. 19th, 1745–6
Let me hear from you, directed as before.

General Howard was finding life in Carlisle increasingly trying. He enlarged upon his difficulties thus to Dr Waugh:

. . . I received two letters from you, and you will easily believe me when I tell you nobody wishes you more speedy success and a quicker return than myself. I don't doubt you would ease me of a great deal of trouble; but the people are so poor and so given to lyes, that I think it is not in the power of anybody to know how rightly to deal with them. . . . I am to provide the garrison in case of an attack—a worse country it could not happen in; people unaccustomed to it; thinking of nothing but their own interest and which way to get most . . . this, with many other disagreeable circumstances, makes me pass my time unpleasantly, and it's hard to do the Government duty, nay impossible, and not disoblige,—the Election town is not my concern at present; I have too much publick duty to have that the least of my thoughts . . .

I am, dear sir,
Yours very faithfully,
(signed) CHAS. HOWARD

Carlisle, Jan ye 20th.

But if the General felt less happy with his lot, Mr Wardale was feeling much better. He too wrote to Dr Waugh on the 20 January, from Netherby:

Revd. Sir,—

Mrs Nicolson insists upon it, it is necessary to write, tho' I have nothing to write about, and I begin to think she's right, for how could you have known that, if we had not told you? . . . As to what's doing at Carlisle, I can give you but little acct. at present, having been here laying in a stock of flesh and spirits for a week past. I think of staying 3 or 4 days longer, in which time I do not fear but I shall lay in a sufficient provision of both for the rest of this winter. Your sister-in-law I find is very angry with the general, chiefly I think because he did not ask her to play at whist one night when he was there. He's represented as a mighty uncomplaisant gentn. I find by the ladies, and I am afraid the evil report will spread further than them. . . .

I am, Revd. Sir,
Your most dutiful and obliged humble servant,
(signed) ROB. WARDALE
Mr and Mrs Nicolson join in compliments to you.

The matter of the bells was satisfactorily settled, but the garrison prisoners had been placed in the cathedral, upon having been removed from the castle after their surrender, and they had made a mess there which caused the Dean and Chapter much annoyance and distress (one can only suspect that the Duke of Cumberland had ordered that they should be put in the cathedral as a deliberate insult to Carlisle, a city of which he entertained the lowest opinion). Prebendary Wilson wrote to Dr Waugh on 27 January 1746:

Revd. Sir,—

No further demand has been made of our Bells; and from your and other letters we are encouraged not to fear any. You may imagine better than I can describe the condition the Rebs. left the Parish Church, for yt was their prison; I was given to understand the damage it suffered wd be made good, but upon enquiry no further power was given than to the cleaning and washing of it. This proves of little use, for the flags being old, spungy, and ill-laid, the earth under them is corrupted; and till that is removed the Cathedral Church will not be sweet, nor will it be safe to have services in it.

The pews . . . are most of them broke to pieces. If you can obtain a power to have this done, and the pews repair'd, you'll merit the thanks of the body.

> I am, Revd. Sir,
> Your obedt servt.,
> (signed) Tho. Wilson

Carlisle, in short, was not a happy place. General Howard made himself less and less popular; according to Mr Nicolson: ". . . no one thing is done to oblige—nay hardly (as it's said) a civil answer given to any body. All the common people most grievously oppressed with soldiers, and the large houses perhaps a single officer, in short things are all conducted in a most strange confused way. . . ." There was indiscreet talk that the General, in his turn, was quite fed up with Carlisle and never designed to stand for Parliament on behalf of the city again: "His father will have him elected at another place without expense or trouble. . . ."

Dr Waugh, in London, met with a "very gracious" reception from high places and was confident that his labours on behalf of his masters would be well rewarded. He spoke to the Bishop of London about the bad state of Carlisle cathedral and received the advice, which he forwarded to Prebendary Wilson, that the best thing to do was to clean up and repair the cathedral "effectually and speedily, and if possible to get an allowance for it afterwards. . . ." The good Chancellor had now so many irons in the fire, so many interests of his own at heart and so many more of other people's, so many requests for assistance, so much assistance to seek, that he scarcely knew which way to turn first. Things in Carlisle were going from bad to worse under General Howard's command and the Chancellor finally, upon 8 February, wrote him a most diplomatic letter:

> Sir,—
> . . . I am sorry I could not come to your assistance at Carlisle, to serve you, being always a pleasure to me: that your situation was not pleasant I could easily conceive, but I have ever found that justice might be done, and people lept in tolerable good humour at the same time, tho' it required some patience and some management to do it. . . . Mr Wilson writes me word that he was given to understand the damage the church suffered would be made good; but that on further enquiry he finds no further power than the cleaning and washing of it, which is of little use, as the

earth under the flags is all corrupted, and that it will not be safe to use the Cathedral till that is removed . . . if you can give any assistance or orders about it you will much oblige me by your good offices therein. . . . Don't be angry that I hint so freely to you what I feel very sensibly; for to do anything that ought to incur your displeasure would be a great affliction to—Sir,

Your most obliged and most faithful and
Obedient Servant,
(signed) JOHN WAUGH

This brought a full salvo from the General:

I stop the post to thank you, Dr. Sir, for yours I received just now, in which you tell me justice may be done and people kept in tolerable good humour, with patience and management; the first part of it I can assure you has always been my view and intention to practise; the latter part, I have endeavoured to copy you as much as I could. Now, Sir, I have told you this, if there are any disobliged at my behaviour since I have the command here, which I don't know there are, they are dirty low fellows that will never want a pretence for a quarrel, and which by experience I have learnt never to make myself uneasy about. If getting the prisoners removed in ten days by application to the Duke of Cumberland and ye Duke of Newcastle, their expences defrayed by the Publick, if quartering five companys in ye suburbs contrary to my orders, and applying to remove six more to other places,—if applying for the Castle to be filled up, or Barracks to be built for a garrison, I suppose that will always be continued here upon ye account of yt neighbourhood; if these things, I say, are hurting the interest and disobliging, I am guilty of them; and since you have called upon me, which I think I did not want, I will finish with telling you, as I am a great scholar, *Nil Conscire sibi, Nullaque Pallescere Culpa*. Mr Wilson never spoke to me about the Church, nor did I ever receive any orders or directions about it; but I hope its well purified and the earth wholesome, because I heard a very loyal sermon there yesterday.

Adieu, dear Sir,
Faithfully yours,
(signed) CHA. HOWARD.

Carlisle, Feby. ye 10th.

According to a letter from Prebendary Wilson to Dr Waugh on 14 February:

... The burning of sulpher and tar had that effect that we had service in the Cathedral on Sunday last, which was well filled, and chiefly by the military. I am not willing of myself to undertake the repairs ... as I cannot yet certainly be informed whether they lay upon the Parishioners or the Dean and Prebendarys: if they do on the latter, I hope they will be effectually and handsomely done. ...

Many persons in Carlisle were investigated by the Government for their Jacobitism and numbers of these wrote to Dr Waugh begging him to put in a word for them with the authorities. One such request came from Edward Backhouse of Uldale on behalf of his brother, the Mayor; it was to Dr Waugh's credit that he did intercede on behalf of the Mayor and, it would seem, succeeded in getting that unfortunate released from custody sooner than might otherwise have been the case.

Another applicant for help, though of a different kind, was a William Hodgson, locally known as Cow Willy. Mr Wardale mentioned this matter of Cow Willy to Dr Waugh in a letter dated 1 March and written from Carlisle:

... Cow Willy came to me on Sunday night, to direct a letter for him to you; there is a deal of stuff in it, but I believe all he wants of you is to put General Howard in mind of a bill for some coals he delivered in to him, which, considering the honest man's loyalty and zeal for the service, and the pains he took and spirit he showed, I believe you will readily do. ...

Cow Willy's letter, written on 22 February, is eloquent:

Sir,—
    I am very sorry to give you this trouble, but hopes you'l pardon me this once. So far as I can learn I am far the greatest sufferer of any in Carlisle, as I had laid most in for the Government's use, and paid all ready money. As soon as ye Ribles got into ye City they were soone informed of what I had done and used me accordingly ... my goods they used at pleasure, and my bank of coals I had laid in, and sign'd them all for the Castle, never doubting, nor in the least thinking, of giving them ye City and Castle so shamefully as was done; after they got possession of my coals they used them all the while in ye Castle and all ye Guards during ye time the Rebells were in England till there return, and about two days before ye Duke of Cumberland obliged them to surrender ye City again they had laid up all

the remaining part of my coals in ye Castle, thinking to have used them if they could have held it longer very provebley, but thanks to Almighty God they were defeated, and my coals hapened to do a great service to our own arme when the City was keept shut up for many days least any of the Rebells escaped. Upon this I applyed to ye Governor for this last quantity yt was found in ye Castle, General Howard who is Governor said if I could bring in a bill well proved of what quantity they got last he 'ould take it with him to London and get me money if it laid in his power, and accordingly he has my bill and is coming up to London. Pray, sir, be so kind as to assist him in what you can, and it will do me a great favour. Sir, were it not for breveity sake I could surprise you with how many dangers I went throw since I soo you for ye cause of my king and country, and of which, if his Majesty were informed, I should not fear being well provided for.

> Sir, your reall friend and
>
> Servant to command,
>
> (signed) WILLIAM HODGSON

Carlisle, Fisher Street, Feb. 22nd, 1745–6

Sir, the bill General Howard has with him contains 120 cartload, at 9 pecks a load, and 4½d a peck, comes to £20 5s 8d; if he happens to mislay, you'l be so kind as to mind him with this, which is a true bill, and I believe he'l remember it, and, without his and your help, I can do but little for myself.

Dr Waugh wrote to Hodgson to say that he would do all that he could to help him and suggested also putting in bills for butter and other goods which had been provided to the castle garrison by Cow Willy. As a result Dr Waugh received an immensely long letter in which Cow Willy described his services to the King; it is too long to give in full here, but part is worth quoting since it throws much interesting light on the true sentiments of the Carlisle Corporation:

It was on a Saturday ye Ribles block'd us up. I had the second gun upon ye tenn gun battre aloted me to my care which I fired upon them with great pleasure, and many times I offred to have a gibet erected and hang the first man that spake of a surrender of the castle to the Ribles, but indeed I ever suspected the town. . . . Upon Tuesday after the Ribles came about the town, I was ordred out at ye Saleport to try what I c'd learn, and at Stanwix I met with a Highland officer, with home I engaged, and took him prissoner, and brot. him my single self in at the Saleport in sight of some hundreds of people, which gain'd me great reputation, but what followed, ye Mayor and Aldermen indeed comited the fellow to preason, but they we'd have nothing to do with keeping of his books and papers, which contain'd the Pretender's comishion to raise men in severell countys, besides a great many letters to persons in divers places in both kingdoms, all w'ch our good Mayor and Aldermen obliged me keep, and when ye town was given to the Ribles they were so kind to me as send there Town Sergent along with the Ribles, and took to sarch my house and got all his books againe, and by this peace of art they saved themselves and ruined me. Emedietly, my wife was sent to the Main Guard, our house plunder'd, my 3 young children left to shift for themselves: this was all ye reward I got from the Coperation of Carlisl for my indevery to save the city, which was more than all there's put together. . . .

General Howard had also been discovering many truths about Carlisle and the intrigues of its Corporation; as he hinted to the Chancellor, "I will be discreet and say no more till I meet you, and then I have a good deal to tell you, for I never knew Carlisle so much as now. . .". What he ultimately divulged to Dr Waugh (if indeed he ever did) we do not know.

Dr Waugh was himself now deep in intrigue of another sort: the Nicolsons together with the Waughs were conspiring to see that it was the Chancellor who succeeded Sir George Fleming at Rose Castle. This is made clear enough by the following letters to Dr Waugh and his wife from Mr and Mrs Nicolson. Unfortunately the Bishop, although constantly ailing, invariably rallied after his bouts of illness. The first of the following three letters is from Mrs Nicolson to Mrs Waugh:

Hawkesdale, Feby. 17th

Dear Mrs Waugh,—

The pleasure of your's I met with yesterday at Rose, on my return from Netherby, where I had been a few days to see a fat ox kill'd that we had every day though in jeperdy, whilst Rebells were in Cumberland, having taken a fancy to that part of Esk for their passing and repassing; and Tom never expected to have had one cut at it, till the Duke once more got between us and danger; so now eats fat beef, and is thankful. The —— you enquire after, (as your friend above did last letter, so good wits jump) is surprizingly well all this winter, and canty; viper broth is a restorer, so something else I much wish for, for indeed I now have hopes somebody will be thought and found the fittest to be sett *there* when the time comes . . . I heartily thank you, dear Madam, for your kind enquiry. My mother, a miracle of her age, has her fevor again, and periodicall headacks, which I have given her bark and brandy for, and she is, I thank God, better. I cannot but say that Dolly has better health and eats better. . .; she has but two soldeirs now, which, indeed, one cannot help being kind to; they left their own homes with great readiness to come to banish the Rebels, and seem honest country men; one of them laments his wife and five children, which he wants to see . . . This poor man has been very ill,—starved;* many of them are this cold weather, with being all night upon guard, and stand many hours, nay days, together as centenals, which just kills them. Great folks will be waited on, let little ones fare how they will; a great many of them are dead in small pox and other distempers.

We sent Dolly barley bread and what things we can, that she may help them out sometimes; these finds their own meat, but she dresses and gives them what little things is wanted to make it ready with. . . . Thankfull we are that not the smallest blot can be laid to our dear friend's charge—not an indiscretion; and pleasure it is to find every one you meet saying how glad they are to hear of his reception at Court. . . . Your and our plate are yet in their safe places I hope, for I reckon your br. will not call for his without Mr Nicolson, and till we hear of the victorious Duke's return, we will let our little sleep a while longer. This is Miss Senhouse's birthday, so we must put on our *caps*, but I warrant they are far from the fashion of the caps you had in hand when you so obligingly wrote; but we will see them on ere long I hope, and I have no fear but to see Miss Waugh advanced some inches nearer the horizon than when I parted from her. . . . My best service waits on her and her sisters. Niece desires Miss Peggy may be sent home, she wants her most sadly, and so does more folks that I cou'd name want to have her prattle. I hope pappa will not forget his *Willydown* when he returns again. I believe you would say I wou'd fain be talking; but Mr Nicolson says I can never leave off whilest a scrap of paper remains un-covered. He and all here are most heartily at your service; and I am,

Dear madam,

Your truely obliged, obedient and affectionate servant,

(signed) E. Nicolson

Mr Nicolson himself wrote to Dr Waugh on 1 March:

* 'starved' in this context used in the Cumbrian sense, meaning nigh frozen with cold.

Reverend Sir,—

As my last may make you expect to hear from me by this day's post, I think it is my duty to write, tho' I've nothing now to say, but fancy all will soon be well again; at least I see no kind of reason to suppose ought else. If it whou'd be otherwise or any alteration happen, you may be sure of the earliest intelligence in my power. . . .

And am your most ob. hble. servt.,
(signed) Jos. NICOLSON

A further bulletin arrived from Mr Nicolson on 3 March;

. . . a foot is till laid up and swelling and great redness talked of, but shoes are buckled, and at times very little lameness showed; I have never seen him eat since (it is industriously avoided) which makes me think stomach is bad; but every other simptom promises length of days, as far as I am able to judge. . . .

In short, Dr Waugh never did become bishop; to reward him for his services in the '45 he was made Dean of Worcester (in addition to his other appointments and livings). Perhaps he had fished too industriously.

On 16 April 1746 Prince Charles' Highlanders were crushingly defeated at Culloden Moor. The Prince was with difficulty persuaded to disguise himself and hide until he could escape to France. His supporters met with degrees of vengeance ranging from butchery to the banning of their native costume. Carlisle was selected as the scene for the main trials and executions; doubtless as dire warning to the citizens.

By May Dr Waugh was in London again, clearly angling after two possible important appointments, which are so discreetly alluded to by his friends that we never discover what they were. Mr Wardale wrote several long letters, largely devoted to inventories of the contents of the cellar at Caldbeck; but he was wearying, not unnaturally, of these domestic duties:

. . . I do not know why, but I long very much to see you, or at least Mrs Waugh and family in the country again, and I cannot very well tell you for what reason; but methinks I am extreamly tired of being housekeeper;

it is not for the trouble of it I am sure, for that is nothing; but I think people look better after their own affairs than either stewards or servants do. But I hope your staying may not be for nothing, though I think the more I wish it the more I fear it. I beg you would excuse this impertinent trouble, and am, Revd. Sir,

> Your most dutiful and obliged
> Humble Servant,
> (signed) ROBT. WARDALE

General Howard was at all events relieved of his wearisome Governorship; he sent a brisk military communication to Dr Waugh:

Sir,—

I writt to you last post to Carlisle, don't know whether you are yett gott thither; this is to acquaint you I received orders yesterday to go as Major-General under Sir John Ligonier for Flanders, with four regiments from hence, and three to joyn us from Scotland, mine one; these are quick transitions we military people are obliged to submit to, I can't say very agreeable, but wherever I go,

> I am Mr Waugh's faithful humble servant,
> (signed) CHA. HOWARD

A sense of real exhaustion now creeps into the remaining letters; the Rebellion was over, anti-climax had set in. Dr Waugh succumbed to stomach trouble and went with his family to Scarborough to take the waters. The Bishop set out upon a tedious round of Days of Visitation. A number of French prisoners arrived in Carlisle; they were welcomed, for "they incommode us very little and spend a great deal of money", according to Mr Wardale. Food prices fell, but everyone was suffering in some degree or other from poor health.

At the end of July 1746 a number of the prisoners taken at Carlisle on its recapture, who had been removed to Lancaster, were sent back to Carlisle in order to be tried at the Assizes. At the end of July, too, there arrived the heads of Captain Berwick and Lieutenant Chadwick, officers of the Prince's garrison, recently executed on Kennington Common; these were placed on the English Gate. On 2 August Mr

Wardale wrote to Dr Waugh, who was still with his family at Scarborough: ". . . We had about forty prisoners brought in yesternight from Lancaster. . . . I do not fear but we shall get these troublesome assizes over much better than we ever expected."

But he was over-optimistic. Altogether there arrived in Carlisle 382 prisoners who for lack of proper room were huddled together in unspeakably overcrowded conditions in the city gaol and the castle. To try the whole 382 of them would have been a task beyond judges and juries, so the prisoners had the option of drawing lots for selection of one out of every twenty to stand trial; the nineteen remaining to submit to transportation. Several accepted these terms. By these means the number standing trial was reduced to 127. The Grand Jury found bills of indictment against them and the hearing against them was then adjourned until 9 September. In the interval between indictment and trial the prisoners were paraded before successive detachments, fifteen at a time, of the citizens of Carlisle, in order that such of them as had been in arms in the town might be identified. The citizens found identification difficult, for, as Mrs Nicolson wrote to Dr Waugh on 8 September, ". . . the prisoners . . . having coats and breeches instead of plads and none, are not so easily known to those who saw them in nothing but dirty pladds. . . ."

On 9 September the court resumed and the trials proper commenced. Very few of the accused were acquitted. The guilty were executed as traitors at Harribee, Brampton and Penrith. The heads of the lairds Macdonald of Tirnadris and Macdonald of Kinlochmoidart were placed on the Scotch Gate, where they remained many years.

On 24 October 1746 Mr Goldie wrote a long letter to Dr Waugh which is the last in this series. In this letter he mused about the virtues of the clansmen now meeting their deaths (which all did with marked nobility): ". . . the executing of too great numbers is shocking," declared Mr Goldie, going on to tell the Chancellor an anecdote which he himself found moving; it may or may not have moved Dr Waugh, who was not a fervent believer in self-disinterest:

> . . . Kinloch Moidart has been represented to me as a plain honest man, and you'll give me leave to relate you a story that moved me somewhat, that I had from an acquaintance of his that went to see him after he was confined

in the castle of Edinr. After the first salutation was over, the gentleman said, "Dear Kinloch; how came you to engage in so desperate an undertaking, which has never had a probability of success. . .?" He replyed, "I, myself, was against it; but, Lord man, what could I do when the young lad came to my house?"

CHAPTER EIGHT

The Carlisle Canal

On 12 March 1823 at seven o'clock in the morning a band began playing music with a strong nautical flavour outside the Bush Inn, Carlisle. Inside sat the members of the Carlisle Canal committee, eating what the *Carlisle Patriot* (forerunner of today's *Cumberland News*) was to describe as a "lavish breakfast". They were in a buoyant and optimistic mood, for theirs was a remarkable achievement; after twenty-eight years of talk by previous canal committees, their committee had accomplished the construction of a canal from Carlisle to the sea and that day would take place the grand opening ceremony.

Carlisle, a flourishing industrial centre by the close of the eighteenth century, had always suffered from poor communications, especially feeling the need of a sea outlet. In 1807, when enthusiasm for canals was approaching its zenith, a canal committee was formed and William Chapman, M.R.I.A.,[1] was asked to submit a preliminary report for a canal between Carlisle and the Solway Firth.

Chapman had already, in 1795, made a survey and report for a Northumberland canal committee upon the possibility of what he called "a line of navigation" from Newcastle-upon-Tyne to the Irish Channel (Solway Firth), via Carlisle. This highly ambitious project, as he frankly confessed in the introductory pages of his survey, had long been "a favoured object" with him. His cherished plans revealed an element almost akin to fantasy; he suggested that the canal and wet dock at Newcastle should be so constructed as to transform that city into "a Peninsula, having water communication to every avenue". At some future date, subsequent to the completion of the main canal, Ullswater would be linked to it; this, he pointed out, would have "various attendant advantages", not least "a free navigation of seven or eight miles in the bosom of mountains abounding with slates of the finest quality in Europe. . .". The Solway outlet to the sea, of this system of waterways, would be Maryport.

He estimated, optimistically, that the cost of constructing the main trunk of the canal would average about £3000 a mile (the entire length of the canal to be about sixty-five miles) with an estimated annual revenue of £17,242, possibly considerably more. At this point he felt it diplomatic to butter the gentlemen of the Northumberland committee by congratulating them upon "being awake to the advantages to be derived from interior navigation" and he went on to predict that, as a result of the canal, Newcastle would become "the Emporium of the north of England".

The survey, when it appeared, was greeted with scepticism. Other experts retaliated with counter-estimates; that the cost of the canal might ultimately be in the neighbourhood of a million, that it would require a hundred locks to get the canal over the Tyne gap alone. The scheme was rejected; Chapman's hopes for realisation of his favoured object were dashed. Then, twelve years later, Carlisle's canal committee asked for a preliminary survey of their canal sceheme, which at least meant that Chapman might see the western section of his dream-project come true.

Yet even this much abbreviated version of his canal was not taken up for a further ten years, when a resuscitated Carlisle canal committee decided, at a meeting on 7 October 1817 with Sir James Graham, Bart., M.P., in the chair, to ask Chapman for a detailed survey of the possible route.

Thus Chapman in 1818 complied with yet another survey and report, proclaiming in its introductory passages that Carlisle could now be the Emporium of the north-west of England. Obviously Chapman had not given up all hope of a canal from Solway to Newcastle, but tactfully conceded that this might be a future scheme, a mere branch "on a smaller scale . . . of the Carlisle-Solway canal". Another branch might continue up the vale of Eden, he added, connecting Penrith, Appleby and Ullswater with the Solway.

The outlet for the Carlisle–Solway canal he now proposed should be at Fisher's Cross, an insignificant coastal hamlet just east of Bowness. The estimated cost of the canal was about £70,000; a small sum, he pointed out, in comparison with the tide of prosperity which would flow to Carlisle as a result of the canal. The canal committee accepted the report, an Act of Parliament was passed in 1819 authorising the canal's construction, the Carlisle and Annan Navigation Company was formed. The final cost of the canal was £90,000; it was eleven miles long and dropped sixty feet by eight locks. Fisher's Cross was renamed Port Carlisle.

The Canal Company issued some charmingly engraved share certificates, depicting crowds of elegantly dressed people attending the opening of the canal basin. Although this ceremony was scheduled, as we have seen, for March, the artist optimistically portrayed the ladies as lightly clad and bearing parasols.

By this lengthy chain of events, then, did the gentlemen of the Carlisle Canal Committee come to be breakfasting at the Bush Inn on the morning of 12 March 1823, while a band beneath their windows serenaded them with "Hearts of Oak" and "The Bay of Biscay-O!" At eight o'clock a cannon was fired at the castle and the colours were run up the castle foremast. At nine the committee departed in carriages for Burgh-by-Sands, where fourteen gaily dressed ships were waiting to sail up the canal to Carlisle. This flotilla was led by *Robert Burns*, followed by *Irishman* (Robert Ferguson & Sons), *Menai* (Messrs Head & Sons), *Crown* (Carlisle Shipping Company), *Miss Douglas* (Carlisle), *John* (Carlisle), *Henry Brougham* (Annan), *Sarah* (Carlisle), *Rosina* (Carlisle) and *Mary* (Liverpool). The rest were coal and peat boats whose names have not been recorded. The flags dressing *Robert Burns* and *Rosina* were made of the first pattern of silk and cotton gingham to be made in Carlisle by John Hewson & Sons some twenty years before.

At ten precisely the canal committee boarded *Robert Burns* and the convoy got under way, *Irishman* (the first ship to be specially built for the canal) second in line, with a band on deck playing more suitably nautical music. The canal banks teemed with people who, we are told, greeted the convoy with "loud huzzahs and the wildest enthusiasm imaginable". At Knockupworth the vessels were saluted by a drum-and-fife band and flags of the Carlisle City Guilds (each of the city guilds had been presented with a half-barrel of beer to further the celebrations). Crowds of people (an estimated 20,000) had thronged to the canal basin; just as in the engraving on the share certificate, although the people were perhaps not quite so elegant and certainly not so summery. Two warehouses at the basin served refreshments; more than a thousand refreshment tickets were sold.

At ten minutes to three *Robert Burns* arrived at the basin, preceded by another band in an open boat; "Hearts of Oak", "Rule Britannia" and then the National Anthem were played as the convoy sailed in, while from an overlooking hillside a salute was fired from two cannon and two six-pounder field-pieces provided by the Board of Ordnance. A second salute was fired as the last ship in the convoy passed the basin entrance.

Carlisle, we are assured, had seen nothing like it within living memory. Everyone had turned out, including a ninety-seven year old bedridden man complete with bed. Unscheduled excitements included the bursting of a gun on board *Menai* (luckily nobody was hurt) and a spectator "who had been too liberal with refreshments" and as a result fell into the canal, thereby getting "a taste of early spring bathing against his will" as the *Carlisle Patriot* put it.

At 4 p.m. the committee, each member carrying a white wand, marched in procession through the streets of Carlisle (preceded of course by yet another band) back to the Bush Inn where, together with some 150 shareholders of the Canal Company, they sat down to "an elegant and sumptuous dinner". Thirty-three toasts were given, with speeches in which a glowing future was predicted for the canal, Carlisle and every one of its citizens. At 9 p.m. the dinner officially came to an end (although several guests carried on with their drinking until the early hours of next morning) and the main party went on to a ball at the Coffee House (now the Crown and Mitre Hotel).

While this elegance was in progress for persons at the top, the lower orders were enjoying themselves too. Messrs Dixon gave their employees free bread, cheese and ale up to the value of two shillings per head. The firm of Slaters, New Mill, gave each workman a shilling and each female worker sixpence with which to celebrate. Messrs Ferguson gave their workers a shilling each and in addition the warpers and warehousemen dined at the Crown in Botchergate while the females attended a tea-party. Nixon's, too, gave their work people a party.

To publicise the efficiency of the new system of transport Messrs Haysham of Carlisle had, on 9 March, imported from Liverpool some raw cotton which reached Carlisle, via the canal, on 12 March, was spun into yarn on the same day, sent to Fergusons the next day, woven into cloth by 15 March and was being worn as a dress by 'a blooming Cumberland lass' on Sunday, 16 March.[2]

Certainly, the canal at first scored some of the success predicted at the gala dinner; canal transport was cheaper and more efficient than land carriage and as a result coal dropped in price from $6\frac{1}{2}d$. to $3\frac{1}{2}d$. per Carlisle peck, while a small local boat-building industry was born to survive, if not exactly to flourish, for the next seventeen years. But the shares issued by the canal company remained persistently and disappointingly low; something was clearly required to give the canal extra commercial impetus. Accordingly a second-hand passage-boat, the *Baillie Nichol Jarvie*, was purchased from Scots owners and let by the canal company to Alexander Cockburn, a local innkeeper, who ran her along the canal as combined passenger boat and species of floating bar; the maiden voyage was on 1 July 1826 when a "good number of passengers had a delightful trip listening to the band provided, enjoying the hospitality of the said Mr Cockburn and inhaling the sea-air" (to quote the *Patriot* once more).

Baillie Nichol Jarvie prospered, under various skippering mine-hosts, until 1834 when she was replaced by *Arrow*, an appropriately named long, or fly, boat, sixty-six feet in length and six feet in breadth. *Arrow* was conveyed overland from Glasgow in a wagon drawn by three horses, the journey taking five days. Once afloat on the canal *Arrow* was towed by two horses, one of them ridden by a boy. The trip from Carlisle to Port Carlisle was advertised as taking one hour forty minutes; passengers could leave Carlisle in the morning and reach Liverpool by sea in the evening.

In *Arrow* the company had made a sound investment, for the service was used by the flocks of Irish and German emigrants at that time leaving for the United States via Liverpool. In 1839 over a thousand Germans passed through Carlisle during the month of June alone. Sir George Head, in his *Notes on a Home Tour Through the Manufacturing Districts of England in the Summer of 1835*, gives an account of a trip on *Arrow*:

> The Carlisle and Annan Navigation Company preserve a communication with Liverpool, by means of the canal cut about a dozen years since from Carlisle, through a flat country, to the Solway Firth; two powerful steamers, the "Newcastle" and the "City of Carlisle", alternately performing the sea voyage. The canal is wide and handsome; the basin sufficiently

capacious for more vessels than at present resort to it; the dimensions of the lighters which attend the port, bringing about a hundred tons up the canal, appear almost *ad libitum*; they are generally so large as to be unable to float with their full freight on board. Any vessel, provided she carries a single mast, is here called a lighter. . . .

Within the last few years persons interested in the locomotive facilities of our canals, and urged in a great degree by the vain hope of competing successfully with steam, have laboured hard to substitute a new description of boat towed by horses; and this object is now certainly performed nearly twice as fast as was wont to be accomplished; not only are boats built with a view of gliding through the water with the utmost possible rapidity, but instead of the heavy breed of lumbering brutes formerly on the towing-paths, old high-blooded hunters are employed, and moreover kept for the purpose in high condition.

The sheet-iron boat, the "Arrow", by which the company convey their passengers to the steamers lying in the Firth is one of these fast vessels. . . . The point of her destination, "Port Carlisle", on the shore of the Solway Firth . . . is . . . just at the commencement of the ford by which people cross over to the Scotch coast at low water. On the opposite coast . . . is the Annan Water Foot . . . and here the steamers touch, both up and down, to land and receive passengers. . . .

I performed a voyage by the "Arrow" down the canal to Port Carlisle, leaving Carlisle at ten o'clock in the morning, towed by a couple of horses; the fare, one shilling and sixpence. The "Arrow" . . . is the best calculated [boat] for moving quick through the water of any I have seen . . . drawing, with forty people on board, and a great deal of luggage, only twelve inches of water; when light, as I was informed, she floats nine inches. . . . On the present voyage we were driven by a postilion . . . the description of animal used was that of a stout, quick post-horse, the pace ten miles an hour; though we were delayed by the locks . . . and expended exactly two hours on the way. . . .

The postilion, added Sir George, rode the hindmost horse, driving the other before him with a gig whip and light rope reins. Whenever it was necessary to detach the horses, "recourse was had to a very neat expedient. . . . By pressing on a bolt, the eye of the trace is instantaneously thrown off the hook, by a contrivance acting precisely like the trigger of a cross-bow."

A great degree of excitement was at first created by the novelty of the conveyance, as well as by the speed, which exceeded that of the old wooden

Old Thirlmere; note 'Celtic Bridge', and Armboth House on left, on western shore. (*George Fisher collection*)

Old Thirlmere, *circa* 1885; looking towards St John's in the Vale and Saddleback. Note the upper and lower lakes and the 'Celtic Bridge'. (*George Fisher collection*)

Old Thirlmere;
the 'Celtic Bridge',
looking towards
Dale Head Hall and
the eastern shore.
(*George Fisher
collection*)

Old Thirlmere;
Smaithwaite
Bridge. (*George
Fisher collection*)

John Peel country, back o' Skidda. (*Abrahams picture—George Fisher collection*)

The Blencathra, *circa* 1900. Centre, John Crozier, Master; to his left Jim Dalton, Huntsman. On far left of group stands George Tickell, later Deputy Master. (*Abrahams picture—George Fisher collection*)

Jim Dalton (at the close of his career as Huntsman and approaching his eightieth year) on the summit of Catbells, with Songstress and Rally. (*Photo: Mayson*)

John Peel's grave. (*Photo: Sylvia Treadgold*)

boat previously on this canal, by just double. Nevertheless, though people were anxious to go on board her, she was, to all appearance, so cranky,—toppling and rolling from side to side so awfully when empty, that folks took a panic, and many declined on any account to venture. Certainly, were she to capsize, there would be little chance of escape, the passengers being all stowed away under an awning, and closed in on all sides, like sheep in a pen; very little, however, is to be apprehended on that score, for she is buoyant as an Indian canoe. . . . A tolerable load on board brings the "Arrow" sufficiently low in the water, when all danger vanishes, and she is perfectly steady. The awning effectually resists the weather; though, as the framework is as light as can hold together, no passenger is allowed to place even the smallest article on the top. . . .

Port Carlisle affords not much choice of amusement; a circumstance to be deplored by those who have the misfortune to remain there waiting for steamers;—however, there is a good-looking hotel called the "Solway Inn," where the traveller may, at all events, calculate upon finding a sufficient supply of gin and tobacco—or, if inclined to be contemplative, he may indulge in an airy walk upon the Jetty, which latter structure extends, though lightly framed, a very considerable way into the Frith.

Sir George's excursion did not proceed all smoothly:

Having arrived in the "Arrow" with an intention of returning with the passengers of the "City of Carlisle", it was some disappointment to find, not only was that vessel later than usual, but to hear that some untoward event had taken place sufficient probably to prevent her arriving that day at all. From the extremity of the jetty, as I perceived the smoke of two steamers instead of one gently ascending on the other shore of the Frith, it was evident that both vessels, the "Newcastle" and the "City of Carlisle" were lying together at Annan Water-foot. By what accident, inasmuch as they plied in opposite directions, they could thus get together, I did not learn. . . . In the meantime the two steamers showed no disposition to move either way, and as it was not the purpose of the commander of the "Arrow" to return to Carlisle without the Liverpool passengers, here we were under the necessity of remaining.

After waiting a full hour the "City of Carlisle" got under weigh, and came safely alongside. . . . The passengers all got out of the "City of Carlisle", expecting immediately to proceed up the canal,—but no such thing. The passengers from the "Newcastle" also were expected to arrive, and till they came he of the "Arrow" refused to budge. Another hour we were doomed to wait; all of which time the "Newcastle" continued to smoke at Annan Water-foot. Disinterested people were busily occupied in the solution of the same problem; namely, why in the name of simplicity, the two vessels having remained so long together, the "City of Carlisle" had not brought over both sets of passengers. . . .

Two small skiffs were at last seen bobbing up and down, and making head slowly towards the Jetty. Both arrived quite full of people, passengers of the "Newcastle", who landed in a highly discontented mood, and marched on board the "Arrow" with bags, boxes and bundles, till there were as many as could obtain seats, and, over and above, more who were obliged to stand at the head and the stern. With this ballast the "Arrow" glided up the canal as steady as a barge. . . .

In June 1836 newly constructed docks were planned at Port Carlisle, so rosy did the future appear. As a result canal shares improved and in 1839 a dividend was paid of 4 per cent, the highest to that date. Indeed it was to prove an all-time high, for in that same year Newcastle and Carlisle were linked by railway, which destroyed all hopes of extending the canal. The new docks at Port Carlisle were opened in 1840, but without avail; in 1845 came the completion of the Maryport & Carlisle railway which, flourishing upon the tide of the booming coal, iron and steel industries of West Cumberland, paid record dividends with which the canal company could not possibly compete. In 1847 the completion of the Lancaster & Carlisle railway established a through service to Liverpool, thereby delivering the canal its death blow. The following year the canal company turned itself into a railway company. The canal was drained, filled in and railway track laid in its bed. The local anglers at least profited, if but briefly, from this step, for the canal when drained produced quantities of pike and eels. One eel, indeed, was so large that the fisherman who caught it was heard to remark that "he was in doubt whether he ought to eat it or suffer himself to be eaten by it". He was advised to send it to the Corporation dinner to be held in Carlisle to mark the end of the thirty years life of the canal.

CHAPTER NINE

The Cherry Orchard of Armboth

"THIS IS GRAND!" exclaimed Dr Fraser, Bishop of Manchester, as he stood on the summit of Raven Crag, Thirlmere, on a fine spring day in 1878, adding, "If Thirlmere had been made by the Almighty expressly to supply the densely-populated district of Manchester with pure water, it could not have been more exquisitely designed for the purpose."

Or so he was reported to have spoken, by his companion Sir John James Harwood, Knight, Councillor and member of the Manchester Corporation Waterworks Committee.

The Manchester Corporation Water Bill (to promote a scheme to turn Thirlmere into a source of water supply for Manchester) was at that time in its progress through the House of Commons and the Corporation Waterworks Committee was engaged in getting up evidence of persons who were to speak in favour of the Bill when it came into the House of Lords; Dr Fraser, one such projected ally, had been accordingly escorted by members of the Waterworks Sub-Committee to view Thirlmere and the surrounding district and, as we have seen from his quoted observation, he came out very strongly in favour of the scheme.

Dr Fraser was, indeed, so moved and softened by the beauties of the scenery as he and Sir John and Mr Hill (the waterworks engineer) walked over Armboth Fells that he spoke freely of his youth, his mother, her excellent domestic economies (his father's death had left the family poor), above all her cooking, her potato-pie and her hot-pot. As a result Sir John, who was a kindly man, arranged that when Dr Fraser that evening sat down to dinner at Dale Head Hall with the

Waterworks Sub-Committee the main item on the menu was hot-pot.

"O Thirlmere!" had rapturised Coleridge on an October morning seventy-five years earlier, "let me somehow or other celebrate the world in thy mirror—Conceive all possible varieties of Form, Fields, & Trees, and naked or ferny Crags—ravines, behaired with Birches—Cottages, smoking chimneys, dazzling wet places of small rock-precipices—dazzling castle windows in the reflection—all these, within a divine outline in a mirror of 3 miles distinct vision!—and the distance losed in by the Reflection of Raven Crag, which at every bestirring the mirror by gentle motion became a perfect vast Castle Tower, the corners rounded & pillar'd and fluted. . . . All this in bright lightest yellow, yellow-green, green, crimson and orange!—The single Birch Trees hung like Tresses of Sea Weed—the Cliffs like organ pipes! and when a little Breath of Air spread a delicious Network over the Lake, all these colours seemed then to float on, like the reflections of the rising or setting Sun. . . ."

The Thirlmere which enchanted the bishop into thoughts of boyhood and hot-pot and the poet into visions of seaweed tresses, castles and floating sunsets, has vanished for ever. The controversy over the destruction, or perhaps more correctly metamorphosis, of Thirlmere was the greatest and most emotional of all such controversies, until the A66 road battle, now waging at this time of writing. The Thirlmere battle lines were drawn up with the vulgar, profit-grubbing Mancunian Goths on the one hand and the sentimental, soft-headed retrogressives on the other (the respective labels affixed by each group to their opposition). "Vulgar Goths!" "Sentimentalists!" crystallised into, "Business men!" "Academics!" and these in turn exploded into, "Waterworks merchants!" "Literary day-dreamers!" These furious exchanges of invective remain imperishably on record.

Basically it was a matter of predisposition and social outlook. Bishop Fraser's eulogising of Thirlmere (and his subsequent spontaneous train of thought) demonstrates very well what manner of man he was, while Coleridge's eulogising of the same lake indicates equally clearly what his reactions would have been had he been alive at the time of the controversy; he had died some forty years earlier, but the school which he represented was the very one which raised greatest objection to the Thirlmere scheme. Who can doubt that he, with his poetic eloquence and pungent journalist's pen would have been in the forefront of those

Fraser that evening sat down to dinner at Dale Head Hall with the

The Thirlmere drama was in every respect Tchekhovian; tragedy interspersed by high comedy, high comedy played against tragedy.

Prior to 1851 Manchester's water supply was very inadequate. In 1874 a scheme was inaugurated for constructing reservoirs in Long-dendale (eighteen miles east of Manchester) and from 1851 onwards Manchester enjoyed water from this source which, in contrast to water obtained, old-style, from "pumps, wells, rainwater stored in cisterns, and the limited resources of the Manchester and Salford Water Works Company . . ." was so "pure and wholesome" that by the end of 1864 Manchester was demanding three times as much water as it had required in 1851 (quotes from Harwood, J. J., *History and Description of the Thirlmere Water Scheme*, Manchester, 1895).

In 1868 Mr. J. F. Bateman, expert adviser to the Manchester Corporation Waterworks Committee, stated that the available supply would only last out eight or nine years from that time. Additional supplies would have to be obtained "if the luxury of a full water supply be maintained and the prosperity of the district be secured by the abundance of water, for personal comfort and the wants of trade."

As a result of this warning the Waterworks Committee on 11 March 1875 passed a resolution that,

> . . . this Committee concurs with Mr Bateman in the desirability of securing a further supply of water . . . and that the Audit Sub-Committee be requested to consider the subject.

At a further meeting the Waterworks Committee heard Mr Bateman's recommendation that a water supply be obtained from Ullswater and Haweswater, either in conjunction with Liverpool or separately. The Waterworks Committee, nothing if not thorough, thereupon visited the Lake Country to see for themselves the actual conditions of waters and watersheds advocated by Mr Bateman. From the first they encountered hostility; as they went from place to place they were "frequently pointed out . . . as the Goths and Vandals who had come to destroy the country. . .". This hostility obviously surprised them.

The tour of inspection was not only conducted under these rather unfriendly conditions, but proved in other ways "generally arduous, and sometimes dangerous". Sir John details one such trying incident:

On the occasion of one of our visits to Ullswater, we left Keswick, and arrived at our destination before noon. We inspected a portion of the Lake, and were much struck by the quality and important character of the residential property on its banks, and the enormous cost that would have to be incurred by raising the Lake should this property be submerged or injured in any way. . . .

As the mountains forming the west watershed of Ullswater are the boundary of the east watershed of Thirlmere, we determined to make full use of the day and return over Helvellyn, and by way of Legburthwaite.

We could only do this by walking or going on horseback, and we were of opinion that we could make a better inspection if we walked. There was, however, one difficulty. Councillor George Booth, one of the party, was advanced in years, and as he could not walk very well, he had frequently to rest, which was the more alarming on this occasion as we had a considerable distance to travel, and night was coming on. For this journey only one horse was hired, as we thought it would be sufficient to carry the luggage, &c. We had perhaps been an hour on the way when Mr Booth required to rest. He was therefore placed on the horse, and not being accustomed to riding had to be partly held on, as well as could be managed by the attendant.

After a while Alderman Grave, who for his age was a good mountain climber, began to be tired, and had to take a turn on the horse, and as the horse could not carry either of these men and the luggage as well, Mr Pape and I had to take charge of the luggage.

We were going but slowly up the mountain when we heard a strange noise in the rear, and found that the horse, with Mr Grave on its back, had walked on a pocket of peat, and sunk above its knees in the bog.

It was a most amusing sight to see Mr Grave holding on to the horse, with his arms round its neck from fear of falling into the bog. We managed at last to get him off, but what to do, or how to proceed to get the horse out, we did not know. The driver did not try for some time to assist it, and it was evident he wanted us to leave him, so that he could return home. After a time the horse was got out, but we had not proceeded very far before we found that Mr Booth would either have to be put on its back again or left behind. By a determined effort we arrived at the top of Helvellyn, when the question was, how and at what point should we descend? Mr Grave said he knew, or had been told, that there was a miner's track leading down to Thirlspot, so we tried to find it, and he went forward with Mr Berrey to descend to a point he thought led to the track. This adventure, however, proved to be a rather disastrous one, as both Mr Grave and Mr Berrey had a fall, and received considerable injury.

Mr Booth, having the horse, would insist on going along the top of the mountain and making the descent at Wythburn; but after getting over Helvellyn Low Man, ready to descend, the driver would not allow the horse to go further. We had therefore to gather up the luggage and do the best we could. We had a very troublesome journey with Mr Booth, but finally arrived at the Nag's Head Inn, Wythburn, after a hard struggle, about ten o'clock at night, where we waited some two or three hours, and then procured a carriage and drove to Keswick.

The Ullswater scheme was abandoned.

On 22 June 1876 Mr Bateman, in a letter to the Manchester Waterworks Committee, suggested Thirlmere as a possible reservoir. The Thirlmere scheme would cost some £170,000 less than an Ullswater one and would not take nearly so much time to execute. "Although a large tract of land would be submerged by raising the Lake . . . there would be little residential injury or damage to ornamental property, and compensation in water would get rid of all the claims of the small mills in the river below," wrote Mr Bateman.

It was thereupon resolved unanimously that,

. . . in the opinion of this Committee it is desirable, if practicable to do so upon reasonable terms, to purchase by private contract the lands and water rights referred to in the report . . . in order to place the Corporation in a favourable position for securing additional supply of water . . . whenever it shall be determined to apply to Parliament for the necessary powers.

That it be referred to the Chairman (Alderman Grave), Deputy-Chairman (Alderman Patteson), Alderman Bennett, and Councillors Booth and Harwood to carry out the foregoing resolution.

To quote Sir John once again:

This step was mainly taken for the purpose of ascertaining as nearly as possible the value of the land and property in the Thirlmere watershed—which, as proposed to be extended, would comprise about 11,000 acres—inasmuch as the Committee were strongly of the opinion that if the difficulty, annoyance, and expense which they had experienced in connection with the Longdendale works were to be avoided in connection with this scheme, and the entire control of the water secured, it was necessary that the whole drainage should be purchased. . . .

This resolution, which was recorded on the Minutes of the Waterworks

Committee, was confirmed by the City Council on the 2nd of August, 1876, and in order to give the Sub-Committee full power to carry the same into effect, the Corporate Seal was affixed thereto. . . .

It must be borne in mind that this was quite an exceptional Sub-Committee, and they were authorised to act in a manner that was very unusual, and could only be justified by the special circumstances at the time. . . .

The self-confessedly exceptional Sub-Committee now proceeded to Thirlmere to, as it were, case the joint. Their reactions to the lake anticipated those of Bishop Fraser. Declared Sir John (doubtless voicing the sentiments of the entire committee), "From the very appearance and character of its surroundings the valley might have been made for the purpose of a gathering ground for water. It is situate in the heart of about the heaviest rainfall in the country. The mountains surrounding it consist of Silurian rock, are exceedingly steep, and are covered with very little verdure, so that the rain which falls flows direct into the Lake, and sometimes 15 or 16 cascades or watercourses can be seen at once running down the mountain slopes, quite pure, and as clear as crystal." He further mused, "The Lake can easily be raised by means of an embankment constructed at the northern end, and across the outlet into St John's Beck."

Thirlmere of those days was about three miles long and a little over a quarter of a mile at its widest part; its greatest depth was estimated at 112 feet and it covered some 330 acres (the level of the lake was ultimately raised 54 feet and the surface area today is 812 acres). The old lake consisted of two parts, called the higher and lower lakes, which were connected near the centre by a very narrow and shallow channel, between Dale Head Hall on the eastern shore and Armboth House (now submerged) on the west; this channel being crossed by a ford and an ancient causeway bridge, described by Sir John as a "rude Celtic bridge". The shores of Thirlmere were remarkably unspoilt, the few buildings thereon being almost exclusively the farmsteads and homes of indigenous statesmen and in no way 'important' or 'ornamental'. The Sub-Committee had no qualms about submerging them, but balked somewhat at the notion of perhaps having to drown Wythburn church, famous for its minute size and for having been extolled by Wordsworth. They toyed with the idea of removing it to higher ground, or perhaps building an exact replica of it somewhere else, but finally it was found possible to leave the church untouched, with the old inn which faced it across the road, the Nag's Head, also unsubmerged, but everlastingly closed and deserted.

The Waterworks Sub-Committee on this inspection of Thirlmere found the natives still unreasonably, indeed almost irrationally, hostile. Says Sir John:

> To show the effect the scheme had upon the people of the district, I may mention that on one occasion . . . our party, proceeding along the road, became separated, some walking before and others a distance behind. Several local workmen happened to be on the road at the time. One of them, engaged in breaking stones, did not know that those who were behind belonged to the party in front. . . . Another labouring man . . . was passing. The stonebreaker attracted his attention and said: "Thoo sees that man theear wid t'white heid" (pointing to Alderman Grave)? He replied, "Yis." "Well . . . he's gitten't intul his heid to tak t'watter oot ot' lake fra here ta Manchester," whereupon the other man laughed and said: "What! Theear's nut munny aneuf in aw t'world as wad dueh't," thus showing the opinion of these poor people respecting the scheme . . . they had a great prejudice against it.

The Sub-Committee endeavoured to gain the necessary particulars respecting the lands and properties at Thirlmere which they had been appointed to purchase, but due to the uncooperative attitudes of the local people very little information could be obtained for some time. Ultimately the services of three persons were secured; namely, Mr David Pape, Mr Thomas Dixon Lancaster, and Mr Henry Irwin Jenkinson. Mr Pape lived at Keswick and was in the habit of frequenting the neighbourhood for the purpose of buying cattle and he had a good knowledge of the value of land in the locality. A valuation of the buildings was made by Mr Lancaster, who was a Keswick builder, while,

> Mr Jenkinson, who had written a very good and popular Guide Book to the Lake District, and lived at Keswick, undertook to obtain what further information was needed. The residents in the neighbourhood were very much against the scheme, and declined to give any particulars; but Mr Jenkinson was supposed to be collecting materials for a Guide Book, and

to be desirous of giving a full description of the places in the new book in order to attract visitors. This resulted in the people becoming very communicative. . . . (Harwood)

Difficulty was also experienced in getting at the rentals or "annual Value" of the various properties, and Mr Charles Birkett, blacksmith of Legburthwaite, the overseer of the district, who had the Township books, did not want to offend any of his neighbours by giving information and for a long time would not allow the Sub-Committee to see them.

A Countess Ossalinsky, who owned about 714 acres on Armboth Fells, five farms (including Armboth House) containing 850 acres, together with a number of sheep and stints, the property having been in the possession of her ancestors for a long period and herself and her family highly respected in the neighbourhood, proved "most difficult and troublesome". The rental derived by the Countess from the property was only a little over £500 per annum, and its value was estimated by the Corporation, after making what Sir John called "a liberal allowance for improvement and compulsory sale", at from £20,000 to £25,000. The valuations made on behalf of the Countess ranged, however, from about £72,000 to over £100,000. Under these circumstances an arbitration under the Lands Clauses Act 1845 was unavoidable. This arbitration did not take place until October 1881 and August 1882; the Committee, said Sir John, was somewhat prepared "for a very large award to the Countess, but every member of the Committee held his breath when the astounding award was announced of £64,447, and £6,000 for the Lake, or in round numbers £70,000 (exclusive of the value of the sheep . . .)"

Sir John stated particulars of this arbitration award in a pamphlet to members of the City Council:

It is quite certain that, if the Parliamentary Estimates are to be exceeded by three or four times the amount, Corporations and Local Authorities will shrink from undertaking works of this nature, which are so necessary to the development of trade and so indispensable to the health and wellbeing of our large centres of industry. It would be a national calamity if property of this kind could not be purchased for purposes such as that for which this is required at something near its market value, and it seems to me that the Corporation have an excellent case upon which to base an appeal to the

Prime Minister of this country for the introduction of a small Bill enabling either party to apply to the Local Government Board for the appointment of an arbitrator.

On the receipt of the award by the Countess, Manchester Corporation took steps, in the Queen's Bench Division of the High Court of Justice, to set it aside, but a compromise between the two parties was effected and the action was not proceeded with. The Association of Municipal Corporations prepared a memorial to the government to introduce a Bill into Parliament for the purpose of amending section 28 of the Lands Clauses Consolidation Act 1845, by vesting in the Board of Trade the appointment of an umpire in relation to the works of Municipal Corporations: the relevant Bill was prepared, introduced into the House and received the Royal assent on 18 June 1883.

The Lord of the Manor of Wythburn, at the time of Manchester's onslaught, was Sir Henry Ralph Vane, Bart., known as Sir Harry Vane after an ancestor whose formidability must (Sir John noted apprehensively) have been considerable, inasmuch as when Cromwell had been about to attack the region he had prayed, " 'From the wiles of the Devil and Sir Harry Vane, good Lord deliver us'." A deputation of the Waterworks Sub-Committee met with their Sir Harry at Hutton Hall and Penrith and ultimately terms of purchase of the manor of Wythburn were arranged, Sir Harry reserving the right of shooting and sporting over Armboth Fells for the remainder of his life.

The Lord of the Manor of Legburthwaite, owner of Lake Thirlmere and the Dale Head estate, Mr Thomas Leathes Stanger Leathes (Thirlmere in early times was known as Leathes Water) proved more obdurate than Sir Harry. It is best to leave Sir John to tell this part of the story:

Mr Leathes . . . was very much opposed to the scheme, and he would not allow us access to his estate or give permission for us to go over the land to see the Lake, and threatened to take very severe measures if any of us were found there. We were, however, very anxious to see what the margin of the Lake was like, and one very wet day Alderman Grave and I went over from Keswick, and to avoid observation we crept on our hands and knees past Dale Head Hall down to the Lake. We had to return to Keswick in our wet clothes, and the consequence was that I was laid up for a week afterwards with a cold, Alderman Grave also suffering for several days.

The Sub-Committee tried approaching Mr Wilkinson of Fisher Place, bailiff for Mr Thomas Leathes Stanger Leathes, but Mr Wilkinson would not give the Sub-Committee any information or help. Things seemed at a total halt, when Mr Leathes fell very ill, dying on 19 June 1876. He was succeeded by his son, Mr George Stanger Leathes who was approached by the Sub-Committee. According to Sir John the new heir had gone

> . . . to Australia when a young man and stayed there for over twenty years, he seemed to have lost all the sentiment which was so manifest in the minds of his father and other members of the family who had remained in this country; and to their credit be it said, we could not help admiring the tenacity with which they clung to this estate and its associations. One could not but be reminded of the story of Naboth, who would not part with his Vineyard, the possession of his ancestors, for money. Mr George Stanger Leathes cared more about his income than the sentiment of living upon the ancestral estate, but so determined was the opposition of the other members of the family to parting with the property . . . that Mr Leonard Stanger Leathes, his brother, in whom vested the succession to the estate in case of failure of male issue to Mr George Stanger Leathes, appeared before the Select Committee of the House of Commons against the Bill. . . .

Part at least of Mr Leonard Stanger Leathes' evidence before the Select Committee, while under examination by his counsel, Mr Maddison, deserves quoting:

Q. The whole estate has been in your family, I believe, for many years?
A. I think the date of the grant is the 7th of Queen Elizabeth.
Q. It came into your family in the time of Queen Elizabeth?
A. Yes.
Q. And there are exclusive rights of fishing over the Lake?
A. That is one of the great advantages and beauties of the Lake. I do not think there is another lake in England where there are exclusive rights.
Q. There was some dispute about your exclusiveness as to fishing, was there not?
A. In my great-grandfather's time, Sir Fletcher Vane contested it. It was tried at the Assizes at Carlisle; but he was defeated, and no other person has questioned those rights but him.
Q. I believe he took other proceedings, did he not?
A. He challenged my ancestor to mortal combat in consequence.

Q. And I think in that he also failed, did he not?

A. Yes.

There could, however, be no challenging of Alderman Grave to mortal combat over Thirlmere in 1879 and even Leonard Stanger Leathes was ultimately persuaded not to oppose the Bill further. The purchase of the Manor and estate was concluded. Mr George Stanger Leathes became tenant for life, instead of owner, of the Dale Head estate. The members of the Waterworks Sub-Committee inspected Dale Head Hall, their newly acquired property, built for the greater part in the first quarter of the seventeenth century; Sir John pointed out to his companions the inscription on a stained glass window over the staircase:

Cristopherus Laythes, hoc Dom. Aedif.

A.D. 1623

Sir John noted that from the windows of the house admirable views were obtained of the upper lake, its rocky promontories, and of Box Holme, a diminutive but picturesque island as he described it. He mused:

The shore of this portion of the Lake is decidedly more attractive than that of the lower part, and there is no reason to think that when the Lake is raised the future higher fringe of woods and fern-covered hillside will be less lovely than the present one; while the disappearance of Box Holme will be compensated for by the creation of two more beautiful islands in the lower Lake. . . .

The vanquishing of the Leathes family was so far Manchester's biggest victory in the battle of Thirlmere but, once more to quote Sir John, "we . . . as yet had not succeeded in making the progress we desired". Cumbrians are skilled stonewallers, in more senses of the phrase than one; the Sub-Committee found the going hard. In addition to the suspicion and obstinacy of the local people themselves, the very countryside seemed to be opposed to Manchester:

One day I called on Mr George Hinde, the owner of the Bank Farm, and found that he had a widowed mother. I promised her that if her son would sell his farm to the Corporation she should not be disturbed, and might reside in the house during the remainder of her days (which she did for three or four years). I often called to see her afterwards, and used to take a packet of tea in my pocket for her. The Sub-Committee urged that I should go with Mr Pape, Mr Lancaster, and Mr Jenkinson to see if we could make any headway as regards this property. We arrived at Wythburn about noon, and after much trouble we succeeded in purchasing it. This farm formed part of a group of houses known as the "City", and consisted of about 39 acres of land, with 24 stints on Wythburn Fells, and a flock of 130 sheep. It was a very important property, as it gave us access to the Lake by several fields coming down to its margin.

It was about half-past three or four o'clock in the afternoon when we had finished, and Mr Jenkinson suggested that as we had never been on the summit of the south end of the Helvellyn Range, and therefore had not seen that part of the watershed, and it being a beautiful, fine afternoon, we might go up and see it . . . it was delightfully clear . . . and as it was moonlight at that time in the evening, we expected to be able to get down the mountain by the light of the moon. As soon, however, as we got to the top a heavy fall of snow commenced, and it began to freeze as I never felt it freeze before or since.

Mr Jenkinson, who was one of the most experienced men in the district, and the best Guide probably in the county, declared that it would be dangerous to attempt to return to Wythburn. We had nothing with us except the clothes we had on, and no refreshments of any kind; but he said it was inevitable that we should proceed on to the other side and make the gradual descent (which was not so dangerous) to Ullswater. We started through the blinding snow, lost our way several times, and Mr Jenkinson had to go forward to assure us that we were not approaching some precipice. We arrived at Ullswater in a terrible plight about nine o'clock at night, having been down in the snow many times through the uneveness of the road. Our friends of course became very much worried about us. We induced a blacksmith, who had gone to bed, to get up and sharpen two horses for us, and drove over Troutbeck Common, which was like one sheet of glass, arriving at Portinscale in a very exhausted condition about two o'clock the following morning.

When accounts of this kind of incident leaked out to the dales people it must have seemed that God was on the side of Thirlmere. If the Waterworks Sub-Committee could only be persuaded to do enough mountaineering. . . ! But the Mancunians were astonishingly hardy and survived all hazards. The day came when Alderman Grave, being chairman of the Manchester Corporation Waterworks Committee at the time of the purchasing, was made Lord of the Manors of Legbur-thwaite and Wythburn, in trust for the Corporation.

The Manchester Corporation Water Bill was given its first reading before the House of Commons in December 1877. The agitation against the scheme now broke forth upon a nation-wide scale; based principally on aesthetic grounds and the need to preserve certain areas such as the Lake District as playgrounds for "the jaded industrial populations of the future". A Thirlmere Defence Association was formed and was supported by a host of people whom Alderman Grave, in a letter to *The Times*, designated as "poets, artists, bishops and sentimentalists". Whereat *The Times* correspondence columns were choked with furious letters in reply, among them a particularly trenchant one from Octavia Hill:

> ... advocates of the scheme ... own that the plan, if adopted, would make considerable alteration in Thirlmere, only they maintain that these altera-tions will be decided improvements upon Nature. For instance Nature, it appears from Mr Grave's letter, has been for hundreds of years at work in the valley, bringing down stones and soil from the mountains. She has filled up the valley at the head and narrowed the Lake in the middle. Her Lake, in fact, contains its own history, written on its shores and surround-ings. Lovers of the Lake Country had been accustomed to consider this formation interesting, but they were mistaken, it seems. Manchester will kindly obliterate the history, submerge the fields. ... Again, some of us liked the sedgy margins of our lakes, where great reeds and rushes grew. ... Here, too, it seems we were wrong, and Manchester will help us by draining or flooding over our lake shore. ...

Satire, fury, indignation, gnashing of teeth, tearing of hair, shedding of tears, all failed. The Bill was passed, the Thirlmere scheme put into operation. The old lake passed inexorably into the realms of the forever lost. The formal ceremony of turning on Manchester's water from the new Thirlmere into the aqueduct took place on 12 October 1894 and was performed by Alderman Sir John James Harwood, now chairman of the Waterworks Committee, in the presence of a large gathering, including many distinguished persons, several of whom had been sworn enemies of the scheme, but who now were silenced; submerged like

Armboth House and Wythburn City, overwhelmed by sheer acreage
of water. At the straining-well and valve house, built to resemble a
small gothic fortress, the Lord Mayor and Corporation of Manchester
were given a cordial welcome by a number of invited guests from the
Lake Country. Canon Rawnsley of Crosthwaite, who had earlier
fought the scheme tooth and nail, opened the ceremonies with a prayer,
after which the Lord Mayor spoke. He was followed by Sir John,
who made a long and witty speech in which he recalled the former
battles for Thirlmere, especially against Cumbria. "You imagined that
we were about to transform all that delighted you into the semblance of
a mill dam, and you fought us stoutly, as Englishmen always fight. Well
we won. . . . We have now completed the works, and today we have
invited you to witness the result of our handiwork. We invite and
challenge inspection. . . . Is there anything hideous in the handsome
embankment we have formed? Is there one of you who thinks that jaded
men and women . . . will be deterred from seeking all they need in this
sequestered region because we have applied the watershed to purposes
of civilisation? No; a thousand times no. . . ."

Sir John, having at last concluded his speech, "upon the invitation of
the Lord Mayor, turned the wheel acting in connection with the
hydraulic machinery, by which the water of the Lake was admitted
into the aqueduct, amidst the cheers of the assembly" (*The Times*).

More cheers, a brief speech by Mr Hill, the engineer, a benediction
by the Bishop of Carlisle (who had earlier led the spearhead of
Cumbria's attack). After this the party drove along the new road on the
west shore of the lake and over the great stone embankment with its
gothic-style architecture, which was then declared open to the public
by Alderman Sir Bosdin T. Leech, Deputy-chairman of the Waterworks Committee. Luncheon was served in the temporary schoolroom
at Bridge End, followed by a plethora of toasts and speeches and a
sonnet composed specially for the occasion by Canon Rawnsley in an
attempt to express what he felt about Sir John, "this true type of strong
Englishman. . .".

> Our generation pass, our names decay,
> The spirit lives—the courage and the skill
> That chains the torrent, that can pierce the hill
> And lead sweet water-floods from far away. . . .

Nearly a century later time and afforestation have concealed the lake's physical scars and visitors unaware of Thirlmere's history do not even realise that they are seeing a new, corporation-made lake. Indeed many people remark that it is the loveliest of all the lakes; invariably going on to say that it is so different from the others that it might be a lake from some other country, or even out of a fairy tale, with its dark pine forests and shadow filled, silver-streaked expanses of water. And they wonder why it is so unlike the other lakes of the region.

And thus they put their fingers on the essence of criticism of Thirlmere. Today, say the critics, Thirlmere, however scenically gratifying to sentimentalists who admire fairy-tale scenery (shades of Alderman Grave! the tables are indeed turned) is completely out of context. The Mancunians who promised Lakeland a new Thirlmere more beautiful than the old one had ever been meant every word of what they said and they searched into the backs of their minds for all that a perfectly beautiful lake meant to them and came up with this nurseryland fantasia by Hans Andersen out of the Brothers Grimm. Which is why, say the critical purists, today's Thirlmere appeals so widely to the undiscerning; it is the reincarnation of everyone's childhood dream of an enchanted lake. But it is never a Cumberland mere.

The Mancunians and their allies respond that modern Thirlmere does in fact more closely resemble the original glacial lake of distant ice-age wrought Cumbria than Leathes Water ever did. Their critics retort that the clock has been put back to a ridiculous distance that results in total artificiality; they point out that the indigenous life of the local community has been completely destroyed, submerged; Thirlmere today is tantamount to a dead lake. The Mancunians demonstrate, backing their argument with figures, that more persons are employed in the Thirlmere catchment area today than ever lived and worked there in the pre-submersion era. Ah! say the critics, but it is not indigenous activity springing from roots based in a community developed over the centuries, part of the region's essential fabric. Today's Thirlmere is instant.

One could report the dialogue interminably, for it is without end, fundamental. As *The Times* observed (20 October 1887): "Disputants who have no common ground can never hope to convince each other."

Echoes from a timeless shrine at sunset reach us; voices, Russian voices, but they might be speaking any language:

LOPAHIN: Forgive me, but such reckless people as you are—such queer, unbusiness-like people—I never met in my life . . .

LYUBOV: What are we to do? Tell us what to do.

LOPAHIN: I do tell you every day. Every day I say the same thing. You absolutely must let the cherry orchard and the land on building leases. . . . Once make up your mind to build villas . . . and then you are saved.

LYUBOV: Villas and summer visitors—forgive me saying so—it's so vulgar. . . .

LOPAHIN: I shall sob, or scream, or fall into a fit. I can't stand it! You drive me mad! . . .[1]

But he won, of course. And the cherry orchard was cut down.

CHAPTER TEN

Legend and Lore

THE QUEST FOR legend and lore in Cumberland greatly resembles the quest for wadd. Each literary source repeats the one preceding it, until the searcher finally unearths an ultimate source which has been buried for so long under a heap of misquoted repetition and misinterpretation that it has become almost obscured.

In the case of Cumbrian legend and lore one is particularly bedevilled by the fact that almost everything written on this subject has been designed for tourist consumption.

The authentic legends and tales were never preserved in writing but were simply handed down by word of mouth, or sung or recited in ballad form, from one generation to the next. A few of the legends were striking enough to be committed to print when tourist time came and, finally, a scholarly attempt was made to preserve some of the ballads,[1] but the great mass of folklore, folk custom, ritual, myth and superstition was indigestible for tourists; thus it went unrecorded and finally passed into oblivion.

The Romantic tourists demanded stock ghosts, phantom coaches, headless ladies, armoured knights and Gothic horrors. They were convinced that the inhabitants of such a wild and remote country as Cumberland must be particularly ignorant, naïve and superstitious. Since there has always been money in catering for the tourist trade, the closing years of the eighteenth and early years of the nineteenth centuries saw a spate of Lake Country legend and lore unleashed upon the ever-increasing Lakeland visitors. There is indication that much of the original crop of so-called ancient legends published at this time was unabashedly embellished, if not downright invented, to satisfy tourist demand.[2] For the same reason the belief was fostered (and in some quarters is still fostered) that the Cumbrian is uniquely superstitious; though in fact the reverse rather seems to be the case.

One of the first to foster the profitable notion of superstitious Cumbria was Robert Anderson, who towards the close of the eighteenth century migrated from his native Carlisle to London where, stimulated by the growing tourist interest in the Lake Country he produced, in 1770, a small book of Cumberland Ballads, in dialect. In his introduction to these he drew a portrait of the Cumbrian people as steeped in belief in "fairies, boggles, brownies and enchantments of all kind". His ballads themselves, obviously based on shrewd and close observance of West Cumbrians, do not bear out Anderson's introductory theme of superstition; the people in his ballads are depicted as lusty, gusty and down-to-earth, much given to hard drinking, feasting, fighting, dancing and courting, as well as addicted to gossiping, scandal-mongering and card-playing. Clay-daubings, weddings, sheep-clippings, cockfights, courtships, merry neets, youth and bounding high spirits, old age and waning powers and fortunes, provide the major themes of his verse; occasionally, but only very occasionally, a random boggle is mentioned, but then merely in passing and never of real consequence.

However, thanks to Anderson, the statement had now appeared in cold print that Cumbrians were a uniquely superstitious people and so, wadd-wise, it came to be repeated henceforth without questioning.

Hutchinson in his 1794 *History of the County of Cumberland* worked hard at the superstitions of the district, reiterating that, ". . . this part of the country . . . abounds in all the *aniles fabellæ* of fairies, ghosts and apparitions. . .". His technique of myth-building is interesting to study. Of Castle Rock in the Vale of St John he wrote: "This massive bulwark shows a front of various towers, and makes an awful, rude and Gothic appearance, with its lofty turrets and ragged battlements. . . . The traveller's curiosity is roused, and he prepares to make a nearer approach, when that curiosity is put upon the rack by his being assured that, if he advances, certain genii who govern the place, by virtue of their supernatural art and necromancy, will strip it of all its beauties and, by enchantment, transform the magic walls. The vale seems adapted for the habitation of such beings; its gloomy recesses and retirements look like haunts of evil spirits. . . ."

It would seem a likely explanation of the origin of this 'myth' that some dalesman (who unwittingly shared his home in St John's Vale with evil spirits) was courteously pointing out local landmarks, including Castle Rock, to the visiting antiquarian, when that gentleman in his picturesque enthusiasm observed that the rock looked so very like a castle that it was difficult to believe that at some time it had not, in fact, been one. To which the dalesman responded, "Oh aye; but when ye gar closer ye'll see that it's nobbut a rock." Result: a report of firm local belief in genii, supernatural art and necromancy and the subsequent birth of Scott's poetic legend of the Vale of St John, "The Bridal of Triermain":

> Where is the Maiden of mortal strain,
> That may match with the Baron of Triermain?
> She must be lovely, and constant, and kind,
> Holy and pure, and humble of mind . . .

Scott as poet was put in his place for ever by Coleridge, in a letter to Wordsworth written from Keswick in October 1810:

> . . . The movement of the Poem . . . is between a sleeping Canter and a Marketwoman's trot. . . . A man accustomed to cast words in metre and familiar with descriptive Poets and Tourists, himself a Picturesque Tourist, must be troubled with a mental Strangury, if he could not lift up his leg six times at six different Corners, and each time piss a canto. . . .

The mysterious Lorenzo Tuvar quoted "The Bridal of Triermain" at length (and it is very, very long) in his book (c. 1850) of Lakeland legends and tales; of which more, later. In this book he repeated Hutchinson, Mackay, Clarke and the romantic rest on Lake Country superstitious belief.

In a talk given on 10 October 1867 to a Cockermouth audience the speaker, Mr Whitfield, M.P., observed (more echoes of Anderson!) that superstitions in the Border country concerning fairies and brownies were more developed, and the belief in spells and enchantments more common, than in many other parts of the country. This was quoted by Daniel Scott in his *Bygone Cumberland and Westmorland*, published in 1899, and has been regurgitated again today by some of our contemporary anthologists of Lakeland lore as an assurance that the people of the Lake Country and the Border are naturally highly superstitious and more prone to belief in fairies, spells, enchantments and fantastic legends than very possibly any other people in the country. So the spirit of Anderson marches on!

Nobody with first-hand experience of a truly superstitious rural community could possibly, in honesty, describe modern Cumbrians as superstitious. The present author spent much of the most impressionable part of her childhood in a remote West Country community which, even in the early nineteen-thirties, was imbued with magic and supserstition; the people did not hide this at all (for superstitious beliefs may sometimes be discreetly concealed from the prying outsider) but openly indulged in every manifestation of faith in witchcraft and fairies. A pinch of salt was always dropped in the fire at churning time so that the fairies would not keep the butter from coming; the bees were informed of every important family event; no creature of darkness, moth, glow-worm, beetle or bat could be handled, lest the person who touched it should find themselves magically glued to the next broomhandle or farm implement that was reached for. Horses' manes must be knotted at certain times in the month; for certain wishes to come true, or unpleasantnesses to be avoided, water must be crossed in the direction opposite to that in which it flowed; to step over a fallen milking-stool was courting disaster. When the cattle got ringworm a witch-doctor was called in preference to the vet. The witch-doctor was a pleasant-faced, rather stout old man who doctored the cows after a certain number of hours had elapsed since human eye had last fallen upon them; the doctoring took place in strictest privacy in an isolated shippen, not even the owner was allowed to be present.

Embedded superstition of this kind seems to have faded into oblivion in Cumberland long before present living memory. It is noteworthy that Dorothy Wordsworth, who certainly had the full confidence of her Grasmere neighbours, although she makes constant allusion in her *Journals* (*c.* 1800) to their quaint sayings and social customs, makes no mention of supernatural beliefs, witchcraft, hauntings or the like. If she had heard of these things she would assuredly have noted them. Old Molly Ashburner would have prattled to Dorothy of boggles[3] and fairies had boggles and fairies been on her mind.

Coleridge, a delighted devotee of Molly, would have quoted her in this context too, as he quoted her other sayings. He, who wandered so widely through the remoter parts of the region and who conversed for hours on end with dalesmen in their own homes, never, in his notebooks and letters, gives any indication that he found these a superstitious people. Quite the reverse: he depicted them, as did Dorothy, as deeply, if unaffectedly, devout in their beliefs; far from naïve and certainly not illiterate, although their reading matter was almost exclusively confined to the Bible and the prayer book.

The best-known and undoubtedly the most influential of the tourist anthologies of Lakeland lore was *Tales and Legends of the English Lakes, Collected from the best and most authentic sources*, by Lorenzo Tuvar; a *nom de plume* which in itself speaks volumes! Published by Longmans, the first edition bears no date, but the mention of a railway at Windermere provides evidence that it appeared after 1847. The copy used by this author and obtained from the Cumberland County library is inscribed, "John Crozier, Riddings 1863".

The introduction makes the purpose and methods of the book very clear:

. . . The last twenty years have witnessed a perfectly new era, as regards access to the Lakes. Railways—the foremost wonder of our teeming age— have now brought nearly every great city and town of our island within a few hours' reach of their Alpine loveliness . . . this beautiful isolation of romantic sublimity . . . is now visited by admiring and increasing thou- sands. The increased and increasing facilities afforded for visiting the un- rivalled scenery of the Lake district naturally excite a corresponding desire to supply the tourist with every incident connected with this interesting locality. The great number of popular publications as Guides and Tours to the Lakes . . . are most of them deficient in their allusion to the history and traditions of some of the more remarkable sites of this romantic region.

To supply this deficiency, in part, is the object of the present Work. . . . In the following pages are narrated a few of the romantic stories the country affords. . . . True, it may appear to be richer in scenery than in legend, and in poetry than romance; but the fact is, its legends and romance have been neglected. The district is highly suggestive of both . . . it contains a mine of *materials* for romance yet almost untouched. . . .

Nonetheless, Lorenzo Tuvar had to scrape the barrel hard to find sufficient picturesque and legendary material for an entire book; indeed of true legends he could only find five (apart from those em- bedded in the Border ballads, mainly derived from Percy's *Reliques*,[4] on which he had a long chapter). These five legends were the hoary old tale of the skulls of Calgarth, the Luck of Eden Hall, the Hart's Horn Tree, Lady Eva and the Giant of Yewdale, and the legend of the Devil and Kirkby Lonsdale bridge. The story of Lord Egremont, the wolf and Wotobank was offered as 'a tradition'. In footnotes were further included the legend of Dunmail and a tale of Scales tarn, described as being of "such great depth, and so completely hidden from the sun, that it is said its beams never reach it, and that the reflection of the stars may be seen on its surface at mid-day". The story of the two immortal trout of Bowscale tarn also received mention. This was very popular with tourists of the time, since it involved an excursion on foot to the tarn; today's motorised tourist would find this trip out of the question.

To pad out the book Tuvar found it necessary to include St Herbert, the hermit of Derwentwater; an assortment of lovers, three pair thwarted and one pair happy; a sprinkling of local minor poets; five long quotations from Wordsworth; the tale of the murder of a servant girl written as a picturesque anecdote; two unfortunate tourists (a young lady in pink ribbons who vanished in the year 1807 and, of course, Charles Gough of Helvellyn); a chapter on Druid temples and Druids; the history of Mary of Buttermere; an account of a dubious affray between Border freebooters in Borrowdale; a brief description of the inscribed rocks at Lowood; another of a once well-known Westmorland eccentric, "Jossy with Whips"; and a section on the annual Derwentwater Regatta. The major part of this material originated from Westmorland; then, as now, the tourist's favoured half of the district. The bulk of the book has nothing whatever to do with true indigenous legend or lore; yet it enjoyed immense popularity and has been consulted for source material by every author since writing on the Lake Country. The book was reissued in 1891 by a Glasgow publishing house; Lorenzo Tuvar was then exposed as "The late Wilson Armistead, author of *The Flora of Liverpool*, etc.".

Somewhere under the great slag-heap of tourist-legend and folklore that has accumulated over the past two centuries lies buried, too deep for much hope of rediscovery and resuscitation, the true ore of the region's myth and magic.

Icelandic mythology must have played an important part in the early legends of the region, but this has become almost obliterated by the superimposition of medieval variation upon the basic theme. The legend of Wotobank, for instance, although of very uncertain ancestry, being more than possibly of tourist inspiration, relates that a lord of Egremont was hunting wolves with his lady and servants when, during the chase, the lady was noticed to be missing and the lord, searching for her, found her lying dead on a bank, being torn to pieces by a wolf, whereat he exclaimed, "Wo to the bank!" The explanation preferred today is that the name Wotobank derives from the Norse god, Wotan.

The region abounds with legends of hunted stags and harts which either could not be caught at all, and therefore must have been enchanted (e.g. the enchanted stag of Borrowdale that was in reality a witch) or were ultimately caught after giving prodigious runs; this variation was a medieval version of the original Icelandic myth of the enchanted beast-witch. The legend of the Hart's-Horn Tree is particularly interesting, amongst the many, because it also carries other implications. Near Penrith, in the area of the former Whinfell Forest, there used to stand an oak which bore the name of Hart's-Horn Tree, owing to the pair of stag's horns which had been nailed to the tree and which had finally become grafted to the tree by the bark growing over their base. The legend attached to these very well authenticated antlers was that in the time of the first Robert de Clifford, about 1333, Edward Baliol, king of Scotland, came into Westmorland and stayed some time with the lord at his castles of Appleby, Brougham and Pendragon. During his visit they ran a stag, by a single hound, out of Whinfell Forest to Redkirke in Scotland and back again to the forest clearing where the stag had first been found. Both animals were totally spent; the stag leaped over the forest paling and died there, but the hound, attempting to leap, fell and died on the opposite side of the paling. As a memorial to this incident the stag's horns were nailed to the oak near by. The hound's name was Hercules, and a popular couplet was based on the celebrated run:

> Hercules kill'd Hart-a-grease,
> And Hart-a-grease kill'd Hercules.

("Hart-a-grease" deriving from a fat hart, stemming from the French *graisse*.)

The famous run may be purely legendary; the antlers, real enough, remained nailed to the tree until 1648, when a Parliamentary soldier broke off one of the branches; ten years later the remaining antler branch was stolen. "So now," wrote Lady Ann Clifford in her diary, "there is no part thereof remaining, the tree itself being so decayed, and the bark of it so peeled off, that it cannot last long; whereby we may see time brings to forgetfulness many memorable things in this world, be they ever so carefully preserved—for this tree, with the hart's horn in it, was a thing of much note in these parts."

In fact, time may have brought to forgetfulness more than Lady Ann realised; it is now thought probable that the antlers were connected with ancient fertility rites which may once have been held in this forest, the story of the Icelandic-myth-based legendary run of Hart-a-grease and Hercules being overlaid upon the pagan fertility rite horns.

The 'barguest' (another Norse derivation), once universally believed in throughout the Lake Country, indeed according to Daniel Scott quite a prevalent belief until late into the nineteenth century, was a fearsome something which haunted the fells, making a terrible wailing noise. It was said that to hear it foretold a death (Kirkby, *Lakeland Words*, 1899). From this interpretation the barguest would seem to have been a species of Lake Country banshee.

One of the few well-authenticated fairies of the region (also found in many other northern countries) was Jack i' the Hob, in Cumberland known as Hob Thross; "a body all ower rough", who came to houses during the night and, if the householders were considerate enough to put out a bowl of porridge or buttermilk on the hearth for him, would finish household chores left undone. If, on the other hand, he found no refreshment left for him, he would break things and make a wanton mess. Mrs Lynn Linton, a local writer and most reliable in these matters, suggests that Hob Thross was still active in the eighteen-sixties in certain parts of West Cumberland.

Boggles, of ancient Icelandic lineage as they doubtless are, possibly never have been taken over-seriously in a region where people are blessed with an acute sense of humour (the boggle story given as Note 3 is typically Cumbrian). "Some believe in them, but most don't," says one informant. "Naturally, more are seen by chaps on way home from t'pub than on the way there." Percy Kelly, discussing West Cumberland boggles, told the author that juvenile conversation in his youth dwelt much on the theme; indeed he was able to provide a list of Workington and Whitehaven boggle-spots, but adult belief in them, at all events in this day and age, was thin, to say the least, he added.

The term "boggle" is not necessarily confined to vaporous visions of the see-through variety; it is also popularly and loosely used for any kind of alleged apparition. The Nordic theme of the demon dog crops up fairly repeatedly throughout the region; the story of the Druggan Hill Dog illustrates well how such superstitions may gain credence. As usual with most ghosts no hard dates are given; we are simply told that many decades ago, or once upon a time, a pedlar who travelled the Plumbland district suddenly disappeared at Druggan Hill and the local community suspected that he had been murdered for the value of his pack and his body buried in a nearby quarry. From the time when this pedlar vanished there appeared a strange, large black dog which for the next twenty years frequented the Druggan Hill neighbourhood; this was popularly supposed to be the spirit of the vanished pedlar and was named the 'Druggan Hill Boggle'.

One cold winter's night the owner of the last house at the Plumbland end of Ponsonby heard loud thudding sounds at the front gate and groaning. At length he summoned the courage to look out and found a neighbour, Joseph Dobieson, lying on the doorstep in a collapsed condition and with his left hand badly lacerated. He was taken indoors and recovered sufficiently to give an account of what had happened to him: at the stile at the foot of Druggan Hill he had fallen over a large black dog which had slunk after him, filling him with dread, so that at last he had turned on the animal to confront it with the cry, "Tha must be t' Druggan Hill boggle!" Whereat his hand had split open and the dog vanished into thin air (a suggested alternative version is that the dog bit him because he scared it and then it ran away). Dobieson's injured hand refused to heal.

In the course of time, during work at the quarry, there was unearthed the skeleton of a man buried in a doubled position; the suspected remains of the pedlar. These were removed to the churchyard for burial and from that time the black dog was never seen again. Moreover, Dobieson's hand was miraculously healed.

There is in Cumberland, comparatively speaking, a dearth of

haunted houses. The worst haunted house in the region, according both to Harriet Martineau and W. G. Collingwood (but the latter may simply have been quoting the former), was the now submerged Armboth House at Thirlmere. Collingwood did not detail the story, but Harriet Martineau did so in her 1855 *Guide to the Lakes*. The daughter of the house, according to Miss Martineau, was to be wed and the wedding-breakfast was being prepared on All Hallowe'en when a breathless stranger arrived to say that the bride had been pushed into the lake and drowned. No further details are given of this murder: a well-known Thirlmere personality whom this author approached on the subject said, "Aye, t'bridegroom did it." This may, or may not be taken seriously. At all events, according to Miss Martineau, each year thereafter on this particular night, lights were seen in the house, all the bells in the building rang, crockery and dishes clattered, the wedding-breakfast table was spread by unseen hands. Meantime, a large ghost dog could be seen swimming across the lake.

Recently, the author was told by a member of the Folder family that, in the old days when Folders were at Stonycroft, Newlands, some visitors arrived there who had left Armboth House very hurriedly after hearing the most remarkable noises: bangings, thumpings, things being thrown about and smashed. They swore that nothing would make them return to Thirlmere.

Mrs Lynn Linton dismissed the Thirlmere hauntings thus: ". . . the haunted house and the terrible ghost-story as reported by Harriet Martineau." It should not, perhaps, be written off so lightly. The ghost dog is one thing; the lights, ringing bells and smashing crockery are quite another matter, coming within the well-recognised category of *poltergeister*. Perhaps Miss Martineau, who was anything but a frivolous personality, had had information about Armboth House that had convinced her that its alleged phenomena should at least be taken seriously enough to receive mention in a book. Unfortunately Armboth House cannot be investigated by modern students of the *poltergeist*!

Another Cumbrian house which makes claim to be authentically haunted is Lorton Hall, anciently a pele-tower and the home of the Dixon family. The present owner and Lord of the Manor, the Rev. J. A. Woodhead-Dixon, fully supports the tale of a phantom grey lady, thought to be the ghost of an eighteenth-century member of the family who was mentally deranged (or perhaps possibly a mongol) and who particularly haunts a certain bedroom and staircase.[5]

Giants, both legendary and in some degree real, have always been a feature of this region. The real giants, exceptionally large and powerful men, would seem to have come particularly from Troutbeck in Westmorland; the most famous of these probably being the great Tom Hickathrift, who has been written of extensively in Lakeland literature. The legendary giants came into the corpus of local lore as an attempt to explain away various stones and monuments otherwise incomprehensible: e.g. the Giant's Thumb, in Penrith churchyard, a tenth or eleventh-century stone cross of Nordic-Christian origin, and the Giant's Grave, also in the churchyard and of the same date and origin, which consists of shafts of two similar crosses, standing fifteen feet apart, with four large hog-backed stones covering the intervening space. The Giant's Cave at Eamont was the scene of an annual festival which continued to be held well into the nineteenth century. Slenderly surviving pagan mythology had this cave as the retreat of a terrible giant, Isir, who dragged men there and devoured them; the early name for the cave was Isis Parlis (Isir's Parlours). Another, later legend merges this with an Arthurian theme; Isis Parlis being the keep of the castle of Tarquin, whom Sir Lancelot du Lac came to slay and destroy. Christian legend became superimposed upon the pagan story of Isir: the caves were said now to have been the refuge of a holy man (of whom details seem to have been lost) and the annual festival of pagan times became a Christian one, the ritual of which has also been forgotten, although the Rev. B. Porteous, one-time vicar of Edenhall, wrote an account of Giant's Cave Sunday in 1850 which Daniel Scott quotes briefly: "Giant's Cave Sunday is still observed, but the custom has dwindled into insignificance, the 'shaking bottles' carried by the children that season being the only remains of what it has been." Unfortunately no description is given of 'shaking bottles'.

It is clear, however, that Eamont must from early Christian times have had pious associations, for in 1425 when New Bridge was built, the Bishop of Durham granted an indulgence of forty days to all persons "truly repenting their sins, and confessing, who should contribute any of their goods given them by God to the building of a bridge over the river Amot, in the parish of Penrith". This bridge, when built, was of stone with a cross with steps or seats all round it and on the top the Dacre arms. A Christian holy man, rather than the giant Isir, would have made Eamont a place of veneration for the Bishop.

Since Cumbrians as a race are tall, and since we have it on reliable record that the region produced some very large men indeed, it is perhaps permissible to surmise that there might have been a genetic strain of exceptional height and girth, possibly originating from Vikings, which produced a breed of comparatively gigantic men. It would be difficult to account otherwise for this very odd record of a giant, found buried at St Bees in the year 1601, just before Christmas-time: ". . . he the said Gyant was four yards and a half long, and was in complete armour; . . . his teeth were six inches long, and . . . he was buried four yards deep in the ground, which is now a cornfield. His armour, sword, and battle-axe are at Mr Sand's of Redington (Rollington) and at Mr Wyber's at St Bees." (Machell MSS., Carlisle).

Cumberland had nearly thirty Holy Wells, several of which would seem to have been in the Penrith district. Well festivals were held at them annually; Skirsgill was a particularly venerated site. Another, near Dalston, was the scene of religious ceremonies on certain Sundays; the villagers would assemble to seek out the good spirit of the well, who was supposed to teach the virtues of temperance, health, cleanliness, simplicity and love.[6] Thus once again was Christian ritual superimposed on what had clearly been a pagan festival in honour of a powerful water spirit.

The ancient festival of Beltain, or Beltan, which was held on May Day, was clearly based upon pagan fire-worship; of this festival little is now known apart from the fact that Beltain fires of rowan wood were lit in the hills at sunrise. Magic fires were also lit on Midsummer's Eve. From these fire-worshipping ceremonies would seem to have sprung the "need-fires" or "neet-fires" (neet cattle being an old term for horned animals), a magic cure, or charm, used in the dales for cattle diseases. All the fires in the village, or valley, were first carefully put out, a deputation going round the houses to ensure that this had been done. Then two pieces of rowan wood were ignited by friction and a fire got going; the afflicted or disease-threatened animals were then brought up to the fire. The scene, we are told, was one of the greatest confusion, with bellowing and uproar, the owners of the beasts anxious that they should get "plenty of Reek". When the fire had been used in one township it could then be transferred to the next, and so on.

The *Patriot* of 25 July 1834 gave mention of need-fire ceremonies in Westmorland: 'A sort of murrain, or pestilential fever, is at present prevalent in the county of Westmorland, the popular remedy for which is the fumigation of the infected animals with the smoke of needfire, accompanied by certain mystic signs." The last recorded case of need-fire in the Keswick region was 1841. It is thought, however, that the fire may have survived for a decade or so longer in some of the more remote dales of the district.

The rowan tree played a very important part in North Country magic; we have already seen that it was invariably used for farm implements, having a particularly important role in the dairy, where it was used as a stick for stirring the cream to counteract bewitchment of the churn. The old wooden butterbowls were also made of rowan wood. Rowan branches were placed above doorways to ward off evil influences.

The Rev. H. J. Bulkeley, once rector of Lanercost, left the following description of a toothache charm (1855): a boy suffering from toothache was taken to an old blacksmith, who prodded the tooth with a rusty nail, then blindfolded the boy and led him into a wood and then, taking the bandage from his eyes, made him hammer the nail into a young oak tree; the boy was then blindfolded again and led out of the wood and made to promise that he would not try to find the tree or tell anyone about it. Blacksmiths, of course, have always been associated with magic properties.

Another cure for pain was to rub, with a stone, the part affected; this operation always took place after sunset and a spell was muttered during the rubbing.

Unhappily most of this folklore, magic and enchantment has been lost: undoubtedly allowed to die as useless, even deplorable, peasant superstition, best forgotten. Our age recognises the vital importance of these things, but it is too late; our Victorian forefathers found old wives' tales and witchcraft subversive to their age of reason and enlightenment.

Mrs Lynn Linton gives a brief list of random superstitions and customs noted as prevalent in West Cumberland at the close of the eighteenth century: "The labouring ox is said to kneel at twelve o'clock on Christmas Eve and the bees at that same hour are heard to sing. . . . To whichever quarter a bull faces in lying on All Hallow's

Eve, from thence the wind will blow the greatest part of the winter.''
Families always kept wake with their dead; Hob Thross was a regular
and anticipated nocturnal visitor in cottagers' homes and farmsteads;
an early breakfast of hack pudding, a dish made of sheep's heart mixed
with suet and sweet fruits, was traditional on Christmas morning;
newly married couples 'laited' (begged) corn from house to house,
with which to sow their first crop, which would yield no grain if the
seed were purchased.

Perhaps some of the most intriguing superstition, or legend, is that
attached to the two famous Lucks of Cumberland; the Luck of Eden
Hall and the Luck of Muncaster Castle. The Luck of Eden Hall (the
Cumberland seat of the Musgrave family) is the best documented, for
it has been on loan to the Victoria and Albert museum since 1926 and
in 1958 the museum was fortunate enough to acquire it.

'The Luck of Edenhall'[7] is a thirteenth-century Syrian enamelled
glass beaker known by this name for at least 230 years. It is some
$6\frac{3}{8}$ in high, the glass of yellowish tint, brilliantly enamelled in red,
blue, green, white and gilt. It has been protected over the centuries by a
leather ('cuir bouilli') case, itself an object of the highest quality and
great rarity. It was made to contain the Luck perhaps as much as a
century after the beaker's manufacture; this case was said, by the
Musgrave family to whom the Luck belonged, to have been the second
one, which experts consider highly probable, since such glasses appear
to have been brought from the Near East originally in wooden cases.
The present leather case, which is decorated by means of stamped and
cut work, was made in the fourteenth century, either in England or
perhaps in the Narbonne region of France. It has IHS on its lid. The
beaker itself is a characteristic Syrian glass of about the middle of the
thirteenth century, of a type attributed to the once famous glass-
making centre of Aleppo. It is probable that it was brought to Europe
by a returning Crusader.

How it came into the possession of the Musgraves of Eden Hall is
shrouded in mystery. The legend, however, says that a party of fairies
were drinking and merry-making round a well near the Hall, called
St Cuthbert's well, when they were interrupted by, version one, a
servant coming from the Hall to fetch water and, version two, some
curious people. The fairies were frightened and fled, leaving the glass

beaker behind them, one of the last of their fleeing party screaming out,

> If this cup should break or fall
> Farewell the Luck of Edenhall.

The mention of St Cuthbert's well in this legend is of interest, since it accords with other facts to suggest that during the Middle Ages the Luck had become associated with the cult of St Cuthbert. Eden Hall lay on the route of the 'Translation' of St Cuthbert's relics from Farne, and had both a church and a well dedicated to him. This association with St Cuthbert is regarded as strong indication that the Luck had been in the Musgrave family since the Middle Ages; possibly one of the family had himself been a Crusader and had returned with it, although there is no record of this.

The Luck's first known mention in literature is in a recension of the so-called Wharton Ballad, made in 1729 by James Ralph, author and one-time friend of Benjamin Franklin. This ballad, called "The Drinking Match at Eden Hall", describes a drinking-match instigated by Philip, first Duke of Wharton (1698–1731) at Eden Hall and the first lines are in imitation of the opening lines of "Chevy Chase", the original Wharton lines running,

> God prosper long our Lord the King
> And also Edenhall.

Ralph changed this to,

> God prosper long from being broke
> The Luck of Eden-Hall.[8]

Francis Douce, the antiquary, visited Eden Hall in 1785 and was shown the Luck, about which he too wrote a poem. Henceforth this mysterious glass appeared in numerous romantic literary works, including Longfellow's translation of Uhland's German ballad of 1834, in which the Luck is imagined as being broken at a feast, with the consequent capture of Eden Hall and death of its lord.

In fact prodigious care was always taken of the Luck, as the following account makes clear; it is initialled W. M. (probably Sir William

Musgrave, a collateral of the Cumbrian family) and appeared in *The Gentleman's Magazine* for August, 1791.

> In an excursion to the North of England, I was easily prevailed upon to see the *Luck of Edenhall*. . . . Antient superstition may have contributed not a little to its preservation; but that it should not, in a more enlightened age, or in moments of conviviality, meet with one *gentle rap* (and a gentle one would be quite sufficient for an *ordinary glass* of the same substance), is to me somewhat wonderful. . . . The late agent of the family had such a reverential regard for this glass that he would not suffer any person to touch it, and but few to see it. When the family, or other curious people, had a desire to drink out of it, a napkin was held underneath, lest any accident should befal it. . . .

The Luck of Muncaster is considerably less well documented, although by its description it would seem to be glass of the same period and origin as the Luck of Eden Hall. It is a glass cup or basin, about 7 in in diameter, ornamented with gold and white enamelled mouldings. It is reputed that when King Henry VI stayed with the Penningtons at their seat at Muncaster Castle in either 1461 or 1464, he gave this cup as a parting gift to Sir John Pennington with the assurance that "the family shall prosper so long as they preserve this cup unbroken".[9]

There is a traditional anecdote (given by Daniel Scott, quoting Roby's *Traditions of Lancashire*) that during the Civil Wars this Luck was buried in a box for safety. When the danger period was over and the box was retrieved from its burying place, it was allowed to fall, and the Penningtons, convinced that the Luck must have been broken, did not dare to open the box to discover whether their family fortunes were ruined, or not. Forty years elapsed before one of them, having noticed no particular ill-luck to be dogging the family, had the box opened and found the Luck intact!

In the castle are two paintings, one showing the King presenting the cup to Sir John Pennington, the other showing His Majesty with the Luck in his hand. In Muncaster Church is a slab inscribed: "Holie Kynge Harrye gave Sir John a brauve workyd glass cuppe . . . whyllys the famylie shold keep hit unbrecken thei shold gretelye thrif." This Luck is still in the possession of the family.

Burrellgreen near Great Salkeld possessed a somewhat more proletarian Luck which, according to Daniel Scott, passed successively into the possession of several families. It was a circular brass dish, of early embossed work, $16\frac{1}{4}$ ins in diameter and $1\frac{1}{2}$ in deep. At one time two inscriptions were decipherable upon it, but constant polishing by proud owners in due course rendered them illegible. One encircled the central ornament, the other decorated the outer rim and was deciphered in 1860 or thereabouts by Mr R. M. Bailey, a London antiquary, as a Latin inscription reading, "Hail Mary Mother of Jesus Saviour of Men".

The legend attaching to this dish was that it had been given long ago by a "hob i' t' hurst" (Hob Thross) to the family then living at Burrell-green, with the caution,

> If e'er this dish be sold or gi'en
> Farewell the Luck o' Burrell Green.

The Luck remained in the hands of Burrellgreen families for many generations and was painted by Jacob Thompson of Hackthorpe. This author has not been able to trace its present whereabouts.

Arthurian legend is encountered in ballad form in Cumberland: for northern tradition maintains that Carlisle was the city of King Arthur and his court, who were in frequent residence there. One of the most celebrated of these ballads tells, in "The Marriage of Sir Gawaine", the story of that gallant knight's marriage with the misshapen lady who subsequently, upon their marriage bed, became fair. The villain of this ballad is the giant of Tearne Wadling. A note to this ballad in Percy's *Reliques* stated that Tearne, or Tarn, Wadling was near Hesketh, on the road from Penrith. Early tradition maintained that a castle had once stood there.)

> ... At Tearne Wadling his castle stands,
>   Near to that lake so fair,
> And proudly rise the battlements,
>   And streamers deck the air.
> Noe gentle knight, nor ladye gay,
>   May pass that castle-wall:
> But from that foule discurteous knight
>   Mishappe will them befall.
> He's twice the size of common men,

> Wi' thewes, and sinewes stronge,
> And on his backe he bears a clubbe,
> That is both thicke and longe. . . .

A ballad of King Arthur's court itself, full of real enchantment, is "The Boy and the Mantle":

> In the third day of May
>   To Carleile did come
> A kind curteous child
> That cold much of wisdome.
> A Kirtle and a mantle
> This child had uppon,
> With brouches and ringes
> Full richly bedone.
> God speed thee, King Arthur,
> Sitting at thy meete:
> And the goodly Queen Guenever,
> I cannott her forgett. . . .
> He plucked out his poterner,
> And longer would not dwell,
> He pulled forth a pretty mantle
> Between two nut shells.
> Have thou here, King Arthur:
> Have you heer of mee:
> Give it to they comely queen,
> Shapen as itt is alreadye. . . .

(A poterner is a poke or a pouch.)

This mantle, explained the boy, would never properly fit the wife that had once done amiss. Queen Guenevere first tried it on: the garment shrivelled and shred from top to toe, finally turning black:

> By my troth, quoth King Arthur,
> I think thou be not true. . . .

The Queen, furious, threw down the mantle and covered with blushes fled to her chamber. One by one the other ladies present tried it on, with similarly dire results: chastity was clearly not a prime virtue at King Arthur's court. At last the mantle was donned by Sir Craddock's lady:

> · When she had tane the mantle
> And cast it her about,
> Upp at her great toe,
> It began to crinkle and crowt.
> She said, Bowe down, mantle,
> And shame me not for nought.
>   Once I did amysse,
> I tell you certainlye,
> When I kist Craddocke's mouth
> Under a greene tree,
> When I kist Craddocke's mouth
> Before he marryed mee.
>   When shee had her shreeven,
> And her sines shee had tolde,
> The mantle stood about her
> Right as she wolde:
> Seemlye of coulour,
> Glittering like gold. . . .

Lady Craddock's constancy was further tried by ordeals of knife and horn, but she survived them triumphantly.

Almost obliterated historical events provide the basis for many legendary tales of the region. One of the most teasing of these concerns the ancient and persistent Buttermere tradition that a battle once took place there.[10] This legend has been used by several authors as basis for highly imaginative stories without any true historical substance whatever. Some say that the battle took place between Romans and ancient British, others that the Normans were here routed by the English after the Conquest, although there is no shred of evidence that either Romans or Normans ever set foot in Buttermere. The indigenous valley legend is that the fight occurred between the men of Buttermere and Borrowdale and a party of Border raiders who had penetrated thus far into the mountains on a cattle rustling expedition. Armistead gives a highly romantic and not very convincing account of the battle, entitling it, "Affray of the Border Freebooters in Borrowdale". According to him the main action took place at the top of Honister Pass and the Border invaders were a party of Grahams. This tale was a great favourite with the romantic tourists and Ackerman had a print showing the fight in progress under Honister Crag.

Buttermere maintains that a very interesting dry-stone structure upon the Scale Beck side of Crummock Water, situated between Far Ruddy Beck and Scale Beck and generally supposed by visitors to be a ruined sheep-fold, is in fact the borran or 'barmekin' into which the local women and children and cattle were placed while the battle was in progress. This structure is circular in shape with a large pile of fallen stones in the centre; its condition has been deteriorating steadily over the thirty years that this author herself has known it and it perhaps might merit expert scrutiny while there is still any of it left.

There was, at the foot of Honister pass on the Gatesgarth side, to the left of the road as one faced the pass, a large flat-topped boulder inscribed, it is said, with foreign lettering and this was always thought in Buttermere to have been some kind of commemoration stone of the above mentioned battle. This stone was well-known locally and is still remembered. At the time the pass was surfaced for motor-cars in the nineteen-thirties the stone disappeared; Buttermere suspected that it had been used for some road construction purpose. Search certainly reveals no trace of it today.

Border frays have provided some of the best legendary material of the region, handed down largely in ballad form. Several of the most stirring feature the Graham clan. The hero of "Hughie the Graham", suggested Bishop Nicolson, was one of the Grahams against whom Bills of Complaint were exhibited to Robert Aldridge, Bishop of Carlisle. The ballad opens:

> Gude Lord Scroope's to the hunting gane,
>   He has ridden o'er moss and muir:
> And he has grippit Hughie the Graeme
>   For stealing the bishop's mare. . . .

Hughie was taken to Carlisle for trial. Lord and Lady Hume spoke up on his behalf, but the Bishop was adamant:

> Were he but the one Graeme of the name,
> He shou'd be hangit high for me.

And hangit high at Harribee was Hughie.

The ballad of "Graeme and Bewick" provides interesting proof that the so-called generation gap is nothing new. Lord Graham and Sir Robert Bewick quarrelled over the merits of their respective sons who were great friends, or 'billies' as the expression then went. The two fathers went drinking together and Bewick taunted Graham with his son's lack of learning:

> Ye sent him to the schools, and he wadna learn:
> Ye bought him books, and he wadna read. . . .

Graham replied,

> My blessing he shall never earn,
> Till I see how his arm defend his head . . .

and insisted that his wretched son must fight either young Bewick or himself. Young Christie Graeme considered the matter: he did not wish to fight either suggested opponent. Finally he decided that God would never forgive him for killing his best friend, but on the other hand, to kill his own father would be a mortal sin. So he forced a quarrel on young Bewick, who mortally wounded him and then committed suicide. His father found him dying,

> "Rise up, rise up, my son," he said,
>   "For I think ye hae gotten the victory."
> "O hald your tongue, my father dear!
>   Of your prideful talking let me be!
> Ye might hae drunken your wine in peace,
>   And let me and my billie be.
> Gae dig a grave baith wide and deep,
>   And a grave to hald baith him and me:
> And lay Christie Graeme on the sunny side,
>   For I'm sure he won the victory."

Long after the actual Border fighting and the ballads that celebrated the frays had faded into antiquity, the children of the Border played games of raids and battles. One of these games, known as Blackthorn, which is recorded as having been played in the streets of Carlisle well into the latter half of the nineteenth century, centred round two bases, some forty yards apart. A boy who volunteered to be the 'catcher' faced the rest, who occupied one of the bases, about fifteen yards from him, and he shouted, "Blackthorn!"

The others replied in unison: "Buttermilk and Barleycorn!"

Catcher: "How many sheep have you today?"

Reply: "As many as you can catch and carry away."

This was the signal for the crowd of boys to race pass the catcher, who tried to catch as many as he could; those he caught then joined his side. This process continued until all were caught; the last one to be caught becoming the next catcher. He had the chance to avoid being catcher if he could get clear past the enemy three times, after which, if he succeeded, he became finally free. The last boy to have been caught next to him then had to become catcher.

Another game, played by both sexes, was Johnny, or Jenny, Lingo. The children formed a ring, with one child standing in its centre and another child running round outside the ring. The child in the centre then called out, "Whoa's that gan roond my stony wall?" Whereupon the following dialogue ensued:

"Only little Johnny (or Jenny, according to the sex of the player) Lingo."

"Mind ye steal nin o' my fat sheep."

"Only one or two."

"Tak one, an' begone."

Then the thief had to try to "steal a sheep"; the leader endeavouring to keep the thief away from the flock.

The most famous children's Border game of all was Watch Webs, or Watch Weds, otherwise known as Scotch and English. A boundary line, the Border, was drawn between the two contending sides and at an equal distance on either side of this Border the two sets of players deposited their caps, jackets and so forth. 'Web', or 'wed', was the name given to a heap of clothes. The game consisted of each side pillaging the store of clothes belonging to the other and when a player was caught he was taken prisoner. The game commenced by "an

Englisher" putting his foot in challenge over the Border and shouting, "Here's a leg in thy land, dry bellied Scot!"

Thus the bloodstained cries of the ancient Border clans found their final echoes in the voices of children playing games and now even these games have been forgotten.

CHAPTER ELEVEN

John Peel and the Blencathra

M ILLOM C OURT B OOK, 28 April 1698, gives this significant entry; "John Tyson of Seathwaite, yeoman, aged 92, saying that for sixty years and upwards he hath been a Hunter of foxes within and upon Ulpha Fells."

Fox-hunting, cock-fighting, horse-racing, wrestling and football were the traditional Cumbrian sports. Fox-hunting here has always been something more than a straightforward sporting diversion arising from the necessity to keep down foxes; it would appear in this high northern country to embody something essential to the regional spirit, part of the old Cumbrian way of life. It is no exaggeration to say that without some knowledge and understanding of fox-hunting in Cumberland there can be no real knowledge or understanding of Cumberland itself.

Hunting with the fell packs differs in several salient respects from hunting in the low country. Hounds are followed on foot. Strangers from the south, casting a superficial and unreflective glance at this Lake Country version of the sport have described it as "the poor man's hunt", presumably under the impression that followers do not ride to hounds in these parts because they cannot afford a mount. The truth is, as the Right Honourable J. W. Lowther (later Viscount Ullswater) observed, during his mastership of the Blencathra foxhounds (1903–19), "A horse would be as much out of place at a meet of a fellside pack as a hippopotamus, and be about as useful".

Fox-hunting in the Lake Country is certainly wholly democratic, it has never been monopolised by the fashionable or the rich; a noteworthy feature of the region has always been an unforced quality of lack of status distinction, master and man here traditionally meeting upon equal terms. The hunt is supported by all members of the dale communities, the local pack is in essence a community project. The only qualifications required in a follower are enthusiasm, energy and stamina, although a monetary subscription, however modest, is appreciated. The *haute monde* of the outside world has not flocked to the fells for sport. The unvarnished observation that the fell-packs are followed on foot over England's highest mountain ranges in all weathers during the winter months perhaps suffices to explain why these hounds have remained a minority attraction.

There is little recorded evidence of the early days of fell fox-hunting. However since this was, from medieval times, a sheep farming region with the fox as a major hazard to young lambs, it is obvious that fox-hunting must here be of ancient origin. Packs for hunting deer as well as fox and hare were maintained, predominantly for sporting reasons, by the old nobility and gentry of the Cumbrian low country; these packs were mounted. In the high country individual dalesmen kept hunting dogs of their own, purely at first for hard motives of fox destruction; over the course of time there grew up a tradition of communal hunting mornings, each man coming to the meeting place with his hound. In this way evolved the old trencher-fed fell-packs, foot followed.

Millom Court Book's entry is evidence of well-established seventeenth-century fox-hunting in the fells, although we do not know whether Tyson was professional huntsman for a gentry-owned pack or, more probably, a forerunner of the great statesmen-huntsmen of the nineteenth century, personalities such as John Peel of Caldbeck and Will Ritson of Wasdale Head. Both of these, being avid hunting enthusiasts, injected into the local trencher-fed packs the lively nucleus of a small string of hounds of their own and by habitual, zealous and highly successful hunting of these packs, developed what were in effect district packs of which they were huntsman-master.

Further evidence of well-established seventeenth-century fox-hunting in the region is found in the *Victoria County History* which tells us that at this date three foxhounds were exported from Keswick to Hertfordshire. All that is recorded of these animals is that after their first run in the south two of them vanished, to reappear in due course back in Keswick!

Fell fox-hunting can have changed but little in spirit and technique since old John Tyson was catching foxes. That he had hunted for sixty years and upwards of his ninety-two, indeed possibly was still hunting at ninety-two for all we know, is not untypical of his kind; as C. E. Benson remarked, middle age in Cumberland starts at sixty or thereabouts. Several of the region's great huntsmen have continued brilliantly in their profession until nearly eighty, one or two have topped that age, finally to expire with their boots on in the midst of a tally-ho. The only significant change, over the years, seems to have been in the foxes themselves.

Today's fell fox tends possibly to be slightly larger and heavier than the average low-country fox and occasionally he may have a sprinkling of grey in his coat. This is some indication that he is descended from the famous so-called greyhound foxes which John Peel hunted, although today's grey-sprinkled animal bears only phantom resemblance to his ancestor who is said to have gained the name 'greyhound' partly because of his colour and partly because of his ability to run. He was also sometimes referred to as the 'Skidda racer', although there is no evidence that he was peculiar to Skiddaw Forest. Clapham[1] tells us (he himself was writing only from hearsay) that the greyhound fox was exceptionally long in the leg, "standing tall" and very strong; considerably heavier than the modern fox. His coat was predominantly a grizzled grey in colour, frequently showing a lot of white about the forelegs. These larger, heavier, stronger foxes gave by all accounts far longer runs than those we get today and did not go to ground as frequently as the modern fox. This greyhound type has now quite disappeared due, it is thought, to penetration of the fells by the smaller, red low-country fox, who by breeding with the greyhound fox has exterminated him as a distinct variety.

This formidable creature, however, would appear to have had an even more formidable progenitor. According to Albert Nicholson (writing in 1906), there was a tradition amongst the old fox-hunters that,

... there was formerly a race of great grey foxes even larger and far fleeter than those we style the greyhound fox in these days. Mr Mayson tells me that his father was in at the death of what he regarded as the last of these giants. It was killed at Bowder Stone in Borrowdale, and weighed 29 lbs.

They are said to have been able to easily outpace the hounds of those days, and that the only way of having a successful hunt was to have a couple of dogs on each top or likely place, and then when one of these great fellows got on the move they slipped them at view when their chance came and so raced them down with fresh hounds, even then seldom having any success.[2]

There is a fascinating quality about these tales of great grey foxes, ever receding into the past, each recession growing larger, greyer, heavier and yet fleeter; at last vanishing as wolves into the mists of Icelandic Cumbria. These vast grey animals are the Moby Dicks of the Cumbrian hunting landscape, luring out the dalesman Ahab who dreams of discovering some last great grey survivor who will rear up from the heather and give the huntsman the run of his life.

The fell fox is hunted on the drag (scent). This means that, whereas in the south hounds are thrown into covert where a fox is known to be lying and from which the pack goes away almost on top of the fox, in the fells hounds have to search for their quarry. Hunting in the fells never starts later than nine in the morning; as the season wears on it frequently starts much earlier. This is in order that the drag may be fresh, picked up not long after the fox has left the dale bottom for the high ground where he lies up during the day, often on one of the heather and bleaberry covered ledges, locally known as 'banks' or 'benks', among the crags. These high altitude haunts of the fox provide little in the way of food for the animal; hence his habit of descending to lower ground under cover of failing light to forage for his dinner. Here, on this low ground, hounds find his drag and from thence work up to where he is lying. The movements of a pack working out a drag through a maze of dry gill beds, heathery ledges and crag buttresses make a subtle spectacle, played against a backcloth of some of the most beautiful scenery in the world.

Although some foxes give remarkably long runs, actual sprinting over the tops by the field is not so frequent as the apprehensive newcomer to the sport envisages. It is a certainty that every hunting morning will begin with a gruelling climb out of the dalebottom but once the sportsman is up he will, if wise, remain aloft, only descending if there is real risk of losing the hunt altogether. The saving grace for footfollowers, as well as for foxes, are the rocky holes or borrans, with which the fellsides abound; to these the hunted fox frequently resorts, which necessitates the putting in of terriers and in some instances (where the rock is mixed with a substance which Cumbrians regard as soil) there may be an attempt by the huntsman and his henchmen to dig out. This business of holing gives the expiring follower a chance to revive and collect his breath for the next frenetic outburst of energy.

The season lasts from October until April, when all fixture hunting stops and the packs confine their activities to going out 'on call', in pursuit of foxes which are lamb-worrying; these are the famous early morning hunts which may start any time after four-thirty in dew and darkness. The dalesman regards it as his traditional right to call upon his local pack in this way; not only for spring lamb-worrying but at any time during the hunting season if foxes raid his poultry.

Early morning hunting on call usually continues until mid-May (it must be remembered that lambing in the high country does not start until the third week in April). There is no recognised cub-hunting in the region, although in practice much of the hunting at the start of the season might correctly be described as such, for many of the foxes then run are eight-month cubs. The best hunting and longest runs come in late winter and early spring; this is the season when foxes are courting and dog foxes travel great distances in search of vixens. A dog fox whose drag is picked up when he has started his journey back to his own country is likely to provide a long, fast run.

Fell hounds hunt three or even four days a week; they have astonishing powers of stamina and endurance. They are smaller and lighter in build than southern fox-hounds. Clapham gives the following definition of a good fell hound:

> Light in frame, and particularly well let-down and developed in hind quarters. Hare-footed, as opposed to the round cat-foot of the standard type. Good neck, shoulders and loin, long in pastern, and ribs carried well back. A good nose, plenty of tongue, and last, but by no means least, pace.

They also tend to be light in colour, since they must be easy to view working on a distant fellside. A good fell-pack does the bulk of its hunting independently, so to speak, of the huntsman. If a pack is running split foxes several hounds may go away after their own fox, have a long run and finally kill entirely without supervision, returning to kennels in ones and twos in late afternoon, wearing self-satisfied expressions.

There are two major mysteries connected with hunting in the fells. C. E. Benson describes the first,

Allusion has already been made to the impractability of the Huntsman controlling the pack; for a man on foot it would be an almost impossible task, if the country were, so to speak, Hyde Park and Kensington Gardens. Now let the visitor walk to the top of Maiden Moor and overlook the fell . . . chaos—ridges, valleys, deep troughs, irregular cloughs, and rock hummocks, the one on which you are standing having the peculiarity of being invariably lower than those around it, so that your view is circumscribed to say the least. Add to this that the moment the hounds have disappeared over the skyline, they may go straight to Thirlmere, the Langdale Pikes or . . . Newlands, and it will be seen that the unfortunate Huntsman . . . has no possible chance of being with them. And yet almost invariably he is— which thing is a mystery.[3]

The second mystery concerns holes. Wherever a fox holes, be it high on the flanks of Skiddaw, or in the depths of a plantation, immediately that the cry for a shovel goes up there will appear, literally from nowhere, as if in obedience to some occult impulse, a muscular individual (hitherto a total stranger to the proceedings) bearing a shovel. He will march briskly up to the hole and without a second's hesitation or word of instruction commence digging. Where he has sprung from, in what manner he knew he was needed, heaven only knows. This thing, too, is a mystery.

The fox-hunting fell-packs of the Lake Country today are the Blencathra, Coniston, Eskdale and Ennerdale, Lunesdale, Melbreak, and Ullswater. The Blencathra, for reasons which will transpire, calls itself the John Peel Hunt. Its country covers the Skiddaw range, Matterdale Common, the Thirlmere side of the Helvellyn range, Armboth and Watendlath Fells, Borrowdale Fells, Derwent Fells, Braithwaite, Bassenthwaite and Uldale Fells, Mungrisedale and Mungrisedale Common; a very large area indeed, much of it John Peel's old country.

Peel, whose ancestors originated from the Border, was born either in 1776 or 1777 (there is no record of the actual date of his birth; his baptism is entered in Caldbeck parish register for 24 September 1777).

According to Peel's biographer, Hugh Machell,[4] who got his information first hand from Peel's children, Peel's grandfather was a farmer and inn-keeper of Ireby, who enjoyed the nickname of 'Old Cock and Bacon', bestowed upon him because he invariably served this dish at his inn on market days. William, Peel's father, was born in 1739, eloping in 1776 to Gretna Green with one Lettice Scott, daughter of prosperous farming folk of Park End, Caldbeck. The couple did not marry at Gretna, however, because they thought that the fee asked was too high; they returned to Caldbeck and were married there in the church on 21 May 1776. William, who had a successful career as horse-dealer and farmer, lived to be eighty-nine, Lettice seventy-six; they had thirteen children, of whom the famous John was the eldest.

John Peel was born in a cottage at the Park End farm and at the age of three weeks was taken by his parents to Greenrigg, Caldbeck, which farm also belonged to his maternal grandparents. John grew up to farming and horse-dealing and we are told that he became addicted to fox-hunting at an early age. In 1797 he eloped with Mary White, then eighteen, daughter of an Uldale statesman; the pair were married at Gretna, their wedding later solemnised at Caldbeck church on 18 December 1797. They had thirteen children in their turn; seven sons, six daughters, of whom eleven survived to attend John's funeral in 1854.

Peel was twenty-two when he began hunting his first pack of hounds; of this pack we have no details. In 1803 he and his wife moved to a farm at Upton, Caldbeck, this farm belonging to John's father. Machell tells us that twelve couple of Peel's hounds were kept by his neighbours and friends, the rest he kennelled in a building next to his house. It would seem that Machell might be overestimating the size of the pack; the early fell packs were much smaller than they are today, and fifteen hounds (not couples, the fell packs are counted by individual animals and not by couples, as they are in the south) was an average size for the old packs. Thus it is reasonable to suggest that twelve hounds came from what was, in essence, the local community's trencher-fed pack, while Peel kennelled some three or four of his own, the assembled body making up a pack which Peel himself regularly hunted. Machell had it on good authority that Peel was in the habit of gathering hounds in from outlying farms on a hunting morning by sounding his horn at an early hour, which was not exactly appreciated by his non-hunting neighbours; thus the line of the celebrated John Peel hunting song, "The sound of his horn brought me from my bed" is not only historically correct, but into it may be read a note of complaint!

Peel certainly had a pack of his own at some later date in his career; it is recorded that it cost him forty pounds a year to keep his hounds. He hunted two days a week; his favourite meets being Skiddaw, Isel, and Messenger Mire. It is clear that he did not really rely upon his farming for a livelihood. He came from a comparatively prosperous farming family and married into such another. In fact, to all intents and purposes, he enjoyed an inherited private income. Upton, as aforementioned, belonged to his father; Ruthwaite, the farm to which he finally moved, belonged to his wife.

The two salient Peel activities were hunting and drinking. Peel was frequently in the state euphemistically described (to Machell) by those who remembered him as 'fresh'. There are anecdotes galore of his freshness at markets, meets, business sessions, on visits to friends, upon the births of his offspring, even on one occasion at a funeral when Peel, then an old man, broke a short silence during the course of the ceremony by standing up and asking in a loud belligerent voice, "Is nobody ga'n to say Amen?" This Peel story comes from a letter sent to Machell by Sir John Mark of Bowscale, Cumberland; Sir John himself having been present at the funeral, which was that of his uncle, Sir George Mark, a hunting friend of Peel.

Sir Wilfred Lawson in his reminiscences wrote:

I have seen John Peel in the flesh, and have hunted with him. . . . No doubt drink played a prominent part, if not the predominant, in these northern hunts . . . I have heard Peel say, when they had killed a fox, "Now this is the first fox we've killed this season, and it munna be a dry 'un!" . . . Words of that kind were the prelude to an adjournment to the nearest public house, where the party would remain for an indefinite time, reaching, I have heard it said, even to two days . . .

At these celebrations, revealingly, the fox's mask used to be dipped into the ale before the drinking began—a species of fox-hunters' sacrament. At length these rites and revelries were concluded and Peel and his acolytes would return to their respective abodes, Peel occasionally enlivening himself with a few 'view halloos' on the way; not only were his long-suffering neighbours roused from their beds by his horn in the morning, but they stood a fair chance of having their well-deserved rest at nightfall shattered by his hollering. No small wonder, perhaps, that some rather hard sayings about him have been handed down to posterity in some quarters, including the brief dismissal by one ancient lady, "John Peel? Owt but a drunken owd taggelt."

At all times, drunk and sober alike, Peel is said to have had a hot, hasty temper and to have been aggressive both in manner and speech. He placed his hunting and horse-dealing activities well before his family interests. A Peel family anecdote concerns the birth of his twin daughters, who were inconsiderate enough to arrive (in 1814) on Rosley Fair day (Rosley being an important horse fair which Peel annually attended). He was anxious to be away, although his wife was in labour. It was pointed out to him that the birth was likely to be a double one, but his reply was, "It disna matter if there be four, I mun gang to Rosley Fair!"

According to some local gossip, assiduously collected by the tireless Machell, Peel's family had suffered at times from financial difficulties arising from his ruinous drinking, especially in his later years. The Peel children themselves, in their adult reminiscences, revealed no bitter memories of life with father; in lean times there had always been plenty of relatives and friends to help them and the enthusiasm for fox-hunting which all, including the girls, seemed to have inherited had compensated for a rather hard life in a decidedly odd household where there was more often than not a bag-fox scratching and smelling in a box in the kitchen and the younger children never composed themselves for sleep at night without first giving a call to hounds, followed by the 'view halloo'.

When Peel's fourth son, Peter, died during the night of 15 November 1840, Peel rose early next morning to hunt for a fox which had been worrying geese. He got his hounds on to the fox's drag and killed it. When he arrived back home he found his kitchen full of relatives, very censorious of him for going hunting while his son lay dead in the house. "Aye, the lad's dead," said Peel. "If he had been alive he would have been with me this morning; but I've got the fox's brush and it shall go in the coffin with him. It'll be a fitting trophy to go on his last journey."

Mr Daniel Birkett of Aighartree, near Caldbeck, a friend and hunting companion of Peel's for many years, who vouched to Machell for
the above story, was nine years of age when first he met Peel. Daniel
was living with his uncle, who had a horse which died. Peel, like all
huntsmen, used to get dead stock from neighbouring farmers to feed
his hounds, so Danny Birkett was dispatched round to the kennels
with news of this dead horse. Peel gave the boy sixpence, observing,
"Ye're a canny lad. Tell your uncle when thoo gars yam that he has to
be sure to have a dead horse for me every fortnight!"

Sir Wilfred Lawson described Peel as,

> . . . a tall, bony Cumbrian, who when I knew him used to ride a pony
> called Dunny, from its light colour. . . . Peel's grey coat is no more a myth
> than himself, for I well remember the long, rough, grey garment which
> almost came down to his knees.

Daniel Birkett's description of Peel ran thus:

> There was no scarlet about the Cumberland huntsman of those days. Peel
> used to wear a grey coat with buttons at the back, what we call a lap coat.
> Tall and straight, a bit of a rough diamond, and as cute and keen a man as
> ever dealt in horse flesh, he had a good heart under his grey coat. . . . He
> rode the shortest stirrup ever I saw a huntsman have; his knees were very
> nearly up with the saddle of the crown cross-breed he usually rode. . . .

A third description has been left us by a Mr G. A. Fothergill who
also hunted with Peel:

> Old Peel always wore a coat of Skiddaw grey (a coarse woollen cloth
> manufactured at Caldbeck, otherwise known as hodden grey), a large
> box-hat, dark-coloured corduroy breeches, and a pair of hunting boots
> without tops, reaching high up the leg.

Fothergill further tells us that Peel carried a whip and a twined horn,
had blue eyes and curly hair which grew in surprisingly long ringlets.
Peel was a fine horseman and besides his passion for hunting was also
very fond of shooting.

Most of this undoubtedly authentic information, derived from named
sources, adds up to a consistent and convincing portrait. The only real

discrepancy occurs when we find Lawson stating that Peel had a "far reaching, yet musical voice" while John Woodcock Graves, Peel's great hunting and drinking crony who wrote the words of the celebrated song, described Peel as having "a girt rough voice and a rough holler".

The reader may be wondering why, when stress has been placed on the fact that the fell packs are foot followed, mention is made of Peel's riding to hounds. Peel, in fact, hunted a very large area, part of which was low country, part high. Since horses were common in the region at that time as a consequence of the ancient tradition of Border service, the practice was to ride in the low country and on the occasion of country meets (or when a fox found in low country ran into the fells) to abandon the saddle. Clear evidence that Peel's hunting was part mounted, part performed on foot, according to the nature of the country hunted, is afforded by this account, from the *Sporting Magazine* for March 1818, of one of Peel's runs:

On March 27th the Caldbeck pack of hounds belonging to Mr John Peel unkenneled a fine old fox in Denton Side, parish of Sebergham, and immediately on gaining the brow of the forest he directed his steps to the mountains, passing near the village of Caldbeck. Reynard's subtlety was soon apparent. He sprang upon the top of a high parapet wall, and ran along its whole length, notwithstanding that the hounds were in full chase. On arriving at the foot of Brag Fell, from the great depth of the snow Mr Peel and two other horsemen were obliged to dismount, and were here joined by several expert pedestrians. Mr Peel's acquaintance with the mountains directed him to a well-known shelter for these animals, Iron Crag. They found that the chase (sic) had been there, but was prevented from taking the ground by the snow, which lay in large masses. Reynard then took an easterly direction, passing over High Pike Carrick, and thence visited the different high mountains in that direction, each of which, no doubt from the cause before mentioned, he found to afford no place of shelter. He was then found to be aiming west again, passing over Saddleback, and approaching Skiddaw. Here the pedestrians came in touch with him, but notwithstanding Mr Peel's knowledge of the district, and his able management of the pack, all exertion was unavailing; for the hounds were found upon Skiddaw, returning from the chase after a persuit of more than eight hours, during which time it is supposed that they ran at least fifty miles.

Riders who took to their own feet were in the habit of either tethering their animals at the most convenient spots available or, preferably, leaving them in the care of persons who had no heart for abandoning the flat to struggle, helter-skelter, over the snowy wastes of Saddleback and Skiddaw. According to Bell, Peel's own mount, Dunny (an exceedingly tough beast, standing about 14·3 hands, "with fairly deep shoulders and very strong loin", said to have come originally from between the shafts of a cart belonging to a hawker named Peter Flynch), followed Peel like a dog across the fellsides. Dunny was trained to wait indefinitely whenever the terrain made it impossible for him to clamber further in the wake of his master. The poor beast would even kneel down to be mounted, if required!

Peel was in the habit of hunting hares at the start of the season, not turning to fox until well into the autumn (he was said to be very clever at finding hares and boasted that on one occasion he had caught a hare single-handed with his whip). His meets were announced by the parish clerk on Sundays after divine service; the clerk would mount on a tombstone in the churchyard and give out dates for hunting fixtures, together with other parish events for the coming week, including sales by auction and "jobs to let". Sunday itself was a very popular day for hunts, since it was the only free day for members of the working population. Certain meets were, so to speak, dedicated to certain groups of the sporting community. Even today the Melbreak Good Friday hunt is referred to as the "quarrymen's hunt", hounds always meeting for this occasion at Buttermere, near Honister slate quarries; the meet of the Eskdale and Ennerdale on Middlefell, Wasdale, upon the first Saturday in November is traditionally the "Salvers' Meet".

The shepherds' meets, held in the back-end, were the great hunting occasions of the statesmen-flockmasters and shepherds. The official business of these meets (which are still held, possibly more restrainedly) was collecting all the stray sheep that had been found on the fells and the return of them to their own flockmasters. But there was always more to a meet than simple business; a fox-hunt was an essential part of the programme. A century ago and earlier such a shepherds' meet might last two days, with a hunt each day and a night's drinking, singing and carousing in between: the shepherds' merry neet. The menu at a merry neet was traditionally "tatie-pot" (a kind of hot-pot composed of layers of mutton, potatoes, bacon and a piece of black-pudding), apple-pie and cheese. This repast was followed by a frequently night-long drinking and singing session. Besides traditional hunting songs, interspersed with view-halloos and whoops, came brilliantly improvised forty or fifty-verse songs, terminating not infrequently with the collapse of the singer, as often from fatigue as from drink; and marvellous tales were told. As well as fox-hunting there was always wrestling, cock-fighting, a "gurning" contest (face-pulling with a horse's collar as frame for the face, the most hideous facial contortion winning the prize) and horse-racing. Accompanying these diversions there was, of course, plenty of betting. The most celebrated of the shepherds' meets were those held at the Traveller's Rest at the summit of Kirkstone Pass; at the Dun Bull, Mardale; the Woolpack Inn, Eskdale; the Kirkstile Inn, Loweswater, and the Mill Inn, Mungrisedale.

Peel's era was one of numerous, small fell-packs, some of which, like Peel's, were fundamentally still trencher-fed packs, some of which were privately owned by members of the local gentry with sufficient time to hunt regularly once or twice a week and means ample enough to permit the maintenance of a few hounds and sometimes to engage the services of a professional huntsman. For instance, Mr John Mayson of Keswick kept, in the opening years of the nineteenth century, a small private pack which was hunted for him by one Fleming who is described as having been "a remarkably fine-looking man with a voice like thunder". A Mr Slack, of Derwent Hill, also kept a similar pack. Another belonged to Mr Joseph Crozier, who settled at Threlkeld in the early years of that same century, marrying Ann Robinson, daughter of an old Threlkeld family. Crozier's first home was at Gate Gill at the foot of Saddleback (or Blencathra, to give the mountain its more romantic Celtic name). Later the Croziers moved to Riddings, on the outskirts of Threlkeld. There John Crozier was born in 1822.

Joseph Crozier's miniature pack of "huntin' dogs" was grandly termed the Threlkeld Foxhounds. Young John, who was raised on fox-hunting, throughout his boyhood hunted frequently with John Peel as well as with the Threlkeld (he was later to say that John Peel taught him how to hunt). Joseph Crozier handed over the hunting and management of his pack to his son when the lad was seventeen years of age, in 1839. John Crozier remained Master of what was essentially the Threlkeld Foxhounds until his death in 1903!

Peel was at one time huntsman (possibly not professionally) to the hounds at Arrowthwaite, the property of Sir Frederick Vane. The record run for this pack was in 1829; starting near Lorton, the pack ran their fox over Wythop Fell, through Embleton, over the Hay near Cockermouth, crossed the Derwent, then ran via Isel, Threapland, Kirkland, Torpenhow, Binsey, Bolton Gate, Westward Park and Faulds, where they killed. The distance is stated to have been seventy miles, over eleven different parishes and Peel said that this fox was the size of a wolf. This, as it happened, was the young Wilfred Lawson's first meet. Lawson became an exceedingly keen follower of hounds, went out frequently with Peel and kept a small pack of his own in due course. In 1850 Lawson and Peel joined forces, hunting their respective packs together as one and after John Peel's death in 1858 Lawson became Master and owner of the entire pack, hunting them as the Cumberland Foxhounds.

John Peel and his close drinking and hunting crony John Woodcock Graves put together the words of the famous song, "D'ye ken John Peel" during a drinking session at the close of a day's hunting in 1832. They were at Graves's house in Midtown, Caldbeck, at the time, close to the Rising Sun (later to become the Oddfellows' Arms), to which the composers are said to have repaired at intervals during their creative labours. The old grandmother was singing Graves's eldest son (then an infant) to sleep with the Border refrain, "Where will Bonnie Annie lie?" Graves set the words of the new hunting song to this somewhat unlikely melody. Shortly afterwards he sang it before an audience at the Rising Sun and the applause and compliments caused John Peel, it is said, to shed tears. "By Jove, Peel, you'll be sung when we're both run to earth!" are Graves's reported words.

In fact the song failed to receive more than regional acclaim until 1869 when William Metcalfe, noted for his choral work at Carlisle cathedral, set the words to new music. In May of that year he sang the song in London at the annual dinner of the Cumberland Benevolent Society and after this the song never flagged in its popularity. Peel was of course by that time dead, while Graves was in the Antipodes.

The original version of the song gave the now sung 'gay' coat as 'grey' (as we have seen, the true colour of Peel's celebrated garment) and Caldbeck for Troutbeck. The errors crept in when, as Machell somewhat scornfully observed in the Peel biography, the song became popular with Cockneys, who knew nothing about hunting in the Lake

Country and indeed did not even realise that John Peel had been a real person!

Graves, on the other side of the world, first in Tasmania, then in New Zealand and Australia and back to Tasmania again, a talented but erratic man who could never settle for long either in occupation or dwelling place, demonstrated how deeply is the passion for a hunt embedded in the Cumbrian spirit. In his roamings about Australia he managed to get together some kind of collection of dogs whenever possible and hunted kangaroos with them, on foot, of course. The people of down-under showed little understanding fo the sport and on one occasion thought that he was shouting 'Murder!' when he, in fact, was simply cheering on his pack in traditional fashion. He endeavoured to make his fortune with a succession of inventions, each of which came to nothing. At last he wrote and got published a protest in the press against cruelties allegedly practised on convicts in Hobart. The authorities at once had him placed in an asylum, as an insane person. He escaped, however, in a manner both typical and ingenious: a local JP who visited him in his confinement had been, in his past, a keen hunting man and he gave Graves permission to paint a mural on the wall of the asylum yard, a mural depicting a kangaroo hunt, in which the JP himself was to feature. To complete the upper part of the mural it was necessary to paint in some sky and in order to paint the sky Graves very naturally required a ladder. A ladder was therefore provided and in no time Graves had escaped over the wall.

He died in Hobart in 1886, at the age of ninety-two, on the banks of an antipodean River Derwent. Besides leaving for posterity the words of the John Peel song he scribbled in pencil on the back of the original manuscript of the verses some notes about Peel's hounds which featured therein: Ruby, Ranter, Royal and Bellman. Ruby, wrote Graves, was "the handsomest and best ever seen, by a Southern sire and clifty clean Harrier bitch . . . with a fine head and deep tongue, which she would give at twenty yards breath and never told a lie." One of Peel's great-great nieces had the honour of being named after this hound. It is worth nothing here too, perhaps, that Ruby (the hound) was walked by a dyer and that on days of important meets he used to dye her sky-blue as a mark of distinction!

Ranter was black and tan, of average tongue, about thirty-five or forty pounds in weight. Bellman was "freckled with patches of black and had good tan chops". Ranter, Royal and Bellman were all by the same mother, Dancer, half beagle, half harrier, and had their mother's musical tongue. Peel used to say that "never was there three like them on God Almighty's ground".

John Peel, at the age of seventy-eight, had an accident in the hunting-field; he is said to have fractured two ribs and to have developed pneumonia, dying a fortnight later. He was buried at Caldbeck; it was estimated at the time that some 3,000 people attended the funeral. His grave is marked by a tombstone bearing motifs of hunting horns, a hound, roses, a portrait of what appears to be a rising sun (the name of his favourite inn), vine leaves and grapes. One definitely detects a Cumbrian sense of humour at work here. The dominant feature is a large, classical urn with flowing draperies, but this has nothing to do with the man buried beneath and is there, one suspects, simply as a gesture to offset the abundant vine motif, the hunting symbols and the rising sun. John Peel would not have recognised a grecian urn had he been shown one, but he would have grasped the implications of the rest of the design without hesitation.

As we have seen, after Peel's death his pack went to Sir Wilfred Lawson. However, John Peel Junior sent his father's favourite hound, Briton, to John Crozier as a keepsake. The blood of this hound could be traced in the Blencathra pack right up until 1900, if not later. According to several reliable sources three more of Peel's hounds accompanied Briton to Threlkeld. Mr Joe Ashbridge of Skelton who today, at eighty-two, is one of the Blencathra's most knowledgeable and enthusiastic supporters, quoting eye-witness evidence handed down to him in a direct line (he is, on his mother's side, a descendant of John Peel), says, "When John Peel died there were a horse and cart in farrier's yard with a net over, and there were four hounds in cart, and they were taken to Crozier at Threlkeld."

John Crozier, who had at first hunted his Threlkeld pack himself, presently employed as huntsman the veteran Joshua Fearon, who died in 1874 at the age of eighty-four, having hunted professionally well into his seventies. He lived to see the Threlkeld, hitherto maintained by Crozier at his own expense, converted into a subscription hunt in 1870 and renamed the Blencathra Foxhounds. Some *cognoscenti* regard Fearon as the founder of the Blencathra. Isaac Todhunter, who followed Fearon as huntsman, had but a brief career with the pack; his successor, John Porter, was Blencathra huntsman for over twenty years but died young, at forty-eight years of age, in 1894, as a result of contracting pneumonia through keeping his wet clothes on at the close of the day's hunting; an occupational hazard of huntsmen. His place was taken by Jim Dalton, who remained huntsman for the next thirty-six years.

During his early years as hunting Master of the Threlkeld John Crozier certainly still rode to hounds when he loused* in low country; his quarry, according to Nicholson, included deer as well as hare and fox. After the renaming of the Blencathra the pack seems to have become strictly foot followed. Hare, again according to Nicholson, was always hunted at the start of the season, to get hounds into condition:

> . . . it was usually about Christmas time before they reckoned to try for the big game, and then the first meet was Barf, which in those days Mr Crozier considered the "smittle spot" for foxes. In later years Skiddaw was a super find. . . .

By the time that Jim Dalton arrived on the Blencathra scene fell fox-hunting had reached the point where it was almost exactly as we know the sport today. Dalton is considered in Lake Country hunting circles to be one of the great huntsmen of all time. There are veteran Blencathra supporters still hunting who went out with Jim Dalton and remember him well. "A very good traveller and one of the best kennelmen ever," recalls Mr Fred Mills of Threlkeld, who has followed the Blencathra for over sixty years. "Jim got eighteen shillings a week when he started, in addition to a cottage, his hunting boots and so on. This was later raised to a pound a week and I believe his wage was increased again before he retired; he certainly deserved every penny of it. His record catch for a season was eighty-four foxes; totals for the season were much less than they are in these days. It was reckoned that if a catch had reached fifteen or sixteen by the New Year, then the going was good."

The record for the present Blencathra huntsman, John Richardson, is 123 foxes in a season; it should be borne in mind that the fox

* Let out the hounds.

population of this country is estimated to have trebled since the nineteen-thirties.

Dalton, who was nearly six feet tall, had as his most celebrated whip Thomas Hutchinson, always known as Tommy Hutch, who on occasion hunted the Blencathra himself, and very well too. Since Hutchinson was about five feet in height, whip and huntsman together provided a somewhat comic spectacle. In spite of his short stature and bandy legs, Tommy could move over the fells at an astonishing speed (it is also recalled that, "He could sup pints of beer, too, as fast as you could draw them"). C. E. Benson, for one, could never get over his experiences with Tommy Hutch and has left us some vivid accounts of what hunting with him was like:

> If we stick to the Whip we shall have plenty of hard work . . . though small, he is mighty tough, and never stops going. When everyone, including the Huntsman, has pulled up near the hounds because there is no obvious necessity for going on, that terrible little man with a command of two or three hounds and terriers, will be seen on the skyline, executing some de-Wet-like movement. . . .

Benson describes in detail one day when a fox went away from Bull Crag, on Maiden Moor, to Gate Crag in Borrowdale. This account of fell fox-hunting at the close of the last century would serve perfectly as an example of a similar hunt today, apart from the fact that Benson's bottom people were in carriages and on bicycles, whereas ours are in motor-cars:

> Long before we catch sight of the hounds again, we know which way they have gone and something of what is happening. The carriages are all trotting up the valley, and bicycle after bicycle shoots across Grange Bridge. A few minutes later we hear the Secretary's most musical cry, cheering on the hounds. What this exact call is, I have never been able to ascertain, and he keeps it a secret, though I have done my best to find out. I once thought of asking him to dinner in the wicked hope of getting it out of him in his cups, but I reflected that by the time I had got a dalesman in his cups . . . I should be under the table, so that any information he might see fit to impart would be rather lost on me.
> We soon see the hounds, stringing in and out, up and down, on Gate Crag and the neighbouring rocks. . . . As we near the crag, we come up

with two local men, one with a hound on a cord, the other with two terriers. They are unrecognised servants of the hunt, who act as whippers-in, or in any other capacity which the moment may require. Soon after our arrival the hounds stop running, and gather round the foot of a broad *couloir*, filled from bottom to top with great boulders. A small grey figure approaches the place and doubtfully inspects it. "Hast whoaled?" comes the cheery voice of an old farmer from the top of the crags. "Ay!" is the reply, "but it's a queer place."

This confounds us. The small, grey figure is the Whip. We left him in Newlands, two miles of solid walking distant, if he had tramped in a direct line; and, as we left him at the bottom of one precipice, and he is now at the bottom of another, it is unlikely that he could have managed that in forty minutes. . . . This is one of the mysteries of the Blencathra Hunt that will never be solved. . . .

Mr Ashbridge, whose first day out with hounds was seventy-two years ago, when he was ten, recalls the occasion with marvellous clarity of detail:

The hounds were cast off on Faulds Brow but did not find a fox until they reached a place called Pow Gill. I remember quite well, for a large fox jumped over the wall quite close to where I was standing and off they went in full cry across Ellerbeck Common. I climbed Bray Fell; we were nearing the top and I was getting left behind when Jim Dalton looked round and on seeing me lagging he said, "Put a lead on that hound and give yon little lad hold of him and it will pull him on." It was a young hound that hadn't got away on the hunt; they called it Butler. No doubt it was getting tired, like me! So they coupled me to it and one of us helped tother. What a trip! We went around the top of Roughton Gill and back down Fellside, but never saw another hound that day. They had gone straight on and finished at Dead Crag on Skiddaw.

After this there was no stopping Joe Ashbridge hunting. He played truant from school whenever he could (Mr Mills also confesses to receiving at least one good hiding for doing the same), the object being of course to have a hunt. "What a man Dalton was! He knew it all. He could even tell in advance what the hunting would be like. He would say of a morning, as we were going along the road, 'Now we'll get out on top, Joe; it'll be a hunt on top today'. And sure enough, it would be."

It is noteworthy that both Fred Mills and Joe Ashbridge agree that their most impressive hunt memories are of the occasions when the Blencathra and the Ullswater had a joint meet on Carrock Fell; this was an annual fixture in those days. Joe Bowman would walk his hounds over from Patterdale to Mungrisedale early in the morning; there would be a grand hunt, lasting the greater part of the day; the two famous huntsmen would then have a drink and a crack together in Threlkeld, "while the hounds waited, both packs all mixed up together. Then it'd be time to go. Jim would say, 'C'me on lads!' and Joe would say, 'Come on there!' and without any fuss whatsoever the two packs would sort themselves out, the Blencathra trotting away after Jim and the Ullswater after Joe."

The Cumbrian zest for fox-hunting (and Cumbrian wit, which is never far under the surface) may perhaps be best expressed in anecdotes of Blencathra followers themselves—anecdotes without doubt authentic, unlikely as they may sound to the southerner. Unfortunately there are so many of these tales, all of them so remarkable, that there is no space for them all here.[5] The character of Cumbrian hunting is well conveyed in a story concerning Mr Ashbridge himself and in a brief account of one Patty, an ardent Blencathra supporter at the turn of the century.

Two seasons back, when Joe Ashbridge was in his eighty-first year, in his excitement during the course of a hunt, he indulged in a sprint up the fellside which resulted in his collapse. Everyone else abandoned the chase to come to the old gentleman's aid. He at length opened his eyes to find the local vicar bending solicitously over him. Mr Ashbridge, without a moment's hesitation said, "Eh-eh, parson, you nearly had another customer that time!" Whereat he got up and resumed his interest in the hunt.[6]

Patty is remembered by Mr Ashbridge as a "wiry, determined little fellow who hunted in winter and poached in summer. He was a grand chap, was Patty. There was one time the Blencathra had a record run; ran their fox from Combe Heights on Carrock to Carlisle cemetery gates. Patty followed the entire distance, nigh on thirty miles it would be, wearing clogs! When he got back home they asked him how many managed to complete the run. 'D'you mean hounds or folk?' said Pat."

The most famous Patty tale of all concerns an occasion when terriers failed to reach a fox which had holed, so Patty went underground himself, clean out of sight. The assembled field on the brink of the hole awaited his reappearance breathlessly; finally Dalton, unable to wait patiently any longer, called down to ask how he was getting on. From the depths came Patty's voice in reply, "Champion! we ha'e baith gotten howld!" Before long Patty surfaced with the fox, the jaws of the animal clamped tight upon one of his arms.

John Crozier, for sixty-four years Master of the Threlkeld-Blencathra Foxhounds, by the end of his life represented for the people of the region something more than mere squire and fox-hunting gentleman. He was a symbol, a relic of their past and they revered him as such. In his old age he used to attend meets in a little phaeton drawn by a grey pony; a small man "with a large white beard . . . he always wore a moleskin hat". He died at last on 5 March 1903 and a period in Cumbrian history died with him. Nicholson has given us a description of his funeral at Threlkeld:

When the morning of the funeral broke with a terribly wild storm of drenching rain, I really think these . . . good folks thought in their hearts it was all in the fitness of things: "Happy is the corpse the rain falls on". . . . Every road to the village was thronged with people . . . many of whom had walked for miles . . . in this awful weather. The idea of "bearing" him was abandoned, and the procession proceeded from the quiet old home he had loved so well down to the village, through lines of sorrowing people standing heedless of the drenching rain. On the coffin were placed his hunting cap, horn . . . and his good oak staff. The impressive scene inside the little church is difficult to describe. Every seat was occupied, and the tall yeomen stood shoulder to shoulder down either side of every aisle, yet many had to remain outside in the storm. The service and address were in perfect accord with the solemnity of the occasion. No words of mine can adequately convey the effect of the singing. . . . This culminated in the final scene when we stood around the grave, and amidst the roar of the storm in the mighty hills as its accompaniment, there rose up the grand old hymn "Oh God our help in ages past. . . ."

The Rt Hon. J. W. Lowther, Speaker of the House of Commons, succeeded John Crozier as Master and remained so for the next sixteen years. Since he had to spend much of his time in the House he had to have a Deputy Master: first Mr Harry Howe, then Mr George Tickell. Parliamentary duties at last forced Lowther to resign his Mastership in

1919; old age obliged Jim Dalton, getting on for eighty, to retire a year later. Fox-hunting on foot in the fells being the healthy profession that it is, he lived until the age of ninety-three.

The Blencathra ultimately returned to the original kennels in Gate Gill of their ancestral pack, the Threlkeld, and they remain kennelled there today. Threlkeld, stretched in a long street at the feet of Saddle-back, with Skiddaw and the region's finest fells spread about it, with quarrying and fox-hunting as its major preoccupations, retains its traditional character, despite an influx of motorised traffic. In the churchyard an unobtrusive four-sided monument bears the names of forty-five outstanding supporters of the hunt:

AROUND THEM STAND THE OLD FAMILIAR MOUNTAINS

A few friends have united to raise this stone in loving memory of the undernamed who in their Generation were noted veterans of the chase, and most of whom lie buried in this churchyard. . . .

The listed names include,

Daniel Walker, of Threlkeld,
    Died Feby 8, 1849, aged 82
Henry Gill, died Jany 28
    1850, aged 61
Ben Graves, died May 26
    1856, aged 75
Wilson Nicholson, died
    Jany 15, 1864, aged 50
James Bainbridge, died
    September 1 1866, aged 82
Mark Fisher, died Dec 16
    1867, aged 81 . . .
Isaac Todhunter of Threlkeld
    died Nov 7, 1868, aged 59 . . .
John Cockbain, died May 5
    1873, aged 89
Joshua Fearon, died June 19
    1874, aged 86
John Hodgson, died Sept 30
    1874, aged 91
Joseph Wilkinson, died
    Dec 15, 1875, aged 87 . . .

These must all have hunted with John Peel. Of the forty-five names listed, fifteen are of octogenarians, fifteen septuagenarians, two were in their ninetieth year, two were in their full nineties. The listed names terminate with,

William Stuart   Died 1902 aged 79

followed by these final inscriptions:

John Porter of High Row Threlkeld
    died May 4 1894, aged 48
    for 26 years Huntsman of the
    Blencathra Hounds
Also of John Crozier of the Riddings
    died March 5th 1903, aged 80,
    for 64 years he was the beloved Master
    of the Blencathra Foxhounds
    And mainly through his instrumentality
    this monument was erected.

The Forest Music is to hear the Hounds
Rend the thin Air, and with a lusty cry
Awake the drowsy echo, and confound
Their perfect language in a mingled voice
                                        Gay

This monument should be visited on a winter's morning, when the Blencathra are hunting on the fell of that name within full view of the memorial stone itself. Standing there, tracing the somewhat lichen-obliterated inscriptions with his finger while the shouts of huntsman John Richardson and the clamour of the pack ring out from the over-shadowing fellside, the visitor feels the very texture of old Cumberland under his hand; and looking up he sees the centuries-long sight of the fox-hunt moving through the dark breast of the mountain, while the tongue of hounds and the huntsman's calls reach him as a living echo of a Cumberland which, though of the past, has bequeathed too much to the present for it to be regarded as extinct.

BIBLIOGRAPHY

The references listed below have been used throughout this book. Those marked with an asterisk are recommended for general reading.

Ackerman,* *A Picturesque Tour of the English Lakes*, 1821.

Bouch, C. M. L. and Jones, G. P., *The Lake Counties (1500–1830). A Social and Economic History*, Manchester, 1961.

Coleridge, Samuel Taylor, *Notebooks*, ed Coburn, Routledge & Kegan Paul.

Collingwood, W. G.,* *Lake District History*, Kendal, 1925; *The Lake Counties*, Warne.

Cumberland and Westmorland Antiquarian and Archaeological Society's Transactions, Old Series (CW) and New Series (CW₂).

Grainger, F. and Collingwood, W. G., *Register and Records of Holm Cultram*, Kendal, 1929.

Housman, J., *A Topographical Description of Cumberland, Westmorland, Lancashire and a part of the West Riding of Yorkshire*, Carlisle, 1800.

Hughes, Edward,* *North Country Life in the Eighteenth Century, vol. ii Cumberland and Westmorland, 1700–1830*, Oxford.

Hutchinson, W., *History of the County of Cumberland and some Places Adjacent*, 2 vols, Carlisle, 1794.

Lynn Linton, E.,* *The Lake Country*, London, 1864.

Lysons, D. and S., *Magna Britannia, vol iv Cumberland*, London, 1816.

Nicolson, J. and Burn, R., *The History and Antiquities of the Counties of Westmorland and Cumberland*, 2 vols, London, 1777.

Parsons, W. and White, W., *History, Directory and Gazeteer of the*

Counties of Cumberland and Westmorland with that Part of the Lake District in Lancashire, etc., Leeds, 1829.

Postlethwaite, J., *Mines and Mining in the Lake District*, Whitehaven, 1889.

Scott, Daniel,★ *Bygone Cumberland and Westmorland*, London, 1899.

Victoria County History, Cumberland.

West, T., *The Antiquities of Furness*. London, 1774.

Wordsworth, Dorothy,★ *Journals*, ed W. Knight, London, 1904.

Wordsworth, William,★ "The Prelude", ed de Selincourt, Oxford.

Wordsworth, William and Dorothy,★ *Letters*, 3 vols, ed de Selincourt: *Early Letters*, Oxford, 1935; *Middle Years*, *1806–1811*; *Later Years*, *1811–1820*, Oxford, 1937.

NOTES

INTRODUCTION

1 First verse of a fragmentary poem found in Wordsworth MSS M and never published during the poet's lifetime.

CHAPTER 1: *High Country, Low Country*

1 Collingwood, W. G., "Mountain Names", CW vol. xviii.

2 *Tacitus on Britain and Germany:* A translation of the *Agricola* and the *Germania* by H. Mattingly. Penguin, 1948.

3 Collingwood, W. G., "Early Roads". CW_2 vol. ix, 217. CW_2 vol. xiv, 29. CW_2 vol. xxiv. Material for this chapter also from the same author's paper on "Packhorse Bridges", CW_2 vol. xxviii. See also Grainger and Collingwood, *Register and Records of Holm Cultram.*

4 Bellhouse, R. L., CW_2 vol. lvi and lviii.

5 Wainwright, A., *A Pictoral Guide to the Lakeland Fells. Book Six, The North Western Fells.*

6 Mr Vickers, in a letter to the author, gives some interesting details of work on the Sty: "In 1930 the Cumberland County Council took over the second-class roads and I was appointed a 'lengthsman', the Sty being part of my length. . . . I built a good part of the gutter. . . . The top part near the gate was already done." Mr Vickers goes on to say that he thinks that his predecessor, Mr Fleming, might have done this work, or it could have been done earlier; thanks to the 1966 floods there is now little trace of guttering left near the gate. ". . . the excess water running down the path worried me a great deal, as I saw visions of hikers being bogged down; I decided to try to channel the water. First I made the channel by removing all the bigger pieces of rock, then I broke up the stones and filled it in on the top. I more or less paved it; the idea was to drain away excess rainfall and preserve the path. This was the only

change; the other work was mainly filling up deep holes left by flooding. . . . The Above Derwent Rural District Council were responsible for the Sty previous to 1930 and they used to contract work out to local farmers (who had the horses and carts necessary). . . . These contractors simply broke up stone and filled in holes left by flood water. . . . With the exception of the gutter the Sty has not been altered in any way since the old days. . . ."

7 Tough, D. L. W.,* The Last years of a Frontier, Oxford, 1928.
8 Bonsall, B.,* Sir James Lowther and Cumberland and Westmorland Elections. 1754–75. Manchester, 1961.
9 Wordsworth, William and Dorothy, Letters, vol. ii, Middle Years.

CHAPTER 2 : Roads and Road-makers of Braithwaite

1 The material for this chapter is drawn from the collected accounts of Braithwaite's road surveyors 1769–1859, now in the possession of the Bowe family.
2 For information on the eighteen sworn men of Crosthwaite, Cumberland, CW₂ vol. xlv.

CHAPTER 3 : In Quest of Wadd

1 B. M. Sloane MS 2487 (an inventory dated 1586 of the equipment and furniture of the Mines Royal at all their establishments in the Lake Country).
2 Collingwood, W. G., "The Keswick and Coniston Mines in 1600 and Later", CW₂ vol. xxviii.
3 For this quoted material on smuggling and smugglers and also for information about the positions of the old adits the author is indebted to Mr J. Moon, F.G.S., of Workington, who is at present working on a new survey of the old mines of the region.
4 Raistrick, A. (ed), The Hatchett Diary of a tour through the countries of England and Scotland in 1796 visiting their mines and manufactories, Bradford Barton, 1967.
5 Forge Mill deeds. The author is indebted to Miss Margaret Birkbeck and Mr David Hodson for access to deeds, documents, records, photographs and much other useful material.

CHAPTER 4 : Statesmen's Progress

1 Material for this chapter from the Skelgill documents and the Grave family.

2 Butler, Wilson, "The Customs and Tenant Right Tenures, etc", CW₂ vol. xxvi.

3 The author is indebted to Mr John Edmondson of Low Snab, Newlands, for the loan of his copy (dated 1849) of *Hodgson's Shepherd's Guide* and also for the very helpful information about salving, p. 108.

4 For information about the region at this time see Celia Fiennes, *The Journeys of Celia Fiennes*, ed Christopher Morris, Cresset Press.

CHAPTER 5: *The Woollen Industry of Millbeck*

1 Kaye, J. W., *The Millbeck Woollen Industry*, CW₂ vol. lviii.

2 Help with the identification of some of the textiles named in this chapter was received from the *Drapers' Record* and the library of the Victoria and Albert Museum.

3 I am indebted to Mr M. Davies-Shiel for generously placing this material at my disposal.

CHAPTER 6: *The First of the Fellwalkers*

1 Material for this chapter drawn from:
Coleridge, Samuel Taylor, *Notebooks*.
Coleridge, Samuel Taylor, *Collected Letters*, ed E. L. Griggs, Oxford and New York, 1956.
Griggs, E. L. (ed), *Wordsworth and Coleridge: Studies in Honour of George McLean Harper*, Princeton, 1939.

2 *A Movable Feast*.

CHAPTER 7: *The Chancellor, the Curate, and the '45*

1 Mounsey, George Gill (ed), *Authentic Account of the Occupation of Carlisle in 1745, by Prince Charles Edward Stuart*. (*Correspondence and Narrative of Dr John Waugh, Chancellor and Prebendary of Carlisle*), Longmans, 1846.

2 Brown, James Walter,* *Round Carlisle Cross*, 9 vols, ed Thomas Gray and Marley Denwood, Carlisle, 1951.

CHAPTER 8: *The Carlisle Canal*

1 See William Chapman's two reports: *Survey and Report on a Proposed Line of Navigation from Newcastle-upon-Tyne to the Irish Channel, 1795*, and *Survey and Report on a Proposed Line of Navigation from Carlisle to the Irish Channel, 1818*.

2 Much useful information for this chapter comes from *The Carlisle Navigation Canal*, Michael Finlay's thesis for Newcastle University.

CHAPTER 9: *The Cherry Orchard of Armboth*

1 Tchekhov, Anton. *The Cherry Orchard*. Act II. Translated by Constance Garnett. Permission to quote from Chatto and Windus and David Garnett.

CHAPTER 10: *Legend and Lore*

1 Professor Child, *English and Scottish Popular Ballads*.

2 The extent to which deception of the Romantic tourists was carried in the Lake Country (and, equally, the extent to which tourists were prepared to be blarneyed) is splendidly illustrated by the tale of the 'old chapel' that was built at Conishead Priory, complete with local geriatric hired to live there as a hermit—to the complete satisfaction of all parties!

3 Boggle—a spirit: the name derived from the Norse *böig*, in turn derived from *böie*, meaning to bend; the idea seeming to be one of a sinuous vapour-like object (Ibsen's Great Boyg in *Peer Gynt*; see the Archers' notes to their translation of the play).

A contemporary Cumbrian's account of how he thought he saw a boggle in Mosedale, Mungrisedale, wonderfully bears out this theme of a vapour-like shape; it is worth noting that the speaker, although he referred naturally to a 'boggle', had no idea that this name derived from the Norse and in the original meant a vapour-like object; he simply knew, instinctively as it were, that this was what a boggle was, and he thought he saw one: "A grey phantom-shape weaving about in t' air, like; very slowly. My hair stood up on my head in horror, I can tell you! But then, just as I was about to turn and run, my nose told me what it was; I smelt muck. And you know, it was steam, like, rising out of a pile of muck that had been raked out of calf-hole; what we call hard muck. The night was bitter cold, and the muck still warm. But it had me gay flaited for the moment like; and I'll not pretend that it didn't."

4 Bishop Percy, Dean of Carlisle, 1778–82, *Reliques of Ancient English Poetry*.

5 There is a detailed account of this ghost in the *West Cumberland Times*, 22 July 1967.

6 Hope, *Church Treasury of History, Custom and Folk Lore*, 1897.

7 The author is indebted to the Victoria and Albert Museum for this information about the 'Luck'.

8 The Ralph version of this ballad is given by Armistead in *Tales and Legends of the English Lakes*, 1891.

9 According to the Victoria and Albert Museum the glass bowl of the Muncaster Luck appears to be Venetian, of a type made about 1500. It is doubtful therefore if it can really have been given by Henry VI to the Penningtons.

10 For Buttermere lore the author is indebted to the late Miss Winnie Burns and, once again, to Mr John Edmondson.

CHAPTER II : *John Peel and the Blencathra*

1 Clapham, Richard, *Foxhunting on the Lakeland Fells*, Longmans, 1920.

2 Nicholson, Albert, "John Crozier of Riddings, Master of Hounds", reprinted from *The Manchester Quarterly*, January 1906.

3 Benson, C. E., *Crag and Hound in Lakeland*, Hurst & Blackett, 1902.

4 Machell, Hugh, *John Peel*, Heath Cranton, 1926.

5 Information for this chapter has been given unstintingly to the author by Blencathra supporters, hunting friends and neighbours, too numerous to be named here individually; to them all she expresses grateful thanks for their assistance.

6 Another authenticated story involving a parson comes from Newlands. The late Joe Wren of Littletown burst into Newlands church one Sunday morning, shouting, "Cut thy good job short, parson; there's cubs on Bullcrag!"

INDEX